JN413640

고득점을 위한 고강도 훈련

고난도 TEPS in TEPS

박기혁 · 정구영 지음

까다로운 TEPS 문법을 완벽 대비할 수 있는 정확한 분석과 해법

2nd Edition

문법 TEST BooK

Grammar

Actual Training 10회분

사람in saramin.com

고난도
TEPS in
TEPS 문법

박기혁

서울대학교 졸업
(전) 중앙데일리 영자신문 객원 논설위원
(현) 와우패스 무역영어 대표강사
(현) 메가스터디 TEPS 강사
(현) 반포 행복한 어학원 대표

정구영

한국외대 영어과 졸업
동양대학교 겸임교수
한영대 영어설교 통역 연구원
강남 YBM e4U 시사영어학원 영어강사

고난도 TEPS in TEPS 문법

저자	박기혁 · 정구영
초판 1쇄 발행	2011년 4월 8일
초판 2쇄 발행	2014년 1월 27일
편집장	강성실
기획 · 편집	박운희, 박혜민, 박문정
디자인 책임	손정수
마케팅 총괄	이종선
마케팅	이태호, 이전희
디지털콘텐츠	이지호, 김정숙
관리	남채윤
출판등록	제 10-1835호
발행처	사람in
주소	121-839 서울시 마포구 양화로11길 14-10(서교동 378-16) 4F
전화	02)338-3555(代)
팩스	02)338-3545
E-mail	saramin@netsgo.com
Homepage	www.saramin.com

※ 책값은 뒤표지에 있습니다.
※ 파본은 바꾸어 드립니다.

ⓒ박기혁 정구영 2011
978-89-6049-240-0 13740
978-89-6049-239-4(세트)

고득점을 위한 고강도 훈련

고난도 TEPS in TEPS

박기혁·정구영 지음

까다로운 TEPS 문법을 완벽 대비할 수 있는 정확한 분석과 해법

2nd Edition

문법

사람in
saram in com

 머리말　　　　　　　　　　　　　　　　　　

이 고난도 문제집은 기존의 문제집보다 난이도가 높은 문제들을 연습하기 위한 것으로서 TEPS에서 진정으로 고득점을 하고자 하는 수험생들을 위해 기획된 것입니다. 모든 공부에는 이론과 실전이 공존해야 합니다. 그래서 이 책은 기본적인 이론 공부를 마친 학습자가 **TEPS의 문법/ 어휘/ 독해** 실전에서 고득점할 수 있도록 기출문제를 바탕으로 실제 시험과 유사한 문제 형태를 유지하되 좀 더 까다로운 수준으로 제작되었습니다.

TEPS는 실용성과 학문성이 절묘하게 결합된 시험으로, 1999년 출범 이래 현재 대한민국 영어 시장에서 완전히 자리매김했다고 평가되고 있습니다. 시행 초기에는 주로 서울대 대학원을 준비하는 이들로 대상이 한정되었으나, TOEIC의 변별력이 떨어지고 TOEFL로 인해 지불되는 로열티 금액이 막대해짐에 따라 그에 대한 반발적인 분위기가 형성되면서 응시 인원이 늘어나기 시작했습니다.

최근에는 외고 등 특목고를 대비하는 상위권 중학생 및 외고 재학생, 대학의 특차전형 입학을 원하는 상위권 중고생, 공기업 취업을 준비하는 대학생, 국가고시 준비생, 로스쿨, 의학 대학원 자격시험(MEET) 및 치과 대학원 자격시험(DEET) 준비생, 신학대학원 준비생 등 다양한 연령대에서 응시하는 시험이 되었습니다.

본 문제집의 내용을 소화한 후에는 수험생 스스로 시사적인 내용이나 학문적인 내용을 다룬 책을 적극적으로 찾아 읽음으로써 단순히 시험 점수를 위한 요령 습득이 아닌 진정한 영어실력 향상을 위해 노력하기 바랍니다.

자신의 꿈을 이루기 위한 발판이 될 TEPS 990점을 달성하는 데 이 책이 좋은 지렛대가 되기 바랍니다. 끝으로 이 책을 출간하는 데 도움을 주신 모든 분들께 감사의 말씀을 전합니다.

저자 일동

TEPS의 구성

TEPS는 청해, 문법, 어휘, 독해 4개 영역에 걸쳐 총 200문항으로 구성되어 있으며 시험시간은 140분이다. 문항반응이론(IRT)에 따라 채점하기 때문에 모든 문제를 맞아도 만점은 990점이고 모든 문제를 틀리더라도 10점은 나온다.

영역	PART별 내용	문항 수	시간/배점
청해 Listening Comprehension	Part I : 문장 하나를 듣고 이어질 대화 고르기 Part II : 3 문장의 대화를 듣고 이어질 대화 고르기 Part III : 6-8 문장의 대화를 듣고 이어질 대화 고르기 Part IV : 단문의 내용을 듣고 질문에 해당하는 답 고르기	15 15 15 15	55분/400점
문법 Grammar	Part I : 대화문의 빈칸에 적절한 표현을 고르기 Part II : 문장의 빈칸에 적절한 표현을 고르기 Part III : 대화에서 어법상 틀리거나 어색한 부분 고르기 Part IV : 대화에서 어법상 틀리거나 어색한 부분 고르기	20 20 5 5	25분/100점
어휘 Vocabulary	Part I : 대화문의 빈칸에 적절한 단어 고르기 Part II : 단문의 빈칸에 적절한 단어 고르기	25 25	15분/100점
독해 Reading Comprehension	Part I : 지문을 읽고 질문의 빈칸에 들어갈 내용 고르기 Part II : 지문을 읽고 질문에 가장 적절한 내용 고르기 Part III : 지문을 읽고 문맥상 어색한 내용 고르기	16 21 3	45분/400점
총계	13개 PART	200	140분/990점

*IRT(Item Response Theory)에 의하여 최고점이 990점, 최저점이 10점으로 조정됨.

TEPS 등급표

등급	점수	영역	능력검정기준
1+급	901-990 361-400 91-100	전반 청해 독해 문법 어휘	교양있는 원어민에 버금가는 정도로 의사소통이 가능하고 전문분야 업무에 대처할 수 있음. 교양있는 원어민에 버금가는 수준의 청해력 교양있는 원어민에 버금가는 수준의 독해력 교양있는 원어민에 버금가는 수준으로 내재화된 문법능력 교양있는 원어민에 버금가는 수준으로 내재화된 어휘력
1+급	801-900 321-360 81-90	전반 청해 독해 문법 어휘	단기간 집중 교육을 받으면 대부분의 의사소통이 가능하고 전문분야 업무에 별 무리 없이 대처할 수 있음. 다양한 상황의 수준 높은 내용을 별 무리 없이 이해할 수 있는 정도의 청해력 다양한 소재의 수준 높은 내용을 별 무리 없이 이해할 수 있는 정도의 독해력 다양한 구문을 별 무리 없이 신속하게 이해할 수 있을 정도로 내재화된 문법능력 다양한 표현을 별 무리 없이 신속하게 이해할 수 있을 정도로 내재화된 어휘력
2+급	701-800 281-320 71-80	전반 청해 독해 문법 어휘	단기간 집중 교육을 받으면 일반 분야업무를 큰 어려움 없이 수행할 수 있음. 일반적 상황에 보통수준의 내용을 별 무리 없이 이해하는 정도의 청해력 일반적 소재에 보통수준의 내용을 별 무리 없이 이해하는 정도의 독해력 일반적인 구문을 별 무리 없이 이해하는 정도의 문법능력 일반적인 표현을 별 무리 없이 이해하는 정도의 어휘력
2급	601-700 241-280 61-70	전반 청해 독해 문법 어휘	중장기간 집중 교육을 받으면 일반분야 업무를 큰 어려움 없이 수행할 수 있음. 일반적 상황에 보통수준의 내용을 대체로 이해하는 정도의 청해력 일반적 소재에 보통수준의 내용을 대체로 이해하는 정도의 독해력 일반적인 구문을 대체로 이해하는 정도의 문법능력 일반적인 표현을 대체로 이해하는 정도의 어휘력
3+급	501-600 201-240 51-60	전반 청해 독해 문법 어휘	중장기간 집중 교육을 받으면 한정된 분야의 업무를 큰 어려움 없이 수행할 수 있음. 일반적 상황에 보통수준의 내용을 다소 이해하는 정도의 청해력 일반적 소재에 보통수준의 내용을 다소 이해하는 정도의 독해력 일반적인 구문에 대한 의미파악이 어느 정도 가능한 문법능력 일반적인 표현에 대한 의미파악이 어느 정도 가능한 어휘력
3급	401-500 161-200 41-50	전반 청해 독해 문법 어휘	중장기간 집중 교육을 받으면 한정된 분야의 업무를 다소 미흡하지만 큰 지장은 없이 수행할 수 있음. 일반적 상황에 보통수준의 내용을 이해하기 다소 어려운 정도의 청해력 일반적 소재에 보통수준의 내용을 이해하기 다소 어려운 정도의 청해력 일반적 구문에 대한 신속한 의미 파악이 다소 어려운 정도의 문법능력 일반적인 표현에 대한 신속한 의미 파악이 다소 어려운 정도의 어휘력
4+급	301-400 201-300	전반	장기간의 집중 교육을 받으면 한정된 분야의 업무를 대체로 어렵게 수행할 수 있음.
5+급	101-200 10-100	전반	단편적인 지식만을 갖추고 있어 의사소통이 거의 불가능함.

이 책의 구성과 특징

● TEPS 고득점을 위한 고강도 훈련 Actual Training

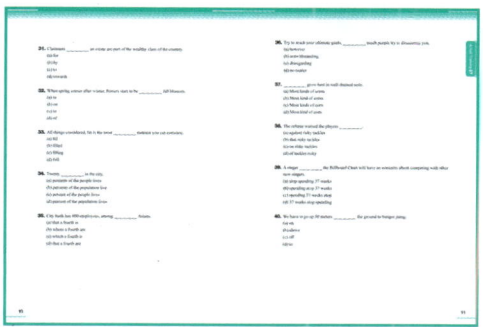

고만고만한 빈출 문제로 구성된 기존의 문제집보다 한 차원 높은 문제들로 정체된 점수를 올릴 수 있도록, 실제 시험과 동일한 문항수로 구성하였다.

● 필요한 내용이 한눈에 쏙 들어오는 해설지

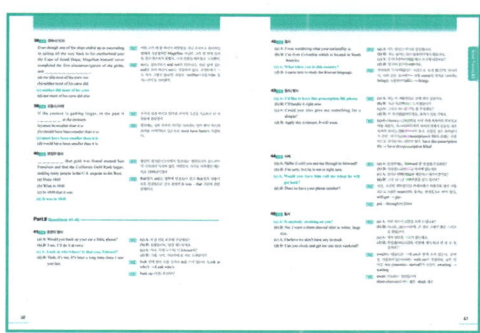

문제와 해설을 나란히 배치하여 고난도 문제의 핵심을 짚어보고, 해설 부분을 가리고 다시 한 번 풀어보거나 각 문제의 유형 tag를 참조하여 유형별 학습을 하는 등 다양한 활용을 가능하게 하였다.

● 고난도 문법 요소를 정확하게 해부한 고난도 point

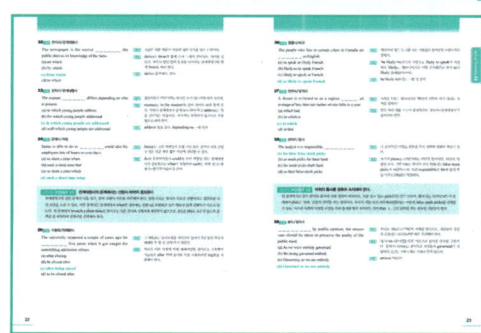

심도 있는 해설이 필요한 문법 요소가 나오는 문제의 경우, 고난도 문제가 되는 이유와 해법을 정확히 분석하여 꼭 알아야 할 50개의 point를 정리하였다.

차례 / Contents

고난도 **Actual Training 01** 9

고난도 **Actual Training 02** 21

고난도 **Actual Training 03** 33

고난도 **Actual Training 04** 45

고난도 **Actual Training 05** 57

고난도 **Actual Training 06** 69

고난도 **Actual Training 07** 81

고난도 **Actual Training 08** 93

고난도 **Actual Training 09** 105

고난도 **Actual Training 10** 117

고난도
Actual Training 01

실제 TEPS 시험의 문항수와 동일하게 구성된 고난도 Actual Training을
제한 시간 25분 내에 모두 풀 수 있도록 노력해 보세요!

Part I

Questions 1-20
Choose the best answer for the blank.

1. A: Aren't you able to drive faster?
   B: Hold your horses, sweetheart! I'd rather _____ than die on the street.
   (a) to delay
   (b) delaying
   (c) be delaying
   (d) be delayed

2. A: What did the eyewitnesses say about the accident?
   B: They insisted that the train _____ at the railway accident last night.
   (a) derail
   (b) be derailed
   (c) was derailed
   (d) should be derailed

3. A: When is a monkey independent of its parents?
   B: Not until a monkey is four years old _____ to display signs of independence from its mother.
   (a) it begins
   (b) does it begin
   (c) and begin
   (d) beginning

4. A: What do you want me to do today?
   B: I would rather that you _____ at home than went out in this blizzard.
   (a) stay
   (b) stayed
   (c) staying
   (d) have stayed

5. A: Did she come to the party last night?
   B: No, she was sick for _____.
   (a) a night
   (b) night
   (c) the night
   (d) nights

6. A: Do you have any idea of the nation's economic future?

B: _____, it is expected to be doomed.

  (a) The way how I look at it

  (b) The way I see

  (c) The way I look at it

  (d) The way in which I look it

7. A: I suppose I like this one. What would be the selling price here then?

B: I guess you're going to like it. _____ $100.

  (a) These pants costs

  (b) This pant cost

  (c) This pair of pants costs

  (d) This pair of pants cost

8. A: Have David and Johnson seen the constellation of Orion yet?

B: _____ awake at night. They are morning people.

  (a) Neither children have been

  (b) Not either child was

  (c) Either child has been

  (d) Neither of the children has been

9. A: Would you mind if I opened the window?

B: _____. It's windy outside

  (a) Yes. Please do.

  (b) I'd rather you didn't.

  (c) I'd be appreciated if you do.

  (d) I appreciated it if you didn't.

10. A: What does the boss have in mind?

B: The employer _____ as soon as possible and without blunders.

  (a) wants the job to do

  (b) wants that the job will be done

  (c) wants that the job would be done

  (d) wants the job done

11. A: This is not the present I _____.

B: Do you want it thrown away?

    (a) have wanted

    (b) have been wanting

    (c) am wanting

    (d) had want

12. A: You are _____ with yourself. What happened?

B: I've won a lottery.

    (a) quite watching pleased

    (b) watching quite pleased

    (c) looking quite pleased

    (d) looking quite pleasing

13. A: I'm having difficulty in running the foreign language institute.

B: When it comes to management, you had better ask _____ it these days.

    (a) one who used to manage

    (b) those who have managed

    (c) those who had been used to manage

    (d) them who would have managed

14. A: It is incredible that you should paint the house yellow.

B: _____, I just spruced it up.

    (a) Being as dreary as

    (b) It being as dreary as

    (c) It been as dreary as

    (d) as dreary as

15. A: Shall I take the red convertible or the white one?

B: It will look nice _____ you may take.

    (a) what the one

    (b) which one

    (c) whichever one

    (d) whatever the one

16. A: Are you sure of your memory of the accident?
   B: Yes. I remember it as clearly _____ it happened yesterday.
   (a) therefore
   (b) as
   (c) so
   (d) as if

17. A: Where did the people from the east settle?
   B: They ultimately went torward the plateau, _____ have supplied plentiful food from generation to generation.
   (a) where
   (b) in which
   (c) whose fertile lands
   (d) on which fertile lands

18. A: I wish that Mr. Smith would act nice to me all the time.
   B: Well, I think that you _____ have made such mean comments about him before.
   (a) ought to
   (b) have got to
   (c) would not
   (d) should not

19. A: Do you happen to know about Java Man?
   B: Certainly. I learned in the archaeology class. _____ Java Man, who lived before the early Ice Age, was the first mankind.
   (a) It is generally believed that
   (b) Generally believed what it is
   (c) That is generally believed
   (d) It is believed generally what

20. A: How did you learn to speak Arabic so well?
   B: As a matter of fact, I _____ in a bakery with plenty of Arabian people. They taught me a lot.
   (a) have working
   (b) had been working
   (c) used to work
   (d) could have worked

Part II

Questions 21-40
Choose the best answer for the blank.

21. The Middle East country had _____ in its deposits as had been expected.
    (a) three times as almost much oil
    (b) much almost as oil three times
    (c) as almost three times much oil
    (d) almost three times as much oil

22. We might miss the plane, _____ we will have to pay an extra fee.
    (a) in that situation
    (b) in which situation
    (c) of which situation
    (d) of that situation

23. The higher the temperature of a molecule, _____.
    (a) the more has it energy
    (b) the more energy has it
    (c) the more it has energy
    (d) the more energy it has

24. To my surprise, no people around us are aware of _____ he was in the civil rights movement.
    (a) how a momentous person
    (b) how a person momentous
    (c) how momentous person
    (d) how momentous a person

25. Morrow did not go to school even a single day, _____ to send his own child to what they call a governmental institution.
    (a) neither he means
    (b) he does not mean
    (c) he neither does mean
    (d) nor does he mean

26. Of all the major problems _____ contemporary people these days, those involved in environmental health will have the greatest effect on their way of life.
(a) being faced
(b) facing
(c) facing with
(d) having faced with

27. The National Assembly has motioned that all foreign citizens _____ their embassy.
(a) living in South Korea registering
(b) live in South Korea be registered with
(c) live in the South Korea has registered
(d) living in South Korea register with

28. The renowned aviator told reporters _____ from seeking to cross the ocean by himself even though other people had failed.
(a) that he had it barely deterred
(b) who had it been barely deterred
(c) that he had barely been deterred
(d) about his having been barely deterred

29. If, through laziness, you read at a slower rate than the rate _____ you are able, there might be great temptation for your mind to wander.
(a) which
(b) at which
(c) through which
(d) with which

30. I hope you submit your work _____ this afternoon. Otherwise, you will get an F for your grade.
(a) lately
(b) later
(c) more late
(d) the latest

31. By 2015, if all goes according to plan, 12 prestigious Western schools _____ branch campuses in a government-financed, 940-acre Global Education City.
(a) will open
(b) open
(c) will have opened
(d) will be opening

32. _____ in history when significant progress was made within a relatively short span of time.
(a) Periods that
(b) Periods have been
(c) Throughout periods
(d) There have been periods

33. They have been offering plenty of useful Web services supplying us with access to _____ for research and development.
(a) online the very best resources
(b) the best very online resources
(c) the very best online resources
(d) online resources the best very

34. In the course of his life, he learned that the robust person does not always win the race, _____ always a loser.
(a) never does the feeble person
(b) neither is the feeble person
(c) does not the feeble person
(d) nor is the feeble person

35. In the multi-cultural _____, it's safe not to worry about explaining the story of Passover because if people don't hear it from me, they'll hear it some other way.
(a) world I live
(b) world which I live
(c) world where I live in
(d) world which I live in

36. Last year, Matt earned _____ who works for a large corporation.
   (a) twice as much as his brother did
   (b) twice more than his brother was
   (c) twice as many as his brother was
   (d) twice as more as his brother has done

37. Jay Ron Philip, _____ one of the greatest composers in the world, wrote his music during the year known as the Gay 90s.
   (a) who many people consider to be
   (b) whose many people consider to be
   (c) whom many people consider as
   (d) what many people consider as

38. The Department of Fine Arts and Architecture has been criticized for _____ required courses scheduled for this semester.
   (a) having not much
   (b) not having much
   (c) not having many
   (d) having not many

39. The palaces in ancient China is so large that the rooms are _____ those of the similar era in other countries.
   (a) four times nearly as large as
   (b) as large four times as
   (c) as four times nearly as
   (d) nearly four times as large as

40. _____ the employees in the factory were making cars.
   (a) Almost all of
   (b) Most all of
   (c) Most of all
   (d) Almost the whole of

Part III Questions 41-45
Identify the option that contains an awkward expression or a grammatical error.

41. (a) A: Honey, what time is breakfast today?
(b) B: I suppose it will be fixed up at seven.
(c) A: Oh, I have a momentous meeting at nine in the morning, which I should be able to make it.
(d) B: I don't doubt that I will make breakfast by the time.

42. (a) A: Are you going to heal me or what, Donald? I only ask, because I'll do it somewhere cleaner I'm going to bleed out.
(b) B: Of course. I'm sorry, I've been busy.
(c) A: Just do it. I've got places to be.
(d) B: Okay, okay. Let's see.

43. (a) A: This is infuriating. I have been waiting for a taxi for over an hour.
(b) B: I heard that a traffic accident took place two hours ago.
(c) A: Can I believe that? Then, that's because I couldn't catch a taxi.
(d) B: Anyway you should get your rear in gear and not be late for the meeting.

44. (a) A: I like another glass of beer, please.
(b) B: With one more glass, that will be ten beers. Aren't you going to have difficulty in making your way home tonight?
(c) A: I believe that beer is a kind of soft drink.
(d) B: You are not vulnerable to beer. What's the secret?

45. (a) A: Do you think it's going to rain?
(b) B: Not for two hours. Perhaps later. How come?
(c) A: I am supposed to go on a hike with George. What do you think?
(d) B: I imagine you had better call off it and go to the cinema.

Part IV Questions 46-50
Identify the option that contains an awkward expression or a grammatical error.

46. (a) What has Canada avoided the plagues that are afflicting everyone else? (b) The short answer is a mixture of good policies and good luck. (c) The main reason for the country's economic resilience is that neither its financial system nor its housing market magnified the recession. (d) And for that regulators deserve a chunk of the credit.

47. (a) Japanese carmaker Toyota's reputation is rapidly declining. (b) The first warning signs of the problems were surfaced in 2007. (c) Its North-American built trucks caused a string of accidents due to their defective gas pedals, but the concern tried to play them down. (d) It seems to forget the lesson that a stitch in time saves nine.

48. (a) As a host of gardeners and farmers know, crossbreeding two wimpy specimens from time to time produces strong offspring. (b) That is an effect which has been known as hybrid vigor and it is common in plants. (c) It also can be found in some animals on the Earth. (d) However, some speculate, it might be lacking European royalty.

49. (a) Corruption experts say that Bulgaria urgent needs protection for whistle-blowers if President Borisov is to stamp out rampant corruption. (b) Last November, a survey by the corruption-rating organization found that 82% of Bulgarians were reluctant to report corruption-related cases because they feared being targeted. (c) Bulgarians still have fresh memories of the old communist dictatorship. (d) That's why "the whistle-blower is all too often seen as a traitor or as being like a police informer."

50. (a) If the LDP seems at the end of the line, the bigger surprise is that it has been lasted so long. (b) It was born of the cold war, free of any ideology save anti-communism. (c) Its business was winning elections and dividing the spoils — and for decades it did that very efficiently. (d) But once communism had collapsed and economic growth had slowed down, the LDP had lost its purpose.

고난도
Actual Training
02

실제 TEPS 시험의 문항수와 동일하게 구성된 고난도 Actual Training을
제한 시간 25분 내에 모두 풀 수 있도록 노력해 보세요!

Part I

Questions 1-20
Choose the best answer for the blank.

1. A: Do you mind my opening the door?
   B: Well, it might get cold with the door _____.
   (a) being opened
   (b) opening
   (c) to open
   (d) open

2. A: Did you see the musical the Phantom of the Opera?
   B: No, but people say it is something _____.
   (a) not to overlook
   (b) not be overlooked
   (c) not overlooked
   (d) not overlooking

3. A: Didn't you forget _____ the door when you left?
   B: Oh, my gosh. I'd better get back home and make sure.
   (a) locking
   (b) to lock
   (c) being locked
   (d) to be locked

4. A: While I was out for a moment, were there any telephone calls for me?
   B: Not _____ I am aware of.
   (a) why
   (b) how
   (c) that
   (d) when

5. A: Is Elizabeth working overtime tonight too?
   B: Yes, she is. She _____ the longest week.
   (a) has
   (b) is
   (c) is being
   (d) has had

22

6. A: What is the0 prospect of the deer diet?
   B: Success in persuading the general public to accept deer as part of its diet hinges on _____ by the mass media.
   (a) how gives away information and recipes
   (b) how well information and recipes are given away
   (c) how information and recipes are given away well
   (d) how well information and recipes give away

7. A: Do you know the reason why John and Judy broke up?
   B: _____ me. I'm not intrigued.
   (a) Search
   (b) Searches
   (c) To search
   (d) Searching

8. A: I like your unique masks. How long have you been collecting them?
   B: Since I _____ a child.
   (a) have been
   (b) had been
   (c) were
   (d) was

9. A: You are supposed to take it easy until you _____ your health.
   B: It's easy for you to say in that you are single. In my case, I have a family to provide for.
   (a) will regain
   (b) will have regained
   (c) regain
   (d) gained

10. A: In case my infirm friend is unconscious after _____ down all of a sudden, what am I supposed to do?
   B: You'd better call 911 Emergency Service.
   (a) being fallen
   (b) fallen
   (c) falling
   (d) felling

11. A: Were you impressed with the Carpenter's performance yesterday?
   B: I was touched to tears lots of times! Everything they sang _____ fantastic.
   (a) to be
   (b) being
   (c) were
   (d) was

12. A: The water in the river _____ during the night.
   B: Don't you know the temperature dropped below zero?
   (a) freeze
   (b) froze
   (c) has frozen
   (d) had frozen

13. A: Do you think the government should continue subsidizing farmers?
   B: I don't mean to sound highly _____ to farmers, but we need to draw the line somewhere.
   (a) unsympathetically
   (b) unsympathy
   (c) unsympathize
   (d) unsympathetic

14. A: Is the attendance rate important?
   B: I guess it is. Those who frequently play hooky are less likely to get high marks _____ on a regular basis.
   (a) as those who is attending
   (b) than those are attended
   (c) than which are attended
   (d) than those who are attending

15. A: Are you insinuating that I am _____?
   B: No, I don't mean to offend you. It's a slip of tongue.
   (a) no cultured
   (b) not that cultured
   (c) none the culture
   (d) such that no culture

16. A: David is confident that he will win the race.
　　B: I'd be amazed if he _____, since the other participants are highly qualified.
　　　(a) wouldn't
　　　(b) could
　　　(c) will
　　　(d) didn't

17. A: _____ the surface of the sun, the temperature is so high that nothing can survive.
　　B: You said it.
　　　(a) Nearby
　　　(b) Nearly
　　　(c) Near
　　　(d) Nearest

18. A: What are you reading now?
　　B: It's about the story about the woodcutter. He _____ his axe to the tree, and began to chop.
　　　(a) lied
　　　(b) lain
　　　(c) lay
　　　(d) laid

19. A: What all of us wish to know about is job security. Are you going to lay workers off?
　　B: Not at all, let me make this _____.
　　　(a) clean
　　　(b) clearly
　　　(c) clear
　　　(d) clearness

20. A: How did your boss find a new employee?
　　B: He advertised _____ on the Internet.
　　　(a) one
　　　(b) to one
　　　(c) on one
　　　(d) for one

Part II

Questions 21-40
Choose the best answer for the blank.

21. It is crucial to remove _____ the way.
    (a) whatever hurdle lays along
    (b) whatever hurdles lie along
    (c) whatever hurdles are lain along
    (d) whatever hurdle is laid along

22. The newspaper is the source _____ the public derives its knowledge of the facts.
    (a) on which
    (b) by which
    (c) from which
    (d) to which

23. The manner _____ differs depending on who is present.
    (a) in which young people address
    (b) for which young people addressed
    (c) in which young people are addressed
    (d) with which young people are addressed

24. James is able to do in _____ could take his employees lots of hours or even days.
    (a) so short a time when
    (b) such a short time that
    (c) so short a time which
    (d) such a short time what

25. The university reopened a couple of years ago _____ for five years when it got caught for committing admission crimes.
    (a) after closing
    (b) be closed after
    (c) after being closed
    (d) to be closed after

26. The people who live in certain cities in Canada are _____ as English.
   (a) to speak as likely French
   (b) likely as to speak French
   (c) likely to speak as French
   (d) as likely to speak French

27. A desert is referred to as a region _____ an average of less than ten inches of rain falls in a year.
   (a) which had
   (b) in which is
   (c) in which
   (d) in that

28. The analyst was responsible _____.
   (a) for their false stock picks
   (b) as stock picks for their fault
   (c) for stock picks their fault
   (d) as their false stock picks

29. _____ by public opinion, the utmost care should be taken to preserve the purity of the public mind.
   (a) As we were entirely governed
   (b) We being governed entirely
   (c) Governing as we are entirely
   (d) Governed as we are entirely

30. After every presentation in this class will be an instant open discussion _____ comments and proposals.
   (a) all students can make for which
   (b) for which all students can make
   (c) can make during which all students
   (d) during which all students can make

31. The world is not all the time _____.
   (a) when we want it
   (b) what we want it to
   (c) what we want to be
   (d) what we want it to be

32. After years of dodging conviction and making the Government seem impotent, John _____ racketeering that includes murder.
   (a) stood convicted with
   (b) to standing convicted with
   (c) stands convicted of
   (d) standing convicted of

33. A few months ago _____ that U. S. forces stationed in the Middle East were releasing several thousand civilian Iraqis.
   (a) had the announcement been
   (b) the announcement was
   (c) it was the announcement
   (d) came the announcement

34. The great ox, _____, survives on Ellesmere Island.
   (a) once hunted almost to extinction
   (b) hunted once almost to extinction
   (c) almost once hunted to extinction
   (d) hunted almost once to extinction

35. One of the best vegetable protein substitutes is the soybean _____ used to make imitation meat products.
   (a) can be
   (b) it can
   (c) that can
   (d) which can be

36. I remember _____ frustrated at the time and as powerless as a very small fish in the sea.
   (a) to feel
   (b) feeling
   (c) being felt
   (d) to have felt

37. Back in the latter part of the 1960s, he wrote a report on smallpox vaccinations, saying that smallpox itself _____ in Europe since 1948.
   (a) has not seen
   (b) had not seen
   (c) had not been seen
   (d) has not been seen

38. _____, pioneers went on to areas still farther west, toward the Mississippi River.
   (a) On account of the years passed
   (b) For the years passed
   (c) The years passed
   (d) As years passed

39. The directors in the commission found the ill-prepared presentation _____.
   (a) chaos and confusion
   (b) chaotic and confused
   (c) to chaos and to confuse
   (d) chaotic and confusing

40. Only after food has been dried or canned _____.
   (a) that it could be stored for later use
   (b) could be stored for later use
   (c) could it be stored for later use
   (d) it could be stored for later use

Part III

Questions 41-45
Identify the option that contains an awkward expression or a grammatical error.

41. (a) A: If you don't mind, I'd like to see you one of these days.
   (b) B: How about the day after tomorrow?
   (c) A: Name the place and time, please.
   (d) B: What does Wednesday at six in front of my office sound?

42. (a) A: In your high school days, who did you have as your chemistry instructor?
   (b) B: Mr. Kim. His class was terrible. I hated it so much.
   (c) A: Oh, really? How come?
   (d) B: He was biased. He would punish the students indiscriminate for no reason.

43. (a) A: Good morning. May I help you?
   (b) B: This camera delivered to me today doesn't work. I'd like to get a refund.
   (c) A: I see. Would you give the receipt to me, please?
   (d) B: Certainly. Here are you.

44. (a) A: You look like a gifted person.
   (b) B: I'm flattered, but I've been awarded to numberless prizes for my English composition.
   (c) A: Oh, really? What is the secret to writing a good essay?
   (d) B: All you have to do is practice.

45. (a) A: Oh, no. I forgot to meet Bill at five. It's already half past five.
   (b) B: Who is Bill? Anyway, call him right now and tell him about this situation.
   (c) A: He's my business partner. The problem is that I lost his business card, so I don't know his phone number.
   (d) B: Then just look him up on the Yellow Pages.

Part IV

Questions 46-50
Identify the option that contains an awkward expression or a grammatical error.

46. (a) Spain, like many European countries, provides protection for those with permanent jobs. (b) It led some employers to expand the use of temporary jobs, which provide fewer benefits. (c) "Most of the job losses were recorded among workers on temporary jobs, many of them are youth," the study stated. (d) For young people, those still in school are excluded from the base.

47. (a) Everyone has a preferred method for treating a hangover that includes Gatorade, greasy food, a Bloody Mary. (b) In my experience, however, none of these work particularly well. (c) So when a bartender recently recommended that I tried coconut water as a morning-after remedy, I was skeptical. (d) However, since I'd been drinking everything else she'd put in front of me, I figured I'd give it a shot.

48. (a) To my surprise, the little juice box seemed to work. (b) I didn't like the sweet taste at first, but I felt noticeably better within an hour. (c) Coconut water, which it is extracted from fruit too young to have formed milk, is low in calories and has no fat and a lot less sugar than most juices. (d) But its most momentous attribute, at least among barflies, is that it is referred to as an excellent hydrator.

49. (a) The proposal takes after one developed through a similar partnership in New Haven. (b) It does away with the shoddy evaluation system which teachers are observed briefly in the classroom. (c) Even the most ineffective ones regularly receive glowing ratings. (d) The new system would require more intensive monitoring and would finally take student performance into account.

50. (a) You might think they would have learned their lesson by now. (b) At the end of 2005 Republicans in the House of Representatives passed a bill that cracked down on illegal immigration. (c) Instead, they did nothing to regularize the position of the 12 million or so people, mostly of Hispanic origin, who were living and working inside the United States without the proper papers. (d) Additionally, the congressmen create no mechanism for allowing people from Mexico and other southern neighbors to work with temporary permissions.

고난도
Actual Training
03

실제 TEPS 시험의 문항수와 동일하게 구성된 고난도 Actual Training을
제한 시간 25분 내에 모두 풀 수 있도록 노력해 보세요!

Part I

Questions 1-20
Choose the best answer for the blank.

1. A: I'm going to be taking a year off next year.
   B: Oh, really? _____ that.
   (a) I wished I will speak
   (b) I wish I could say
   (c) I wish I should have said
   (d) I wished I might speak

2. A: What are you waiting for?
   B: Michael _____ ring me at 2 o'clock in the afternoon. That was one hour ago.
   (a) is supposed to
   (b) has been supposed to
   (c) was supposed to
   (d) is supposing to

3. A: You know about Mr. Kim?
   B: I know. He's a cool guy. _____ the blame, the dissident leader asked leniency for his party officials involved in fishy dealings.
   (a) Stressed that he is willing to shoulder
   (b) Stressing his will to shoulder
   (c) To stress his willing to shoulder
   (d) Stress to his willing shouldered

4. A: I feel really restless because my grades for this semester will be announced tomorrow.
   B: Why _____ now? If you had done your best, the grades would not be bad.
   (a) worried
   (b) worry
   (c) concerns
   (d) concern

5. A: My father's car broke down again on the road. So he had it towed.
   B: Well, I suppose that it's high time he _____ a new automobile.
   (a) buy
   (b) buys
   (c) bought
   (d) had bought

34

6. A: I cannot remember my father hugging me in my childhood, _____ sit on his knee.
   B: If my memory serves me right, you were not alone.
   (a) neither will I
   (b) nor would I
   (c) neither did I
   (d) nor did I

7. A: How was your trip to Thailand? Was it fantastic?
   B: It was more intriguing than I believed it _____.
   (a) will be
   (b) would be
   (c) had been
   (d) had to be

8. A: What are the scientists studying?
   B: They are currently studying _____ exist.
   (a) the way which such rodents as hamsters
   (b) how rodents such as hamsters
   (c) in which such rodents as hamsters
   (d) to the way in which such rodents as hamsters

9. A: What is it about Dennis _____ so compelling?
   B: He's so cool.
   (a) what you find
   (b) that you find
   (c) who you find
   (d) who you finding

10. A: How far had Brian and Hutch gone _____ they ran out of gas?
   B: It was only a few miles.
   (a) while
   (b) when
   (c) long before
   (d) after

11. A: Do you believe that you'll pass the bar exam?

B: _____ my best, and I'll be an attorney some day.

    (a) Under no circumstance I will do

    (b) Under no circumstances will I do

    (c) Under any circumstances I will do

    (d) Under any circumstances should I do

12. A: Oh, my gosh. It's too late. I've got to be leaving now. I enjoyed it very much. Thank you for your invitation.

B: Nice _____ you today. See you later.

    (a) to meet

    (b) to have met

    (c) to meeting

    (d) having met

13. A: Is Amy also working on tomorrow?

B: If my memory serves me right, she has _____ off.

    (a) every other days

    (b) every another day

    (c) every other day

    (d) every once in a while

14. A: Didn't you used to believe that your job is cut out for you?

B: Yes, but as time goes by, I feel sick and tired of it. And I _____ commuting at the moment.

    (a) have hated

    (b) have been hating

    (c) am hating

    (d) hated

15. A: What a good smell! It smells like orange.

B: Yes, I just cut _____.

    (a) orange

    (b) the orange

    (c) many orange

    (d) an orange

16. A: Good evening, Mr. Park. My name is David Lynn.
   B: How do you do? Susan _____ a lot about you.
   (a) had said to me
   (b) has talked me
   (c) has told me
   (d) had spoken to me

17. A: Would you please explain to me what anarchism is?
   B: Anarchism is a term describing a group of doctrines _____ significant uniting feature is the belief that government is both inimical and noxious.
   (a) in that
   (b) since
   (c) whose
   (d) and

18. A: What did you do after the hurricane had passed through?
   B: The strong winds _____, we began to assess the damage.
   (a) being abated
   (b) abating
   (c) having abated
   (d) to abate

19. A: What are the results of the archaeological excavations?
   B: Excavations in several places on the east bank of the Euphrates River have disclosed an ancient community that _____ later reconstructions of the city of Babylon.
   (a) had laid beneath
   (b) had lay beneath
   (c) had been lying under
   (d) had been laying under

20. A: Boy, rumor _____ he will be fired for his scandal.
   B: Serves him right. He has not managed well.
   (a) has that
   (b) has it that
   (c) that has
   (d) that it has

Part II

Questions 21-40
Choose the best answer for the blank.

21. Mr. White, the former General and the incumbent Secretary of Defence, _____ embezzlement and fraud.
    (a) charged with
    (b) had been charged of
    (c) has been charged with
    (d) is being charging of

22. The more stress you are under, _____ develop cancer.
    (a) the likely you are more to
    (b) the more you likely are to
    (c) the more likely you are to
    (d) the likely more you are to

23. The ban-on-crude-oil-import policy would push petroleum prices in the country _____ the world level.
    (a) almost up to ten times
    (b) up to ten times almost
    (c) up to almost ten times
    (d) almost ten times up to

24. Of all the things edible, flour is the one _____ food for more people than any of the other grain crops in America.
    (a) it provides
    (b) that providing
    (c) provides
    (d) that provides

25. Much of _____ about the behavior of porpoises has come from observations made at Sea World in Florida.
    (a) which said
    (b) which is said
    (c) what said
    (d) what is said

26. Certain fish eggs include droplets of oil, _____ to float on the surface of the water.
   (a) allowing them
   (b) allows them
   (c) they are allowed
   (d) this allows them

27. No one knows exactly how big China's Internet police force is these days, although estimates run as high as 40,000. But _____, its sophistication is less than ever.
   (a) whatever its scale
   (b) however it's scale is
   (c) however its scale
   (d) whatever it's scale is

28. The sports complex was built just _____ from my office.
   (a) five mile away
   (b) five miles away
   (c) on five miles away
   (d) in five mile away

29. Elizabeth's grandfather, Henry Tudor, became King Henry VII of England in 1485. He _____ his son Henry VIII in 1509.
   (a) was succeeded in
   (b) was succeeded to
   (c) was succeeded by
   (d) succeeded to

30. It is not a religion _____ tenets almost everyone would think inordinate.
   (a) which
   (b) what
   (c) that
   (d) whose

31. Some children like to read _____ during their spare time.
   (a) that kinds of book
   (b) that kinds of book
   (c) that kind of book
   (d) those kind of books

32. _____ the off-shore drillers had located the oil field, they prepared its development.
   (a) Until
   (b) If
   (c) What
   (d) Once

33. The Consumer Price Index has been listing _____.
   (a) how much costs every car
   (b) how much does every car cost
   (c) how much every car costs
   (d) how much are every car cost

34. According to the research, _____ is essential for the development of robust bones and teeth.
   (a) the calcium
   (b) that calcium
   (c) calcium
   (d) though calcium

35. _____ people use social space reflects their social relationships and their ethnic identities.
   (a) The way in which
   (b) It is the way
   (c) Which is the way
   (d) Which way is

36. Congressmen eager to promote a piece of legislation no doubt _____ whenever their bill languishes in committee.
   (a) seeming to feel thwarted
   (b) seem to feel thwarted
   (c) seems to feel thwarting
   (d) seems to feel thwarted

37. Grounded on the assumption that light is made up of color, the post-impressionists came to the conclusion _____ not really black.
   (a) was shadows that
   (b) which was that shadows
   (c) that was shadows
   (d) that shadows were

38. Even though one of his ships ended up in succeeding in sailing all the way back to his motherland past the Cape of Good Hope, Magellan himself never completed the first circumnavigation of the globe, and _____.
   (a) nor did most of his crew too
   (b) neither most of his crew did
   (c) neither did most of his crew
   (d) nor most of his crew did also

39. If the cosmos is getting larger, in the past it _____ at the moment.
   (a) must be smaller than it is
   (b) should have been smaller than it is
   (c) must have been smaller than it is
   (d) would have been smaller than it is

40. _____ that gold was found around San Francisco and that the California Gold Rush began, making many people in the U.S. migrate to the West.
   (a) Since 1848
   (b) What in 1848
   (c) In 1848 that it was
   (d) It was in 1848

Part III Questions 41-45
Identify the option that contains an awkward expression or a grammatical error.

41. (a) A: Would you back up your car a little, please?
(b) B: I see. I'll do it at once.
(c) A: Look at who's here! Is that you, Edward?
(d) B: Yeah, it's me. It's been a long time since I saw you last.

42. (a) A: I was wondering what your nationality is.
(b) B: I'm from Colombia which is located in South America.
(c) A: What takes you to this country?
(d) B: I came here to study the Korean language.

43. (a) A: I'd like to have this prescription fill, please.
(b) B: I'll handle it right now.
(c) A: Could you also give me something for a pimple?
(d) B: Apply this ointment. It will work.

44. (a) A: Hello. Could you put me through to Howard?
(b) B: I'm sorry, but he is not in right now.
(c) A: Would you have him call me when he will get back?
(d) B: Does he have your phone number?

45. (a) A: Is anybody awaiting on you?
(b) B: No. I want a short-sleeved shirt in white, large size.
(c) A: I believe we don't have any in stock.
(d) B: Can you check and get me one next weekend?

Part IV Questions 46-50
Identify the option that contains an awkward expression or a grammatical error.

46. (a) Holding teachers responsible for student performance is now all the rage. (b) So, let's make a simple thought experiment in the sports world. (c) Imagine an amateur baseball league in which team owners dictate whose bats players use. (d) The owners seek to single out the utmost, but the research on bats is so poor, they might choose the worst.

47. A tree trunk shattering in the wind can sound very much like a lightning strike. (a) I braced for the worst when I heard that sound the other day while lying in bed at home. (b) My thought was the tree was about to crash down, pounding my garden into rubble but thankfully, that did not happen. (c) When I pulled back the shade, I found that the wind had wrenched off a massive branch and lowered it deftly into the neighbor's yard with no real property damage to speak. (d) A sharp-eyed tree surgeon would have pointed at it and have it condemned.

48. (a) According to statistics recently released by the Bureau of Statistics, people aged 65 or older now account for more than 20% of the population in each of 30 rural cities. (b) This is a fresh reminder of the rapid pace on which the nation's population is going gray. (c) The lowest fertility rate in the world makes the whole thing seem horrible. (d) But productive solutions are unlikely as long as we view this problem with horror.

49. (a) In one of the most heated general elections ever, the British Conservative Party won over the ruling Labor Party. (b) But the Conservatives failed to win a majority, forcing to form a coalition government. (c) As a result, it left British politics in flux for some time. (d) After the voting tally came out, leaders of political parties insisted on a major say in the formation of the next government.

50. (a) Probation is a device to deter future crimes in imposing penalties on crimes committed in the past. (b) But it was managed in the same way as other penalties. (c) So the Constitution Court find it unconstitutionally for raising the hazard of double jeopardy and excessive penalty. (d) I am not comfortable with the idea of reinstating probation.

고난도
Actual Training
04

실제 TEPS 시험의 문항수와 동일하게 구성된 고난도 Actual Training을
제한 시간 25분 내에 모두 풀 수 있도록 노력해 보세요!

Part I

Questions 1-20
Choose the best answer for the blank.

1. A: Is it possible for your dream to come true?
   B: Certainly, the time will surely come when my dream _____ true.
   (a) comes
   (b) will come
   (c) will have come
   (d) coming

2. A: I'm surprised to hear that the actor died of lung cancer.
   B: The doctor insisted that he _____. The actor ought to have followed his advice.
   (a) had not smoked
   (b) should not have smoked
   (c) not smoke
   (d) did not smoke

3. A: I was so angry that I took the boss by the collar.
   B: You went too far. _____ your shoes, I would not have done that.
   (a) I had been in
   (b) I should have been on
   (c) Had I been in
   (d) Were I with

4. A: Do you remember of our boarding school days?
   B: Sure. I wish we _____ to get to know one another better in the time we had.
   (a) will be able
   (b) would have been able
   (c) were able
   (d) had been able

5. A: What is the merit of Glacier National Park?
   B: Extensive forests, _____, abundant wildlife, and beautiful waterfalls are among the attractions of Glacier National Park.
   (a) it has spectacular mountain scenery
   (b) the mountain scenery is spectacular
   (c) spectacular mountain scenery
   (d) and the spectacular scenery of the mountains

46

6. A: Jason, what did you do yesterday?
   B: _____ snowy, I went out to make a snowman with my son.
   (a) Being
   (b) As being
   (c) It being
   (d) Having been

7. A: Bob, how's your lawsuit going?
   B: Since I have _____, I am confident that I will win the case.
   (a) many evidence
   (b) a number of evidences
   (c) much evidence
   (d) the number of evidence

8. A: Do you happen to know about the South Korean miners and nurses who were sent to West Germany in the 1960s?
   B: Of course. _____ their home substantial money back home, but they saved earnings as well.
   (a) Not merely were they remitting
   (b) Not only they were remitting
   (c) Not only did they remit
   (d) Not merely they remit

9. A: Will my dream come true?
   B: If you try your best, you can _____.
   (a) do who you want
   (b) be whoever you want to be
   (c) be anyone whoever you want to be
   (d) do anything whatever you want to

10. A: Do you help him?
   B: He is not poor, _____ need I help.
   (a) but
   (b) and
   (c) nor
   (d) neither

11. A: As I told you, I urge you _____ for your health.

B: Thank you for your advice, but that's easier said than done.

(a) to have worked out on a regular basis

(b) walking out on a regular basis

(c) to work out on a regular basis

(d) on a regular basis to walk out

12. A: How much do they cost?

B: I don't know how _____.

(a) much cost these shoes

(b) do these shoes cost

(c) does these shoes cost

(d) much these shoes cost

13. A: Elizabeth is naughty. It wouldn't be easy to deal with her at the party.

B: Don't forget. Elizabeth is going to be accompanied _____ seniors.

(a) with three other

(b) with other three

(c) by other three

(d) by three other

14. A: Are you going to the Art Center to see Rossini's opera?

B: No, the price of the tickets is _____ high for me.

(a) too far

(b) so much

(c) far too

(d) too much

15. A: _____ fantastic magician, Mike always works hard to create a new trick.

B: I agree, he is trying to be beyond man's ability.

(a) Which

(b) Because

(c) A

(d) Also

16. A: In this shop, _____ credit card?
   B: No, only cash is available.
   (a) has the item covered in
   (b) is the item covered with
   (c) is the item covered by
   (d) does the item cover to

17. A: What do you think about the renowned novel?
   B: The more I read, _____.
   (a) the better I got bored
   (b) the more I got boring
   (c) the worse boring I got
   (d) the more bored I got

18. A: How long will you stay at Jane's house?
   B: I will stay at her house for _____.
   (a) a few days more
   (b) three more days
   (c) more three days
   (d) more a few days

19. A: Do you by chance know the woman who is smiling?
   B: She is the new United States of America _____. She is going to address the audience.
   (a) the Ambassador in South Korea
   (b) the Ambassador at the South Korea
   (c) Ambassador on the South Korea
   (d) Ambassador to South Korea

20. A: Do you know how many people are starving around the world?
   B: Yes, I do. _____ ten million people in the world are in peril of starvation.
   (a) An estimated
   (b) The estimated
   (c) Estimated
   (d) Estimating

Part II

Questions 21-40
Choose the best answer for the blank.

21. Gerry Brown is considered by most art critics _____ greatest landscape painter in the United States of America.
    (a) to be
    (b) as he was the
    (c) that he was the
    (d) as the

22. As predicted by American historian Arthur Schlesinger, the 1980s were supposed to be followed by something _____: giving all for the cause.
    (a) close resembles its 1960s
    (b) closely resembled the 1960s
    (c) closely resembling the 1960s
    (d) close to resemble its 1960s

23. An ostrich's egg is such an efficient structure for protecting the embryo inside _____ not easy to break.
    (a) as is
    (b) that
    (c) and is
    (d) that it is

24. _____, Richard Johnson is also well renowned for his prolific biography of well known politicians.
    (a) A prominent American novelist
    (b) He is a prominent American novelist
    (c) A prominent American novelist who is
    (d) Despite a prominent American novelist

25. In contemporary politics it is as momentous to define _____ as it is to define what you are. This is especially true in a country as congenitally moderate as the U.S.
    (a) who you are not
    (b) who you are not
    (c) what you are nor
    (d) what you are not

26. So as to grow vegetables properly, farmers have to know _____.
   (a) what each vegetable requires
   (b) that each vegetable requires
   (c) whether each vegetable's requirements are
   (d) that is required by each vegetable

27. James was so altruistic in youth that he used to strip the very coat from his back and donate it to unwashed vagrants, along with _____ country home.
   (a) keys of its
   (b) keys on its
   (c) the keys in his
   (d) the keys to his

28. There was _____ of the burglar than the fingerprint on the gun.
   (a) no clearer evidence
   (b) no most clear evidence
   (c) no more clear evidences
   (d) not the clearest evidences

29. _____, concentrate on your test that was given by your instructor.
   (a) For being seated
   (b) When to seat
   (c) While seated
   (d) During seating

30. Five years after the September 11 attacks, books _____ of the shocking events are beginning to be published.
   (a) deepen greatly that our comprehension
   (b) deepening great our comprehension
   (c) that greatly deepens our comprehension
   (d) that greatly deepen our comprehension

31. Once America was the great exporter of trends — not just fads, like multiple earrings, but whole new life-styles _____ characteristic garments and substances of choice.
(a) involved
(b) involving
(c) involved in
(d) to involve

32. Delivery time from the sender to the receiver is _____ a few seconds, even from one country to another.
(a) no more than
(b) no fewer than
(c) as much as
(d) no less than

33. In the early 19th century one of the prestigious schools, the University of Michigan became the first state university _____ by a commission elected by the voters of the state.
(a) to have managed
(b) it was managed
(c) having managed
(d) to be managed

34. Nowadays there are about 5.3 million university graduates in India who are out of work, _____ behind by the increasingly strict demands of the tech-driven economy.
(a) leave
(b) be left
(c) having left
(d) having been left

35. The two capitalists made out that _____ they divorced themselves from communists, they became at risk of losing not just their souls but their political viability.
(a) if
(b) even though
(c) unless
(d) since

36. One of George Bernard Shaw's _____, Pygmalion, was related to the story that formed the rudiment for the musical 'My Fair Lady.'
(a) most famous work
(b) most famous works
(c) the most famous work
(d) the most famous works

37. _____ not fully supported by the local government in Liverpool county.
(a) Homeless are
(b) Homeless is
(c) The homeless are
(d) The homeless is

38. Art attempts to take something invisible, something spiritual, and _____: art shows people images of the people.
(a) making it possible
(b) make them possible
(c) make it visible
(d) take it visible

39. The first _____ during the last period of the dinosaurs' reign.
(a) flowers are plants appearing
(b) plants have flowers appeared
(c) plants flowers were appeared
(d) flowering plants appeared

40. _____ of his childhood home in Anchorage, Alaska, supplied the inspiration for one of his most popular novels.
(a) Remembering
(b) Memories
(c) It was the memories
(d) He remembered

Part III Questions 41-45
Identify the option that contains an awkward expression or a grammatical error.

41. (a) A: This office is getting too smaller for our growing business.
  (b) B: You're telling me. We need to consider moving somewhere.
  (c) A: Precisely, but what place do you have in mind?
  (d) B: Yeah, I've already talked to a real estate agent.

42. (a) A: I'm sorry for the loss of your employer. Does anybody know the reason why he killed himself?
  (b) B: In his suicide note he mentioned about too many blunders he had made in his life.
  (c) A: All of us make errors, but I suppose that we don't have to punish ourselves by resorting to extreme measures.
  (d) B: I see eye to eye. I wish he had made out that.

43. (a) A: Do you have the time to talk with me?
  (b) B: Yes, I do. Why do you want to have a talk?
  (c) A: I got two complimentary tickets.
  (d) B: Really? You made my day.

44. (a) A: I'm considering purchasing a vehicle.
  (b) B: How come? You are right down the street from your company.
  (c) A: Some day I may need one.
  (d) B: There seems no point on having a car if you don't actually need it.

45. (a) A: I'm too busy to do this. Could you help me with my assignments?
  (b) B: I will try to do as much as I can.
  (c) A: I am confident that you are adopt at everything.
  (d) B: Don't overestimate me.

Part IV Questions 46-50
Identify the option that contains an awkward expression or a grammatical error.

46. (a) Despite the often heated national debate, the majority of Americans are still in favor of the death penalty. (b) According to a recent study, approximately 65 percent of Americans still think that the death penalty looks appropriate for crimes such as first-degree murder. (c) More than 80 percent of Americans wanted the death penalty given to Timothy McVeigh. (d) It is the man killed hundreds in the Oklahoma City bombing.

47. (a) In the house of a well-to-do Italian, nine o'clock at night finds the larder as bare as though the place were uninhabited. (b) Provision is bought only in the exact quantity needed. (c) The refuse of the well-heeled man's kitchen is carefully stored by the cooks. (d) One of their main jobs is selling the leftover to dealers in "second-hand" food.

48. (a) It is nothing new that young people face difficulties finding jobs. (b) You don't have to look at jobless numbers to see how youth unemployment is widespread, because there are so many unemployed young people around us. (c) Official statistics show that youth unemployment is over 8%. (d) Some analysts put the number of people out of work at 4 million.

49. (a) Japan Inc. shrugged when Samsung Electronics surpassed Sony in operating profits for the first time in 2001. (b) But in retrospect, that was a prelude to what was later known as the Japanese disease. (c) Japan Airlines, Japan's national air carrier, which declared bankruptcy, still flies jets despite falling demand. (d) Sony finds it lagging behind Samsung and Apple more often than it would like.

50. (a) South Korea's recent nuclear plant deal with the United Arab Emirates is so astounding that few Japanese want to bring up the topic. (b) Not long ago, many Japanese thought Japan was leaving South Korea in the dust in high tech while the gap in general-purpose technologies has narrowed. (c) But now they think otherwise. (d) Japanese officials say that nuclear reactor by South Korea highly competitive both in price and technology.

고난도
Actual Training
05

실제 TEPS 시험의 문항수와 동일하게 구성된 고난도 Actual Training을
제한 시간 25분 내에 모두 풀 수 있도록 노력해 보세요!

Part I

Questions 1-20
Choose the best answer for the blank.

1. A: Do you think I need a diet?
   B: Well, _____ you are exercising every day, it is probably not necessary.
   (a) although
   (b) despite
   (c) supposed
   (d) providing

2. A: What's happening here?
   B: Don't disturb yourself. I _____ it under control.
   (a) had had
   (b) have
   (c) have been
   (d) am having

3. A: When did the criminal begin to open his mouth?
   B: Only after they got him a lawyer _____.
   (a) started to talk he
   (b) he started to talk
   (c) did he start to talk
   (d) he did start to talk

4. A: Should I wear the first jacket or the second?
   B: _____ feels more comfortable.
   (a) Whichever
   (b) That
   (c) Which
   (d) What

5. A: Did your boss acknowledge your new business suggestion?
   B: No, he _____ see it my way.
   (a) mightn't
   (b) shouldn't
   (c) mustn't
   (d) wouldn't

6. A: What do you think of Mr. Park as a doctor?
   B: He is _____ I've met.
   (a) as a competent doctor as
   (b) as competent a doctor as
   (c) most competent doctor that
   (d) a very competent doctor

7. A: The tickets to the World Cup have sold out. Will we never get to see the match now?
   B: No, I _____.
   (a) suppose we'll not so
   (b) don't suppose we will
   (c) suppose we will
   (d) don't think it not suppose

8. A: You look really into this project.
   B: Do you think so? Our department _____ the highest sales ever.
   (a) is devoted to recording
   (b) is devoted to record
   (c) is devoting to record
   (d) is devoting to be recorded

9. A: Why didn't you tell me you were going to watch a movie?
   B: I _____ you if you had been willing to pay attention to me.
   (a) had told
   (b) was telling
   (c) would have told
   (d) would have been told

10. A: Should I apply for the internship at Citibank?
    B: It _____.
    (a) will try not to cost you
    (b) will try to cost you not
    (c) won't cost to try you
    (d) won't cost you to try

11. A: Sunny, _____?

B: Barack Obama. I believe he is an eloquent speaker.

(a) you vote for whom

(b) for whom did you vote

(c) for whom you vote

(d) whom did you vote

12. A: Do you think you were right to dump her?

B: No, I _____ .

(a) shouldn't have never

(b) shouldn't

(c) shouldn't have

(d) shouldn't have been done

13. A: Have you ever experienced doing something you didn't want to?

B: Luckily no, _____ so upset.

(a) or would I be

(b) or I would be

(c) nor would I be

(d) nor I would be

14. A: Who left the door open?

B: Sorry, I _____ have left it open.

(a) will

(b) should

(c) need

(d) must

15. A: If you have any doubts on the veracity of this report, please contact me.

B: OK, but I'm certain _____ .

(a) of it

(b) that it is

(c) of that

(d) to have it

16. A: Did she decide to take the better position?
B: No, but I'd hoped _____.
(a) her to taking it
(b) she takes it
(c) her to take it
(d) that she would take it

17. A: Do you remember we _____ soccer after school?
B: Yes. I miss those days.
(a) are used to playing
(b) used to playing
(c) used to play
(d) are used to play

18. A: How was the party?
B: It was a disaster. _____, it rained all day.
(a) Which is more
(b) What is worse
(c) Which is worse
(d) That is more

19. A: What are you going to do if you win the Lotto?
B: I have never thought about it, but I _____ around the world.
(a) would travel
(b) would have traveled
(c) might travel
(d) might have traveled

20. A: Are you interested in buying this building?
B: I wish I had _____ more money in my bank account.
(a) a little
(b) a few
(c) few
(d) little

Part II

Questions 21-40
Choose the best answer for the blank.

21. In Israel, _____ of workers are women.
(a) a estimated 40 percents
(b) an estimated 40 percents
(c) a estimated 40 percent
(d) an estimated 40 percent

22. _____ aren't fond of peanuts since all of them have allergies to them.
(a) Jefferson family
(b) The Jefferson family
(c) The Jeffersons family
(d) Jeffersons families

23. He _____ a graduate of Seoul National University and worked for Samsung before coming to Nokia.
(a) was
(b) is
(c) has been
(d) had been

24. George is a best-performing salesman _____ Mercedes-Benz.
(a) for
(b) in
(c) at
(d) into

25. Once _____, the semiconductor chips are assembled in all sorts of electrical devices.
(a) to produce
(b) produced
(c) were produced
(d) they have produced

62

26. _____ fishing continues to threaten fish's survival significantly, their greatest virtual threat is habitat loss caused by water contamination.
   (a) Unless
   (b) Since
   (c) While
   (d) Because

27. It was Marilyn Monroe's sexiness, combined with her excellent acting performance, which made her _____ presence.
   (a) such renowned a on-screen
   (b) renowned such an on-screen
   (c) on-screen renowned such a
   (d) such a renowned on-screen

28. John can barely change the fluorescent light, _____ repair a chair.
   (a) yet
   (b) furthermore
   (c) much less
   (d) even so

29. _____ without passing the Highest Civil Service Examination.
   (a) Not a single judge can be appointed
   (b) Can a single judge not be appointed
   (c) A single judge can be appointed
   (d) No single judge cannot be appointed

30. Classifying people _____ similar consumer behavior may help marketing research companies to establish their strategies.
   (a) to
   (b) with
   (c) for
   (d) within

31. A number of _____ of the North and South poles have begun to minimize environmental pollution.
   (a) countries in the regions
   (b) countries in the region
   (c) country in the regions
   (d) country in the region

32. Calculus, _____ refined and mathematical symbolic system, can reduce complicated problems to simple terms.
   (a) it is a
   (b) that it is a
   (c) a
   (d) is a

33. Scarcely _____ his room when his girlfriend came into his room.
   (a) had he cleaned up
   (b) did he clean up
   (c) he did clean up
   (d) he had cleaned up

34. Ever since the 1930s, archaeologists have believed that the Tigris and Euphrates valley in ancient Mesopotamia (now Iraq) was the 'cradle of civilization,' _____ around 8000 B.C., people first settled in villages to cultivate wild grain and domesticate animals.
   (a) which
   (b) when
   (c) where
   (d) with which

35. The value of money was determined by the value of the material _____ it was made, such as silver and gold.
   (a) by which
   (b) of which
   (c) what
   (d) from which

36. The professor gave an assignment to students to write _____.
   (a) a paper of three pages
   (b) a three pages paper
   (c) a paper of three page
   (d) a three paper pages

37. In the 2nd half of the 18th century, Andrew Webster opened the Wilderness Trail and made _____ the first settlements in the rural countryside.
   (a) possibly it was
   (b) as possible
   (c) possible
   (d) it possible

38. _____ given a bonus to commemorate the 50th anniversary.
   (a) All personnels was
   (b) All personnels were
   (c) All personnel was
   (d) All personnel were

39. _____ is how international students can do so well in courses given in a foreign language.
   (a) That I find interesting
   (b) What I find interesting
   (c) Why I find interesting
   (d) What I find it interesting

40. _____ about the reason why he attempted to steal the money, the criminal answered he hasn't paid his rent for several months.
   (a) When inquired
   (b) When inquiring
   (c) Having inquired
   (d) Having inquiring

Part III

Questions 41-45
Identify the option that contains an awkward expression or a grammatical error.

41. (a) A: What do you think of the technical trainer?
(b) B: He's obviously very knowledgeable, but I don't think he knows how to communicate with us very well.
(c) A: Oh, really? How do you say that?
(d) B: I can't understand the jargons he uses.

42. (a) A: Did you meet her? How was it?
(b) B: It was really good. We had dinner and afterwards walked around the park.
(c) A: Really? You must be happy. You wanted to meet her for a long time.
(d) B: I guess I am a lucky man.

43. (a) A: What do you want for dinner tonight?
(b) B: I've been craving noodles.
(c) A: Noodles? Thai or Chinese?
(d) B: Both sounds good. Which do you prefer?

44. (a) A: I'm hungry now. When are we going to eat?
(b) B: Oh, I didn't know it was time to eat dinner. I reserved a restaurant.
(c) A: Really? What name is under the reservation?
(d) B: My father's name, James Park.

45. (a) A: Can you be a more careful driver?
(b) B: Well, I am trying to drive smoothly.
(c) A: Are you? I think you are making sudden stop at every traffic light.
(d) B: Sorry, I will be more cautious.

Part IV

Questions 46-50
Identify the option that contains an awkward expression or a grammatical error.

46. (a) Arabic ranks six in the world's league table of languages, with an estimated 186 million native speakers. (b) It belongs to the Semitic group of languages which also includes Hebrew and Amharic, the main language of Ethiopia. (c) There are many Arabic dialects. (d) Classical Arabic — the language of the Qur'an — was originally the dialect of Mecca which is now in Saudi Arabia.

47. (a) The third most popular buzzword, right after downsizing and outsourcing, is teamwork. (b) "Easy," you say, "I've been playing on teams for years." (c) You might be surprised, therefore, to find out that what it takes to win on the sports field might not be the same as what's required to field a winning team at work. (d) Take this quiz to see how suited you are to being an effective team member.

48. (a) Animal behavior can be explained how they act to preserve their genes in the population. (b) It can be used to explain why a lioness will nurse not only her own young, but the young of her close genetic relatives in the pride. (c) It can also be used to explain why a new dominant male lion will kill cubs in the pride that do not belong to him. (d) Killing the cubs causes the nursing females to come into heat faster, thereby giving the male lion an opportunity to get his genes into the population much faster.

49. (a) One traditional icon of St. Patrick's Day is the shamrock. (b) This stems from an Irish tale that tells how St. Patrick used the three-leafed shamrock to explain the Trinity. (c) He used it in his sermons to represent how the Father, the Son, and the Holy Spirit could all exist as separate element of the same entity. (d) Though originally a catholic holy day, St. Patrick's Day has evolved into more of a secular holiday.

50. (a) We have changed our name to Allstream Inc., from AT&T Canada, signaled our new status as a fully independent leading communication solutions. (b) The name, Allstream, embodies how we deliver leading communication solutions by demonstrating collaboration, responsiveness and flexiblity with all stakeholders. (c) Shortly, you will receive detailed information about our new brand and the benefits Allstream can bring to your business. (d) If you have any questions, please feel free to contact me anytime.

고난도
Actual Training
06

실제 TEPS 시험의 문항수와 동일하게 구성된 고난도 Actual Training을
제한 시간 25분 내에 모두 풀 수 있도록 노력해 보세요!

Part I

Questions 1-20
Choose the best answer for the blank.

1. A: What is the characteristics of the Roman conquest of the Greeks?
   B: The experts say that it is marked by _____.
   (a) Roman plunder of works on a massive scale of art
   (b) a massive scale of Roman art works on plunder
   (c) art works of Roman scale on a massive plunder
   (d) Roman plunder of art works on a massive scale

2. A: Why does he look so tender with her?
   B: Didn't you know? He _____ her last month.
   (a) married
   (b) got married with
   (c) married to
   (d) got married

3. A: Are you two relatives?
   B: Yes. Mom says he is _____ from me.
   (a) many times removed
   (b) many times moved me
   (c) removed many times
   (d) moved many times

4. A: What's the most famous tourist site in this country?
   B: _____ was built hundreds of years ago and it attracts so many tourists.
   (a) The Queen Castle of England's
   (b) The Queen of England's Castle
   (c) The Queen of England Castle's
   (d) The Queen Castle of England

5. A: I have recovered quickly from the injury _____ my mother has nursed me devotedly.
   B: That's good news.
   (a) in case
   (b) what if
   (c) unless
   (d) now that

6. A: Why didn't you confirm the meeting schedule to me?
   B: I _____. Check your voice mail.
   (a) do confirm
   (b) did confirm
   (c) confirm
   (d) had confirmed

7. A: Who _____ broke into the office?
   B: I have nothing to do with this incident.
   (a) was it
   (b) have done it that
   (c) did it that
   (d) was it that

8. A: Is it true Sam's new book has become a best seller?
   B: Yes, _____ that the publishing company has asked him to write a book again.
   (a) his book was so famous
   (b) famous was his book so
   (c) his book was famous so
   (d) so famous his book was

9. A: Why did they call him down for not coming?
   B: They believe he _____ met Jennifer, his talkative girlfriend; othewise, he should be here by now.
   (a) could have
   (b) must have
   (c) would have
   (d) should have

10. A: Can you break this $1 bill into smaller money?
   B: I am extremely sorry but I don't think I have _____.
   (a) the enough changes
   (b) enough change
   (c) an enough coin
   (d) enough coin

11. A: Let's finish playing hide and seek. It's time to go. Where are you?
   B: _____!
   (a) Here am I
   (b) Here I am
   (c) Here is me
   (d) Here me is

12. A: I am sorry to say, he only has a few days left.
   B: It might not have got to this stage, _____ diagnosed a little earlier.
   (a) if he were
   (b) if he has been
   (c) had he been
   (d) had he

13. A: How are your new part-time workers doing in their job?
   B: I am considering the possibility _____ the job myself.
   (a) doing
   (b) do
   (c) of doing
   (d) to do

14. A: How is the business going?
   B: Not so good. Actually, I don't see _____ any worse.
   (a) how anything could get
   (b) how something could get
   (c) something could get how
   (d) anything could get how

15. A: What's wrong with her?
   B: She _____ since she fought with her boyfriend.
   (a) had been upset ever
   (b) ever has been upset
   (c) was being upset ever
   (d) has been upset ever

16. A: Look, the sky over Korea, especially in autumn is very, very blue.
   B: _____.
   (a) So it is
   (b) It is so
   (c) So is it
   (d) Me, either

17. A: I like the jeans in this clothing store.
   B: _____ way too high.
   (a) These pairs of jeans values
   (b) This pair of jeans value
   (c) This pairs of jeans values
   (d) These pairs of jeans value

18. A: Is there _____ for me to fit in?
   B: Sure, I think you are the last one.
   (a) a space
   (b) the space
   (c) space
   (d) spaces

19. A: Beijing is trying to be _____ one of the cities to take charge.
   B: I think it must be.
   (a) chosen for
   (b) choosing
   (c) chose
   (d) chosen as

20. A: Maybe some kind of an electrical storm or something is coming?
   B: That _____. The sky's just as blue as anything.
   (a) doesn't seem likely
   (b) seems to be likely
   (c) seems like
   (d) is to seem likely

Part II
Questions 21-40
Choose the best answer for the blank.

21. _____, she curbed almost all of the unnecessary spending.
    (a) To satisfy making ends
    (b) Made ends meet
    (c) To make ends meet
    (d) Satisfying ends meet

22. Clark didn't register for the class, _____.
    (a) being afraid and worried taking a martial art class
    (b) being for fear to taking a martial art class and being worried
    (c) being fearful to taking a martial art class and tired
    (d) for he was afraid and worried to take a martial art class

23. Whether he accepts our offer or not is _____.
    (a) a matter of tasting
    (b) a matter of taste
    (c) a tasting matter of
    (d) a taste of matter

24. Today, we _____ the seriousness of air pollution.
    (a) are discussed
    (b) will discuss about
    (c) discussed about
    (d) will be discussing

25. During the first year that she and I were neighbors, our conversations turned frequently to two points of poetry: the power of exciting the sympathy of the reader by a faithful adherence to the truth of nature, and the power _____ of novelty through imagination.
    (a) to give the interest
    (b) of giving the interest
    (c) to give interest
    (d) of giving interest

26. Analysts said today's trading was typical of end-of-year trading, _____ did not indicate what is to come next year.
(a) and
(b) but
(c) furthermore
(d) that

27. They are debating what _____ the causes of air pollution.
(a) comprises
(b) is comprised of
(c) comprises of
(d) comprises in

28. The Internet _____ user rate in Korea, reaching eighty percent of the entire population according to the recent survey.
(a) have an incredible
(b) had an incredible
(c) has an incredible
(d) has incredible

29. The Monsoon Company _____ when the auditors released the results.
(a) closed
(b) be closed
(c) closing
(d) will close

30. Grameen believes that charity is not an answer to poverty _____ it creates dependency and takes away individual's initiative to break through the wall of poverty.
(a) and
(b) so
(c) since
(d) provided

31. _____ thousand Korean soldiers took part in the Vietnam war.
   (a) Several
   (b) Few
   (c) Every
   (d) Many

32. _____ of carbohydrates, at least three should be from whole grain foods.
   (a) Among six of the eleven daily servings
   (b) Of the six to eleven daily servings
   (c) Daily serving of six to eleven
   (d) With serving daily six of eleven

33. He was able to pay $1000 a month into an installment savings account when he was _____.
   (a) in the office
   (b) in office
   (c) in the bank
   (d) at bank

34. Technological improvements in the industry, combined with significant reductions in the expenses associated with transport, _____ to remove these commodities more efficiently and at a much lower cost, resulting in an extraction rate that many experts consider to be unsustainable.
   (a) has made possible
   (b) has made it possible
   (c) have made possible
   (d) have made it possible

35. The price has gone up higher _____ for much better service.
   (a) to pay
   (b) paying
   (c) paid
   (d) pay

36. In plenty of animals, _____ involves reflex action or involuntary response to stimuli.
   (a) almost the behavior
   (b) almost behavior
   (c) most behavior
   (d) the most behavior

37. Take _____ if you'd like to visit the downtown art gallery.
   (a) Ivy Lane bus
   (b) the Ivy Lane bus
   (c) some Ivy Lane bus
   (d) a Ivy Lane's bus

38. All of the activities that students do in the language study camp are _____ an assistant's supervision.
   (a) in
   (b) under
   (c) within
   (d) with

39. Make sure you _____ of the risks relating to this option.
   (a) are fully apprised
   (b) fully apprised yourself
   (c) fully apprising you
   (d) fully apprise you

40. After a crime case is reported, the police investigate the suspects and _____.
   (a) photograph and fingerprint them
   (b) photograph, fingerprint them
   (c) photograph and fingerprint themselves
   (d) photograph, fingerprint themselves

Part III Questions 41-45
Identify the option that contains an awkward expression or a grammatical error.

41. (a) A: May I ask who you were talking to?
(b) B: She's the professor for which class I couldn't attend during summer vacation.
(c) A: Why can't you attend the class?
(d) B: I am planning to do an internship.

42. (a) A: Do you need any help?
(b) B: It'd be grateful if you could move this box on second floor.
(c) A: Sure. Anything else?
(d) B: No, that's enough for now.

43. (a) A: Where are you going?
(b) B: I'm going out to meet my friends.
(c) A: I wouldn't go out if I were you since it's raining cats and dogs. When are you coming back home?
(d) B: It doesn't matter. I will be back until 8.

44. (a) A: You look so pale. What's wrong with you?
(b) B: You are, too, if you had eaten rotten food like me.
(c) A: That's a pity.
(d) B: I have to go see the doctor.

45. (a) A: How is your grade for this semester?
(b) B: It's not as good as I thought. I don't know that I've done wrong.
(c) A: I suggest you meet the professor and ask about your grade.
(d) B: I agree. I should go and see her.

Part IV
Questions 46-50
Identify the option that contains an awkward expression or a grammatical error.

46. (a) People perceived as the most likely to succeed might also be the most likely to crumble under pressure. (b) A new study finds that individuals with high working-memory capacity, which allows them to excel, do worse on simple exams. (c) The pressure causes verbal worries, like 'Oh no, I can't screw up.' (d) Negative thoughts take up space what would otherwise be pondering the task at hand.

47. (a) This is to confirm that Mark Stephens was employed by the City of Drisdale and served as a Building Inspector for 8 years. (b) During his tenure of employment, he displayed a unique ability to identify and solve problems. (c) He ensured that structures built in Drisdale were constructed in a manner which guaranteed they were safe to live and or work in. (d) Countless times, Mark had to perform his tasks despite physical strains.

48. (a) The Civil War between the states of north, where capitalism had developed on the basis of wage labor, or the southern states, where capitalism was based on the slave labor, became transformed into a revolutionary war. (b) It was thanks to this terrible war that the U.S. definitively won its national unity. (c) It also allowed the democratic and independent road of the development of capitalism to triumph over the oligarchic and dependent road. (d) Hence, the current United States exists.

49. (a) Easter is an annual festival observed throughout the Christian world. (b) The date for Easter shifts every year within the Gregorian Calendar. (c) The Gregorian Calendar is the standard international calendar for civil use. (d) In contrast, it regulates the ceremonial cycle of the Roman Catholic and Protestant churches.

50. (a) Cambridge University has announced that it will be introducing a scholarship program to encourage women in the engineering program. (b) $500,000 has been set out over the next five years to be awarded to first-year university women which show promise in engineering. (c) Cambridge hopes to re-balance the ratio of men and women in the program, from its current imbalance of eight to one. (d) Many women have shied away from pursuing an engineering degree due to the intimidation of a male-dominant field.

고난도
Actual Training
07

실제 TEPS 시험의 문항수와 동일하게 구성된 고난도 Actual Training을
제한 시간 25분 내에 모두 풀 수 있도록 노력해 보세요!

Part I

Questions 1-20
Choose the best answer for the blank.

1. A: Ken is always of good manner _____ anyone annoys him.
B: I know. He seems to be out of this world.
   (a) even though
   (b) as if
   (c) even
   (d) as

2. A: Do we have to go to Namsan as part of the tour schedule?
B: No, we don't _____, the guide said.
   (a) have
   (b) have to
   (c) have to go
   (d) have to go it

3. A: _____ of the new strategy.
B: Sure. It is a brilliant idea!
   (a) You seem to approve
   (b) It seems you to approve
   (c) You seem to be approving
   (d) It seems you are approving

4. A: Is she watching the movie with you?
B: I couldn't talk her _____ with me.
   (a) to go
   (b) of go
   (c) into going
   (d) that she go

5. A: Why are you so sad?
B: I have an assignment but I am _____.
   (a) behind two days
   (b) behind schedule two days
   (c) two days behind
   (d) two days behind schedule

6. A: _____ came to the party.
   B: You must have had a lot of fun.
   (a) Many a students
   (b) The many students
   (c) A great many students
   (d) Many a great students

7. A: When I watched the ceremony with the _____, I was too nervous.
   B: Me, too. I hardly remember the winner of the ceremony.
   (a) authority figure present
   (b) present authority figure
   (c) figure authority present
   (d) authority present figure

8. A: You don't need to prepare anything in advance since the registration process will _____ the program here.
   B: That's cool.
   (a) facilitated by
   (b) facilitate by
   (c) be facilitating by
   (d) be facilitated by

9. A: Finally, I succeeded in joining the company that I have always prayed for.
   B: _____.
   (a) That's a good news
   (b) That's good news
   (c) It's a good news
   (d) It's the good news

10. A: Why didn't you take part in the farewell dinner in the Ritz Carlton hotel?
   B: Because I had _____ to finish.
   (a) too much assignment
   (b) a lot of assignments
   (c) many assignment
   (d) a assignment

11. A: I don't want him _____.
   B: But he is always late to work and has embezzled the company's money.
   (a) to discharge
   (b) discharged
   (c) to be discharging
   (d) to been discharged

12. A: I took my parents to Thailand during the summer vacation.
   B: That _____.
   (a) must be nice
   (b) must having been nice
   (c) must have been nice
   (d) must have nice

13. A: Those convertibles look luxurious. Do you know _____?
   B: I heard that they are not as expensive as they look.
   (a) how much cost them
   (b) what do they cost
   (c) they cost how much
   (d) what they cost

14. A: How come _____ all the risk?
   B: That's because no one else will take it.
   (a) did you try to take
   (b) did you try taking
   (c) you tried to take
   (d) you tried taking

15. A: How are you doing these days?
   B: _____ better days.
   (a) I had had
   (b) I've had
   (c) I'd have
   (d) I had

16. A: Finally, we are here on schedule.
   B: What you did was very reckless. We _____ gotten into a car accident!
   (a) would
   (b) might have
   (c) should
   (d) must have

17. A: Why has he changed so much?
   B: I don't know. He is not _____.
   (a) what he was
   (b) who he used to
   (c) what he would be
   (d) what he is

18. A: Our player has been sent off.
   B: The team will have to operate _____.
   (a) a player shortly
   (b) a player short
   (c) a short player
   (d) a shortly player

19. A: When Henny stayed in Boston, he used to play _____ on weekends.
   B: Yes. We joined together.
   (a) baseball
   (b) a baseball
   (c) the baseball
   (d) baseball game

20. A: He told me he loved me, _____ was a pure fabrication.
   B: Really? That's a big surprise.
   (a) as
   (b) that
   (c) who
   (d) what

Part II

Questions 21-40
Choose the best answer for the blank.

21. _____ no one has any further inquiries, I would like to conclude today's session.
(a) Notwithstanding
(b) Considering
(c) On condition that
(d) Just in case

22. Nevertheless, critics of globalization claim that the beneficiaries of IT are _____ the developed nations and that the inhabitants of developing countries are deprived of the advances in IT.
(a) those living in
(b) ones living in
(c) those living
(d) ones living

23. Steven Jobs is currently the CEO of the company _____ he was once fired.
(a) which
(b) whatever
(c) by which
(d) of which

24. When people first meet a person, they must see him _____, and not judge by his appearance.
(a) as he is
(b) what he is
(c) from he is
(d) as is he

25. The rent fee for the apartment _____ by 10%, which forced the tenants to move out.
(a) was increased
(b) has increased
(c) had increased
(d) has been increased

86

26. The cars _____ delivered at the port today will arrive next week in Los Angeles.
   (a) have
   (b) just
   (c) were
   (d) itself

27. If someone asks me a question, I will answer him _____.
   (a) at some circumstances
   (b) under any circumstances
   (c) on certain circumstances
   (d) in no circumstances

28. _____ his death that he was acknowledged as a great poet.
   (a) Not until it was
   (b) That was not until
   (c) It was not until
   (d) Not until it were

29. Meet me _____ to see the musical which begins at 7 o'clock.
   (a) of Oxford Street
   (b) on the Oxford Street
   (c) along Oxford Street
   (d) on Oxford Street

30. The game was _____ moving in the Beijing Olympics I want to visit there.
   (a) so
   (b) such
   (c) that
   (d) very

31. Claimants _____ an estate are part of the wealthy class of the country.
(a) for
(b) by
(c) to
(d) towards

32. When spring comes after winter, flowers start to be _____ full blossom.
(a) in
(b) on
(c) to
(d) of

33. All things considered, fat is the most _____ nutrient you can consume.
(a) fill
(b) filled
(c) filling
(d) full

34. Twenty _____ in the city.
(a) percents of the people lives
(b) percents of the population live
(c) percent of the people lives
(d) percent of the population lives

35. City bank has 600 employees, among _____ Asians.
(a) that a fourth is
(b) whom a fourth are
(c) which a fourth is
(d) that a fourth are

36. Try to reach your ultimate goals, _____ much people try to discourage you.
   (a) however
   (b) notwithstanding
   (c) disregarding
   (d) no matter

37. _____ grow best in well-drained soils.
   (a) Most kinds of corns
   (b) Most kind of corns
   (c) Most kinds of corn
   (d) Most kind of corn

38. The referee warned the players _____.
   (a) against risky tackles
   (b) that risky tackles
   (c) on risky tackles
   (d) of tackles risky

39. A singer _____ the Billboard Chart will have no concerns about competing with other new singers.
   (a) atop spending 37 weeks
   (b) spending atop 37 weeks
   (c) spending 37 weeks atop
   (d) 37 weeks atop spending

40. We have to go up 50 meters _____ the ground to bungee jump.
   (a) on
   (b) above
   (c) off
   (d) to

Part III Questions 41-45
Identify the option that contains an awkward expression or a grammatical error.

41. (a) A: Did you know that the rate of suicide of young men is the highest in Korea among the OECD countries?
(b) B: Really? It is a striking fact.
(c) A: What do you think about it?
(d) B: It's a shame that such many people lose their lives when they are young.

42. (a) A: This dress is too small for me.
(b) B: Really? Where did you purchase it?
(c) A: At the department store.
(d) B: Do you have a receipt? You need it when you are getting a refund.

43. (a) A: For how long have you been living in this city?
(b) B: I was born here.
(c) A: How is the city? I'm planning to move to this city.
(d) B: I think you need to consider moving a little bit more since I want to get out of this bored city.

44. (a) A: How did you do on your test?
(b) B: It was so terrible that I don't want to think about it.
(c) A: Was it that bad?
(d) B: I was so upset and frustrated that I cried all night for a week.

45. (a) A: Do you overcome the hard times?
(b) B: No, not yet.
(c) A: I knew it. You look depressed.
(d) B: I think I might go see the psychotherapist.

Part IV

Questions 46-50
Identify the option that contains an awkward expression or a grammatical error.

46. (a) A heap of debris taken from quarry trash in Mexico has yielded a stone block inscribed with that researchers believe is the oldest writing ever found in the New World. (b) Researchers say the serpentine block dates back almost 3000 years and was created by people from the Olmec civilization. (c) Broken pieces of pottery and ground stone made the experts believe the block and its text date to the Lorenzo phase. (d) This period was 400 years earlier than any previous writing in the Western Hemisphere.

47. (a) When I'm interested in something, I might spend so much time immersed in it that I forget to eat or sleep! (b) The autistics share these characteristic with me, becoming obsessed with what the world might see as unimportant things. (c) When I am immersed in an obsession, it is absolutely wonderful. (d) Time seems to stop, and nothing bothers me while I'm pursuing my "obsession."

48. (a) The roots of a tree make it strong because they bring water and food from the soil to the tree. (b) The tree's roots help it stayed straight in wind and rain. (c) A human being's roots come from his or her culture. (d) One generation passes them on to the next.

49. (a) When you're ready for the closure that only a divorce can provide, we can give you a reliable and affordable alternative to high priced lawyer fees and mind-numbing do-it-yourself divorce kits. (b) Our experienced team of legal professionals has prepared thousands of divorce documents which have been accepted by courts across the country. (c) If you and your spouse cannot agree on the terms of the divorce, you need to consult a lawyer. (d) However, if you are among the 90% of Canadians who divorce is uncontested, our services are ideal.

50. (a) Why does the most sophisticated communications technology suffer the most primitive forms of advertising? (b) Internet banner ads are little more than billboards flashing at us with garish, distracting messages. (c) Pop-ups are like carnival callers trying to muscle you into their show. (d) One of the most unique benefits of the Web is that they give individuals tremendous autonomy and freedom.

고난도
Actual
Training
08

실제 TEPS 시험의 문항수와 동일하게 구성된 고난도 Actual Training을
제한 시간 25분 내에 모두 풀 수 있도록 노력해 보세요!

Part I

Questions 1-20
Choose the best answer for the blank.

1. A: I think these shoes are really pretty.
B: You can _____ if you want.
    (a) put on them
    (b) put it on
    (c) put on it
    (d) put them on

2. A: Do you think I have to confess that I like her?
B: I'd prefer _____.
    (a) it you did
    (b) if you didn't
    (c) it you didn't
    (d) it if you didn't

3. A: Do you want to drink some water or juice?
B: _____, thank you.
    (a) Either does well
    (b) Either will do
    (c) each one is good
    (d) each will be fine

4. A: Where is my key?
B: Is _____ you're looking for?
    (a) this on which
    (b) this which
    (c) this the thing which
    (d) which this

5. A: What am I supposed to do when my meeting is interrupted by an unexpected visitor?
B: Do not show displeasure. Just whisper to the person with whom you are talking, and _____.
    (a) left
    (b) leaving
    (c) leave
    (d) having left

6. A: I saved $1000 a month for 10 years and finally I bought _____.
B: Great! I really wanted to buy that cabin too.
    (a) a two-stories mountain cabin
    (b) a two-story mountain cabin
    (c) the two-stories mountain cabin
    (d) the two-story mountain cabin

7. A: How is your new girlfriend _____?
B: She is prettier and has a great body.
    (a) contrasted with your ex-girlfriend
    (b) contrasted with ex-girlfriend
    (c) contrasting with ex-girlfriend
    (d) contrasting with the ex-girlfriend

8. A: Where did I leave my bat?
B: _____ at home.
    (a) Yours are
    (b) Yours is
    (c) Your one is
    (d) Your ones are

9. A: I heard that he got a position at Samsung at the first half recruitment.
B: I take _____ that he can have many opportunities to succeed.
    (a) as promising job
    (b) it as a promising job
    (c) as promising a job
    (d) it a promising job

10. A: We had _____ we could have a party outside.
B: Really? I should have gone there.
    (a) a very good weather
    (b) very good weather
    (c) such a good weather
    (d) such good weather

11. A: Jerry, are you the one who glued Robert to his chair?
B: What do you mean? Under no circumstances _____!
  (a) will I do such mean thing
  (b) will I do such a mean thing
  (c) I will do such a mean thing
  (d) I will do such a means

12. A: Boss, there is _____ waiting in the room.
B: I will be there in a minute.
  (a) a Mr. Park
  (b) the Mr. Park
  (c) Mr. Park
  (d) the Mr. Park's

13. A: What are you _____ these days?
B: Nothing much, just helping out my father's business.
  (a) up to
  (b) up at
  (c) doing up
  (d) do

14. A: Should we do some more work or leave some work for tomorrow?
B: Let's call it a day, _____?
  (a) shall we
  (b) should we
  (c) will we
  (d) would we

15. A: What's the result of the meeting?
B: Dentists agree that brushing your teeth three times a day _____ and a more attractive smile.
  (a) promote good dental health
  (b) should promote good dental health
  (c) promotes good dental health
  (d) should promote dental good health

16. A: How is the class? There is a rumor that the professor is _____ picky.
   B: I think he is OK except for his tedious talk.
   (a) sort a
   (b) sorts of
   (c) sort of
   (d) a sort of

17. A: When is the plane for Seoul departing?
   B: It _____ 14:30 over the electronic display. Please refer to it.
   (a) is announced
   (b) says
   (c) said
   (d) announced

18. A: What's the situation on TV?
   B: While the farmers are trying to increase pesticide use, government _____ its use prevent natural disasters.
   (a) controls on
   (b) control for
   (c) control on
   (d) controls for

19. A: This is ridiculous. I have been waiting for the bus for over an hour.
   B: I heard a traffic accident _____.
   (a) took place in
   (b) have been taken place
   (c) to be taken place in
   (d) took place

20. A: About how many people are coming to the concert?
   B: _____ 10,000 people are lined up to enter the concert hall.
   (a) Approximate
   (b) An estimated
   (c) The estimating
   (d) Approximated

Part II

Questions 21-40
Choose the best answer for the blank.

21. The new decision will make North Korea to prepare for and _____ the shortage of food supplies.
(a) confront for
(b) confront
(c) confront to
(d) confront with

22. Theorists typically proposed some sort of sudden and violent catastrophic event, _____ a collision of the Sun with another stellar body or comet.
(a) while
(b) but
(c) so
(d) such as

23. Weather lore represented _____ a haphazard collection of proverbs derived from stories of personal experience.
(a) much more than
(b) little more than
(c) a little more than
(d) a few more than

24. _____ accumulate the vast volumes of data required to create an accurate picture of the weather, contemporary meteorologists employ a wide range of devices.
(a) In order to
(b) In pursuance of
(c) In contrary to
(d) In conclusion to

25. This is one _____ houses that they are selling off.
(a) of them
(b) of those
(c) of this
(d) of their

26. The criminal must have broken into our house by the window, _____, how else would he get in?
   (a) if not
   (b) if he were not
   (c) if he's not
   (d) were it not

27. All members are compelled _____ the rules of the conclave.
   (a) to conform
   (b) to conform to
   (c) conforming
   (d) to conforming to

28. _____ of the accuracy of computer models with respect to the state of the atmosphere, they would be of limited value without some means to estimate future weather patterns based on the information.
   (a) Regardless
   (b) Although
   (c) In spite
   (d) Nonetheless

29. Few vitamins and minerals are absorbed so fluently in our body _____ are those made in natural foods.
   (a) that
   (b) as
   (c) which
   (d) than

30. Our company would like to confirm our decision _____ the catering service from your company.
   (a) in purchasing
   (b) for purchasing
   (c) to purchase
   (d) purchasing

31. The critics suggested many opinions, _____ is often the case.
   (a) what
   (b) that
   (c) who
   (d) as

32. The Pope _____ in the meeting on New Year's day.
   (a) wished well everyone
   (b) wished everyone well
   (c) everyone well wished
   (d) well wished everyone

33. Neither these gold rings nor this pearl necklace _____ with my crown.
   (a) goes
   (b) go
   (c) becomes
   (d) become

34. Ben and Jenny, _____ much younger than Michael, were not allowed to see the performance with him.
   (a) who
   (b) are
   (c) both
   (d) whose

35. The very book I wanted to read being at a loss to break through the struggle _____ "The Gulliver's travels."
   (a) is
   (b) are
   (c) were
   (d) was

36. I was too sad of my friend's death to do _____ as playing golf leisurely.
   (a) any such a thing
   (b) any such thing
   (c) such any a thing
   (d) such any thing

37. The manager suggests _____ or we might be moved away.
   (a) us that we get rid of bad customs
   (b) that we get rid of bad customs
   (c) us to get rid of bad customs
   (d) that we might get rid of bad customs

38. The salary raise in the motor company was $8,000 per year, _____.
   (a) double the payment of last year
   (b) the payment double of last year
   (c) the double payment of last year
   (d) the last year double payment

39. Tom, a twelve year old boy, invented a godget _____ can bring rain when activated. Actually, it was just a piece of junk metal.
   (a) who he said
   (b) when he said
   (c) which he said
   (d) he said it which

40. _____ today did I realize she had a boyfriend, so that made me stop chasing her.
   (a) Hardly
   (b) However
   (c) Notwithstanding
   (d) Not until

Part III

Questions 41-45
Identify the option that contains an awkward expression or a grammatical error.

41. (a) A: What happened last night? Did you fail the breathalyzer test?
(b) B: Unfortunately yes.
(c) A: How you are going to tell your father about it?
(d) B: I don't know. I might not tell anyone and solve the problem.

42. (a) A: The doctor told me to lose weight to stop to snore.
(b) B: I need a diet, too.
(c) A: What are you going to do?
(d) B: First of all, I might reduce the amount of food I ingest everyday.

43. (a) A: Are you going somewhere?
(b) B: Yeah, I decided to move to a new studio apartment.
(c) A: Is the studio apartment equipped with all the household goods?
(d) B: No, not yet. I need to buy some furnitures.

44. (a) A: Excuse me. You need to show me your identification to see this movie.
(b) B: What is that necessary?
(c) A: Since this movie is an X rated movie, people under the age of 18 are not allowed to watch it.
(d) B: I guess I should choose another one.

45. (a) A: Did you choose your food?
(b) B: Not yet. What would you recommend?
(c) A: We specialize in steaks.
(d) B: Then, I would like my steak rarely to cook.

Part IV

Questions 46-50
Identify the option that contains an awkward expression or a grammatical error.

46. (a) "I would describe it as a reinvention and a move away from the work I've done in the past," says Hilary Duff, in a description of her newest album. (b) Just a child herself, at 19, Duff hardly seems capable of 'reinvention.' (c) However, given her remarkable fame and constant media attention, anything from dyeing her hair to a slight wardrobe change warrants some degree of Hollywood news coverage. (d) For someone so young with so much media hype, Duff appears surprisingly ground and modest about her music.

47. (a) PD Ports wants to build a new deep-sea container terminal on Teesside that would bring goods directly to the North from the Far East. (b) If that happens, it can reduce road congestion in the South and revitalize the economy of the Tees Valley. (c) But Felixstowe, Harwich, and Thamesport, have already submitted applications to the government, which said it was ready to approve Thamesport and would make a decision about the others soon. (d) If all three are approved, Teesport's plans become unviable because of the port capacity shortage in the UK will have been met.

48. (a) The microclimate is the variations in localized climate around a building and a building's microclimate is affected by its orientation, the location of neighboring objects, and the surrounding landscape. (b) It has a very important impact on both the energy and environmental performance of a building. (c) The microclimate can also determine the shape of the building and it sits on the site. (d) For an ideal site, you would want to maximize solar access to the south facade as solar energy is greatest and most intense from the south.

49. (a) Teachers need the ability to understand a subject well enough to convey its essence to a new generation of students. (b) The goal is to establish a sound knowledge base on which students will be able to build as they are exposed to different life experiences. (c) The passing of knowledge from generation to generation allows students to grow into useful members of society. (d) Good teachers are able to translate informations, good judgments, experiences, and wisdoms into a significant knowledge of a subject that is understood and retained by the student.

50. (a) When Sam Walton founded Wal-Mart more than 40 years ago, his stores were chaotic, with goods piled high on tables and the company's success rested on "Mr. Sam's" formula of scouring the marketplace for the best prices and keeping a relentless rein on expenses. (b) The stores charged unparalleled low prices and crowds flocked to them. (c) But the retailer, recognizing the importance of efficient systems, also led a technology revolution, installing computerized ordering and distribution that others quickly imitated. (d) Little would have imagined that Wal-Mart would become such a controversial issue as it has become today.

고난도
Actual Training
09

실제 TEPS 시험의 문항수와 동일하게 구성된 고난도 Actual Training을
제한 시간 25분 내에 모두 풀 수 있도록 노력해 보세요!

Part I

Questions 1-20
Choose the best answer for the blank.

1. A: How is the party?
   B: _____ be better.
   - (a) Couldn't
   - (b) Shouldn't
   - (c) Mustn't
   - (d) Wouldn't

2. A: Oh, my gosh! My purse _____ gone!
   B: Don't you remember where you last left it?
   - (a) was
   - (b) be
   - (c) had
   - (d) has

3. A: Why did you go home so early last night from the party?
   B: I had to finish my assignment but I returned home _____.
   - (a) drunk
   - (b) drunken
   - (c) being drunken
   - (d) to be drunken

4. A: I'm disappointed with the new representative _____ in my constituency.
   B: Tell me about it.
   - (a) to have elected
   - (b) electing
   - (c) elected
   - (d) to be elected

5. A: Mmm. The food _____ delicious!
   B: Don't you dare touch it before your sister comes home.
   - (a) is smelling
   - (b) smells
   - (c) smelling
   - (d) has smelled

6. A: What's the matter with your car?
   B: I don't know _____ it — all I remember is parking it in front of my house.
   (a) what has happened to
   (b) whether it has happened to
   (c) whatever has happened
   (d) what it had happened

7. A: What is the assignment for today's class?
   B: You need to write _____ by this Friday.
   (a) paper
   (b) lost of paper
   (c) any paper
   (d) some papers

8. A: I really don't like this kind of weather. It's so humid!
   B: You _____ as well get used to it since we are going to be staying here for another year.
   (a) should
   (b) could
   (c) might
   (d) need

9. A: Do you have any idea where we are?
   B: _____ me. I have never been here before.
   (a) Beating
   (b) Beats
   (c) Beat
   (d) Beaten

10. A: How _____ more pairs of shoes are necessary?
   B: A hundred would be enough.
   (a) many
   (b) a large number of
   (c) by far
   (d) a plethora of

11. A: I got free tickets to the baseball game tonight! Do you want to join us?
　　　B: Thanks, but I'd rather stay home _____.
　　　　(a) than going out
　　　　(b) than go out
　　　　(c) than to go out
　　　　(d) than to going out

12. A: What's the earliest and most primitive link in mythology?
　　　B: It was surely that of hunter and prey with _____ the fatal role of victim.
　　　　(a) humans possibly playing
　　　　(b) playing possibly humans
　　　　(c) possibly humans playing
　　　　(d) possibly playing humans

13. A: I heard that you were sick for a week! Have you gotten _____ better?
　　　B: I'm fine now.
　　　　(a) lots
　　　　(b) very
　　　　(c) some
　　　　(d) any

14. A: What did they serve for the official dinner?
　　　B: The authorities prepared _____ for us.
　　　　(a) authentic Chinese food
　　　　(b) Chinese authentic food
　　　　(c) authentically Chinese food
　　　　(d) Chinese authentical food

15. A: How do you think of him or his company?
　　　B: He is expected to get a good deal of income, if not _____.
　　　　(a) many as again
　　　　(b) as many again
　　　　(c) again as many
　　　　(d) as again many

16. A: Why are you busy working even on weekends?
B: I need _____ more money for traveling eastern Europe during this summer vacation.
(a) some
(b) any
(c) a few
(d) a lot of

17. A: How could you find these nice cooks?
B: Once I decided to, I advertised for _____ in the classified news.
(a) ones
(b) them
(c) they
(d) those

18. A: I knew he couldn't pay back the debt he got for using a credit card.
B: You're right. _____ he couldn't reimburse the money.
(a) No denying is that
(b) It is not to deny that
(c) Not to deny there that
(d) There is no denying that

19. A: What's the lesson of this story?
B: _____ well-established system can collapse.
(a) Even more
(b) Even the most
(c) The most even
(d) More even

20. A: What should I do if I can't carry the luggage?
B: You can ask me for help at _____ times.
(a) all
(b) much
(c) some
(d) any

Part II

Questions 21-40
Choose the best answer for the blank.

21. Hyundai Motors announced in the press conference that its car _____ first in 1975.
    (a) has manufactured
    (b) had been manufactured
    (c) has been manufactured
    (d) was manufactured

22. The professor provided me with a lot of tips for my paper, _____ was quite unnecessary.
    (a) many of which
    (b) many of them
    (c) much of which
    (d) much of what

23. Please pay attention to the presentation given, _____ will be of interest to you.
    (a) for which I'm confident
    (b) what I'm confident
    (c) which I'm confident
    (d) that I'm confident of

24. Animals which _____ to produce a lot of offspring show a tendency to breed early.
    (a) have been evolved
    (b) have evolved
    (c) evolved
    (d) evolves

25. _____ continue to pollute the ocean with all forms of contamination such as plastic containers remains a mystery to environmentalists.
    (a) People that
    (b) Why people
    (c) Those people that
    (d) Although people

26. In the past, it was considered adequate for a building _____ during an earthquake, now insurance companies and even clients are demanding buildings that will be able to maintain their structural integrity through an earthquake and remain sound after the earthquake.
   (a) not to collapse
   (b) not to be collapsed
   (c) to not collapse
   (d) to not be collapsed

27. The theory of Adam Smith is that, _____ intact by government, competition in the market will bring benefits to the greatest number of people.
   (a) were left
   (b) if left
   (c) if that's left
   (d) it is left

28. When I went to the lost and found, the assistant asked me _____ I had when I checked in at Incheon Airport.
   (a) how many baggages
   (b) how much baggage
   (c) how many bags of baggages
   (d) how many pieces of baggages

29. The second crusade, _____ enough, was defeated severely.
   (a) not prepared to fight
   (b) preparing not to fight
   (c) prepared not to fight
   (d) would prepare to fight

30. _____ she didn't like to play the piano for her children.
   (a) Not that
   (b) No that
   (c) Not because
   (d) No because

31. _____, the Russian chemist Dmitri Mendeleev also used a tabular method to group all known elements (sixty-five at the time) into vertical columns based on their chemical properties in the order of ascending atomic weights.
(a) Worked contemporaneously
(b) Worked contemporaneous
(c) Working contemporaneous
(d) Working contemporaneously

32. _____ scientist, Einstein, discovered the neutron in the nucleus of an atom, which was actually the beginning of nuclear physics.
(a) There is
(b) It is
(c) The
(d) It is the

33. The researchers found _____ counterfeited.
(a) surprising facts to be
(b) surprising facts being
(c) it surprising facts to be
(d) it surprising facts being

34. We should stop clearing wilderness land for construction, _____ the deer population keeps decreasing.
(a) otherwise
(b) even if
(c) supposing
(d) however

35. By and large, the first half of our youth _____ studying, and the other half by constantly working.
(a) are spent
(b) were spent
(c) become spent
(d) is spent

36. _____ are the indigenous people of Australia.
   (a) The Aborigines
   (b) The Aborigine
   (c) An Aborigine
   (d) Aborigine

37. The labor union argued that the recent deaths of the workers _____ if the previous recommendations by the union had been accepted by the company.
   (a) might be averted
   (b) should be averted
   (c) could have been averted
   (d) should have been averted

38. Pope Peter said, "I will not accept any forceful method _____."
   (a) anything
   (b) no matter what
   (c) what matter is
   (d) however

39. I can swim quite a long distance, _____.
   (a) but neither can John
   (b) and so John can
   (c) but John can't
   (d) or so John may

40. The new production line, starting last year, proved to be a little less profitable than we wished it _____.
   (a) would be
   (b) should be
   (c) would have been
   (d) should have been

Part III

Questions 41-45

Identify the option that contains an awkward expression or a grammatical error.

41. (a) A: I have a very important meeting tomorrow at 8 o'clock in the morning.
(b) B: Wow. You must get up early.
(c) A: Of course. Can you give me wake-up call at six tomorrow morning?
(d) B: Sure, I will arrange that for you.

42. (a) A: I think it is a terrific idea to design a T-shirt to promote good teamwork.
(b) B: I will create the design then.
(c) A: OK. Should we have anything special written it on?
(d) B: No, just a good picture would be fine.

43. (a) A: We need to do a great deal of things to get a job.
(b) B: I agree. Where should we start from?
(c) A: What do you say about signing up for a foreign language institute?
(d) B: OK. Let's get moving.

44. (a) A: Where did you learn to speak English so well?
(b) B: I just studied myself while watch CNN.
(c) A: You must have tried very hard.
(d) B: Not really. I can just have a basic everyday conversation in English.

45. (a) A: Can we get a non-smoking table?
(b) B: I'm sorry. It's full right now.
(c) A: Then we will wait because neither of us smoke.
(d) B: OK. I will get you a seat as soon as possible.

Part IV

Questions 46-50
Identify the option that contains an awkward expression or a grammatical error.

46. (a) The course of American history was drastically changed by the Vietnam War. (b) The American policies on foreign affairs, domestic policies and cultural and social history were greatly changed by this event. (c) The Vietnam War was a military attempt by the US to halt Communist aggression in Southeast Asia. (d) In January 23, 1973 the US and the North Vietnamese agreed to cease-fire arrangements.

47. (a) The peasant is the class of character most commonly represented smoking. (b) There are countless examples of low-life smokers in Dutch 17th-century art. (c) Tobacco, with its mind-dulling narcotic capacities, was ideally suited to such representations. (d) His character ranged from naive, earthy simpleton to diligent worker to aggressive brute.

48. (a) We've noticed that your contact information has changed. (b) When you read this email, please let us to know your new address and telephone number as soon as possible. (c) You can do this by visiting our Web site, by calling our toll-free phone number or by writing. (d) If you write to us, please be sure to sign the letter and include your social insurance number.

49. (a) A new study shows mechanical heart pumps designed for adults may be used in children whose bodies are large enough to accomodate the devices. (b) The ventricular assist devices maintain heart function in critically ill patients while they are waiting for a heart transplant. (c) Researchers examined the cases of 99 children who received a mechanical heart pump between January 1993 and December 2003 and their prognoses were very promised. (d) Seventy-eight percent of the cases successfully adapted to the transplanted organ.

50. (a) As for women, one shouldn't drive alone at night and always try to avoid areas where there are few people. (b) Buddy's creator, Sheilas' Wheels, launched the blow-up man for the purpose of women making feel less nervous about driving at night. (c) Women who don't like driving alone at night can purchase a blow-up to place in the passenger seat. (d) When they are finished with the "Buddy on Demand," they can deflate it by flicking a switch and the "passenger" is even small enough to fit in the car's glove box.

고난도
Actual Training
10

실제 TEPS 시험의 문항수와 동일하게 구성된 고난도 Actual Training을
제한 시간 25분 내에 모두 풀 수 있도록 노력해 보세요!

Part I

Questions 1-20
Choose the best answer for the blank.

1. A: Bill, don't forget you lend me a chemistry book.
   B: I don't have it _____ at school.
   (a) as I miss the book
   (b) missed the book
   (c) as I missed the book
   (d) cause I had missed the book

2. A: How did you do on your presentation?
   B: It was close. I couldn't get the computer _____ at first.
   (a) to work
   (b) working
   (c) to working
   (d) work

3. A: Pass me that salt, _____?
   B: There's another one beside you.
   (a) won't you
   (b) can't you
   (c) will you
   (d) couldn't you

4. A: A drug addict was killed.
   B: Where is the dead body of the _____ guy?
   (a) murder
   (b) murdered
   (c) murdering
   (d) murderer

5. A: Excuse me, but do you _____ a ten dollar bill?
   B: I'm sorry. We don't have any cash at the moment.
   (a) have enough changes break
   (b) have enough change to break
   (c) have enough a change break
   (d) have change enough breaking

6. A: What are you planning to do after graduation?
   B: Well, when I _____ under-graduate school, I plan to study more.
   (a) will graduate
   (b) will have graduated
   (c) graduate
   (d) have graduated from

7. A: Which school _____ ?
   B: Actually, I work now.
   (a) have you been in
   (b) have you attended
   (c) did you go to
   (d) do you go to

8. A: Any news on the next conference?
   B: I heard that the conference _____ next year.
   (a) is held
   (b) is to be held
   (c) is to be hold
   (d) holds

9. A: Will you join us today at the baseball park?
   B: No, I can't. I have an appointment with John _____ we can go to the fish market.
   (a) so that
   (b) unless
   (c) if only
   (d) even if

10. A: How long has it been since _____ your science textbook?
   B: Over a year.
   (a) had you last opened
   (b) you last opened
   (c) you have last opened
   (d) last you open

11. A: Mike, what's going on with your teammates nowadays?
B: Never worry. I _____ control.
   (a) have it under
   (b) am having them under
   (c) have been them over
   (d) had had it over

12. A: How many candles do I have to light up?
B: I _____ 10.
   (a) believe she has just reached
   (b) just believe she reached to
   (c) just believe she has reached
   (d) believe she has reached to just

13. A: The inauguration speech was fantastic, don't you think?
B: Yes, especially the part where the president emphasized how the strengthening elementary education policy is crucial if no child _____.
   (a) is left out
   (b) is to be left out
   (c) is to left out
   (d) lefts out

14. A: What, _____, solutions do you have for this matter?
B: I will have one as soon as possible.
   (a) if ever
   (b) nonetheless
   (c) if any
   (d) nevertheless

15. A: John and I had a big fight yesterday.
B: Again! Are you guys at the point where you are too upset with each other _____ have a normal conversation?
   (a) that you can
   (b) that we can
   (c) to be able to
   (d) unable to

16. A: What did you do when the monitor blacked out?
B: _____ no time, I wrote down what was coming out of the speakers.
(a) There being
(b) Being
(c) Having been
(d) As there is

17. A: I really appreciate _____ the time to explain everything to me.
B: Anytime.
(a) you will take
(b) your taking
(c) you taken
(d) you being taken

18. A: What do you have to do in the afternoon?
B: I must peruse _____ as the first assignment of the class.
(a) chapter one
(b) first chapter
(c) chapter first
(d) the chapter one

19. A: What happened? You are so early and you don't look good.
B: I _____ everyone at the prom because of a silly action that I did.
(a) laughed at
(b) was laughed at
(c) was laughed by
(d) was laughed at by

20. A: There is a rumor that you are being dispatched to Vietnam?
B: Are you sure? I thought you _____ as a suitable person.
(a) consider
(b) considered
(c) were considering
(d) were being considered

Part II   **Questions 21-40**
Choose the best answer for the blank.

21. I studied as hard as I could everyday _____ fail.
(a) in order not to
(b) in order to not
(c) in not order to
(d) not in order to

22. When I entered his study, I _____ in the breeze over the window.
(a) have been seeing swayed
(b) saw a beech tree sway
(c) have seen a beech tree swayed
(d) was seeing a beech tree have been swayed

23. You haven't been sleeping for days. You should get some sleep _____ much reading you have to do.
(a) no matter
(b) despite
(c) however
(d) regardless

24. One reason that the coach was fired was he said beforehand that even a _____ against Brazil would be tough.
(a) draw
(b) drawing
(c) drawal
(d) drawer

25. Surprisingly, although most age groups are known to be influenced by the new H1N1 virus, _____ affected.
(a) the aged is least
(b) the aged are least
(c) least the aged is
(d) least the aged are

122

26. After he passed his bar examination, his credit was _____ as before.
   (a) twice
   (b) more than twice
   (c) twice as much
   (d) twice more

27. The demonstration against war was supported by _____ from all over the world.
   (a) a million people
   (b) millions people
   (c) a million peoples
   (d) millions of peoples

28. She has studied English since she was ten years old, and _____ of English.
   (a) it seem she is a now good speaker
   (b) now it seems she is a good speaker
   (c) now she is a good she seems speaker
   (d) it is a good she seems speaker now

29. We just have to leave grandma's coat beside the door, and she _____.
   (a) dresses
   (b) dresses herself
   (c) gets dressed herself
   (d) dresses her

30. When I traveled around the world, _____ to go with me, I had to go alone.
   (a) as there being no one
   (b) there being no one
   (c) as is no one there
   (d) there is no one as

31. Stella sometimes tells you stories some would rather you _____ about.
  (a) don't know
  (b) didn't know
  (c) hadn't known
  (d) haven't known

32. _____ the MOSFET and its characteristics according to the studies in the conference?
  (a) What is
  (b) What are
  (c) How come
  (d) How about is

33. It is important to work hard in your job; it is _____ to take care of your family.
  (a) equally as importance
  (b) equally to importance
  (c) equally importance
  (d) equally of importance

34. He still works in the company as an understrapper _____ he always wanted to quit.
  (a) which used to say that
  (b) that he used to say that
  (c) what he used to say
  (d) he say used to

35. My mother objected _____ at my house.
  (a) to my friends sleeping over
  (b) to my friends to sleep over
  (c) my friends sleeping over
  (d) my friends to sleep over

36. _____ last night's terrible fire was started by a notorious arsonist.
 (a) It is believed that
 (b) They had believed that
 (c) It believes that
 (d) They believe as

37. I won't be _____ the mid-term exam if the exam starts early.
 (a) prepared to taking
 (b) prepared for taking
 (c) preparing to take
 (d) preparing for taking

38. A class action lawsuit is a type of lawsuit in which claims of many people are decided in a single case, meaning that you _____ try to win the case with the best lawyers, although quite costly.
 (a) have got
 (b) would have to
 (c) might as well
 (d) may well

39. When I was sick from food poisoning, I blamed my friend because she never visited me _____ my favorite snacks.
 (a) bring
 (b) to bring
 (c) without to bring
 (d) without bringing

40. The cute Korean girl completed her performance on the ice far more wonderfully than _____ figure skater and won the gold medal.
 (a) another
 (b) any other
 (c) each
 (d) any

Part III **Questions 41-45**
Identify the option that contains an awkward expression or a grammatical error.

41. (a) A: How much time do we have left?
(b) B: About an hour.
(c) A: An hour? We must hurry.
(d) B: Yeah, the time just seems to have been disappeared

42. (a) A: Who did you choose to go to the dance party?
(b) B: I think Mary is the proper partner for me.
(c) A: Mary? I didn't get it. You must be kidding me.
(d) B: Seriously. I have a crush on her.

43. (a) A: Did you know that Joe committed suicide in the army?
(b) B: That is very astonishing. What made him so foolish?
(c) A: I know nothing at all. I find that hardly to believe.
(d) B: I think he lacks filial piety to his parents.

44. (a) A: How was the presentation in your class?
(b) B: It was fantastic, which made every student interesting in the presentation.
(c) A: That's good news.
(d) B: Now, I am confident in giving a presentation.

45. (a) A: Are you coming to the airport to see Jenny off?
(b) B: Sure. I will go, and maybe one of my friends is coming along.
(c) A: Who's coming with you?
(d) B: As far as I know, John has. Do you know who he is?

Part IV

Questions 46-50
Identify the option that contains an awkward expression or a grammatical error.

46. (a) In the early 1900s, the company wasn't known by its familiar fowl moniker and sold other foods in addition to tuna. (b) But fortune shined on it when it became the first food company to can 'light tuna.' (c) The mildly flavored fish became the company's trademark product, and its owners sought a catchier name for their canned fish. (d) When asked about the flavor of the new light tuna, many customers remark, "it tastes like chicken," so the company began to market the light tuna as 'Chicken of the Sea'.

47. (a) Depending various biological and social factors, from insects to fish to small mammals and even humans scientists are finding examples of excellent fatherhood. (b) Some creatures have evolved adaptive qualities that ensure the male is raising his own offspring. (c) Female giant water bugs, for example, cement their eggs onto the dad's back immediately after they mate. (d) For weeks, the male cares for his bug eggs, stroking them with his hind legs.

48. (a) Marcel Proust said: "The only true voyage, the only Fountain of Youth, would be found not in traveling to strange lands but in having different eyes." (b) He also said, "In seeing the universe with the eyes of another, of a hundred others, is seeing the hundred universes each of them sees, which each of them is." (c) Whilst I agree with him in part, I think that traveling in strange lands is the eyes of another person. (d) Growing beyond one's origins necessitate the departure from one's origins in every sense of the word, particularly in the physical sense.

49. (a) The Puritans were not susceptible to the charms of poetry. (b) The strenuous life of the pioneer left little time for cultivating any of the arts. (c) The spirit of New England was too serious and too stern to permit indulgence in what was merely pleasant or beautiful. (d) What the Puritans were not without imagination, however, is abundantly proved by the forceful figures and impassioned rhetoric of the prose writers.

50. (a) We are so exciting you and your family will be coming to stay with us over the holiday season. (b) I wanted to let you know that we would like to pick you up at the airport, but we don't have your flight number, please call us as soon as possible with your travel plans. (c) June is really looking forward to meeting her cousins and Rob and I really want to hear about all you have been up to with that business of yours. (d) 985-1132 is Rob's cellphone, which is always with him, so you can reach us there too.

고난도 TEPS in TEPS 문법 TEST BooK

고득점을 위한 point를 정확히 알려주는 학습서

TEPS 고득점을 위한 Actual Training
고만고만한 빈출 문제는 그저 그런 성적을 낳을 뿐이다. 한 차원 높은 고난도 문제가 실전 경쟁력을 높인다.

전략적인 학습을 유도하는 유형 표시
각 문제에서 묻는 문법 요소를 표기한 유형 분류 tag를 활용하여 자신의 취약 분야에 대한 전략적 학습이 가능하다.

고난도 문제의 핵심을 꿰뚫는 고난도 point
기본적인 해설에 덧붙여 심도 있는 '고난도 point' 해설로 고난도 문제 해법의 핵심을 제시한다.

ISBN 978-89-6049-240-0 13740
978-89-6049-239-4(세트)

₩15000

고득점을 위한 고강도 훈련

고난도 TEPS in TEPS

박기혁·정구영 지음

까다로운 TEPS 문법을 완벽 대비할 수 있는 정확한 분석과 해법

2nd Edition

문법
ANSWER BooK

Grammar

Actual Training 10회분 & 해설

사람in

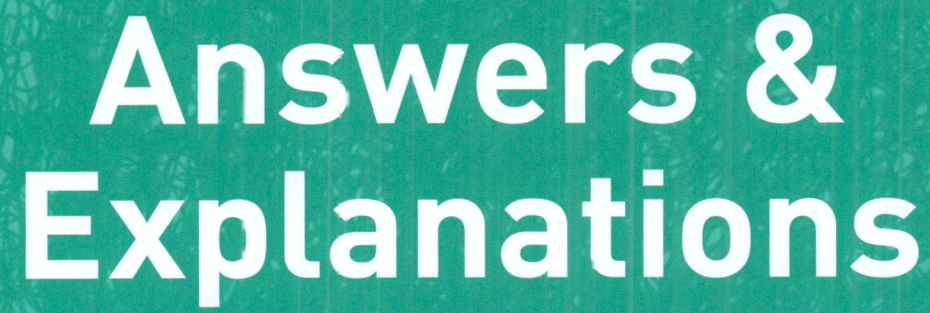

고난도 Actual Training 01

1. (d)	2. (c)	3. (b)	4. (b)	5. (c)	6. (c)	7. (c)	8. (c)	9. (b)	10. (d)
11. (a)	12. (c)	13. (b)	14. (b)	15. (c)	16. (d)	17. (c)	18. (d)	19. (a)	20. (c)
21. (d)	22. (b)	23. (d)	24. (d)	25. (d)	26. (b)	27. (d)	28. (c)	29. (b)	30. (b)
31. (c)	32. (d)	33. (c)	34. (d)	35. (d)	36. (a)	37. (c)	38. (c)	39. (d)	40. (a)
41. (c)	42. (a)	43. (c)	44. (a)	45. (d)	46. (a)	47. (b)	48. (d)	49. (a)	50. (a)

Part I Questions 1-20

1 유형 부사 rather/ 수동태

A: Aren't you able to drive faster?
B: Hold your horses, sweetheart! I'd rather _____ than die on the street.
(a) to delay
(b) delaying
(c) be delaying
(d) be delayed

해석 A: 더 빨리 달릴 수 없어?
B: 진정해, 자기야! 길에서 죽느니 차라리 늦겠어.

해설 would rather A than B는 'B하느니 차라리 A하겠다'라는 의미로 A와 B 모두 동사원형을 쓴다. 목적어가 없으므로 타동사의 수동태 형태인 (d)가 정답이다.

어휘 Hold your horses. 흥분하지 마, 진정해.
delay 연기하다, 미루다

2 유형 시제의 일치/ 수동태

A: What did the eyewitnesses say about the accident?
B: They insisted that the train _____ at the railway accident last night.
(a) derail
(b) be derailed
(c) was derailed
(d) should be derailed

해석 A: 목격자들이 그 사고에 대해 뭐라고 말했어?
B: 어젯밤에 기차가 철로에서 탈선했다고 했어.

해설 주절의 동사가 insist이지만 that 이하의 내용이 단순 사실을 전달하는 것이므로 시제 일치에 따라 과거형을 쓰거나 그 이전 형태인 과거완료형태를 써야 한다.

어휘 eyewitness 목격자 derail 탈선시키다

3 유형 not until~ 도치/ 수일치

A: When is a monkey independent of its parents?
B: Not until a monkey is four years old _____ to display signs of independence from its mother.
(a) it begins
(b) does it begin
(c) and begin
(d) beginning

해석 A: 원숭이는 언제 부모에게서 독립하니?
B: 네 살이 되어서야 비로소 어미에게서 독립하려는 기미를 보이기 시작해.

해설 문두의 not until로 보아 다음에 나오는 주절의 주어와 동사가 도치된다는 것을 알 수 있다. begin은 일반동사이므로 주어 앞에 does가 먼저 나와야 한다.

고난도 POINT 1   도치 구문을 알아두자.

도치와 같은 특수 구문을 묻는 문제가 매 시험마다 출제되므로 자주 출제되는 구문을 알아두는 것이 좋다. Not until은 자주 출제되는 도치 구문으로, 부정어가 문장 앞에 나올 때 뒤에 나오는 주어와 동사가 도치되는 경우이다. 이때 주의할 점은 until이 이끄는 절이 아닌 아닌 주절에서 도치가 이루어지고 동사가 be동사가 아닌 일반동사일 경우 조동사(do, does, did)가 먼저 나오고 '주어+동사원형'의 순으로 나온다는 것이다.

4 유형 would rather 가정법

A: What do you want me to do today?
B: I would rather that you _____ at home than went out in this blizzard.
(a) stay
(b) stayed
(c) staying
(d) have stayed

해석 A: 오늘 내가 뭘 했으면 좋겠니?
B: 네가 이런 눈보라치는 날에 밖에 나가느니 집에 머물러 있는 게 좋겠어.

해설 would rather 뒤에 that절이 와서 가정법을 나타내며 현재 사실에 대한 내용이므로 과거동사가 적합하다.

어휘 blizzard 눈보라

5 유형 정관사 the

A: Did she come to the party last night?
B: No, she was sick for _____.
(a) a night
(b) night
(c) the night
(d) nights

해석 A: 그녀는 어젯밤에 파티에 왔니?
B: 아니, 어젯밤에 아팠대.

해설 '어젯밤'이라는 특정한 때를 가리키므로 정관사 the와 함께 쓴다.

6 유형 the way+절

A: Do you have any idea of the nation's economic future?
B: _____, it is expected to be doomed.
(a) The way how I look at it
(b) The way I see
(c) The way I look at it
(d) The way in which I look it

해석 A: 국가의 경제적 미래에 대해 어떻게 생각하십니까?
B: 제가 보기엔, 암울한 것 같습니다.

해설 자동사 look은 목적어를 바로 취할 수 없으므로 (d)는 정답에서 제외되고, 관계부사 how의 경우 the way와 연달아 나올 수 없으므로 (a) 역시 답이 아니다. (b)의 경우, see는 타동사이므로 뒤에 명사가 나와야 하는데, 없으므로 오답이다. 자동사 look이 목적어를 취할 수 있도록 전치사 at과 함께 쓰인 (c)가 제대로 된 형태이다.

어휘 doomed 불운한

7 유형 복수명사/ 수 일치

A: I suppose I like this one. What would be the selling price here then?
B: I guess you're going to like it. _____ $ 100.
(a) These pants costs
(b) This pant cost
(c) This pair of pants costs
(d) This pair of pants cost

해석 A: 이게 좋겠는데요. 여기서 파는 가격이 얼마지요?
B: 마음에 드실 겁니다. 이 바지는 100달러입니다.

해설 바지는 항상 pants, 복수형으로 쓰지만 바지 한 벌을 뜻하는 a pair of pants는 pair에 초점을 맞추어 단수 취급하므로 this pair of pants 역시 단수동사를 취한다.

8 유형 대명사 neither/ 수 일치

A: Have David and Johnson seen the constellation of Orion yet?
B: _____ awake at night. They are morning people.
(a) Neither children have been
(b) Not either child was
(c) Either child has been
(d) Neither of the children has been

해석 A: David와 Johnson은 지금까지 오리온 별자리를 본 적이 있니?
B: 그 애들 중에 누구도 밤에 깨어 있질 않아. 아침형이거든.

해설 neither가 형용사로 쓰일 경우 단수명사와 단수동사를 취하고, 대명사로 쓰일 경우 복수동사와 단수동사 모두 가능하다. They are morning people.이라는 내용으로 보아 (c)는 적절하지 않다.

어휘 constellation 별자리 awake 깨어 있는

고난도 POINT 2 동사가 나오면 수 일치를 살펴봐야 한다.

이 문제는 neither의 쓰임새와 연관하여 뒤에 나오는 동사의 수 일치에 관하여 함께 묻고 있다. 선택지에 동사가 나올 경우 주어에 따라 수 일치가 되는지를 살펴보아야 한다. 특히 주어가 A of B의 형태로 나올 때, 둘 중 어떤 것이 주어인지를 파악하여 정답을 골라야 한다.

---

9 유형 would rather 가정법/ 시제 일치

A: Would you mind if I opened the window?
B: _____. It's windy outside.
(a) Yes. Please do
(b) I'd rather you didn't
(c) I'd be appreciated if you do
(d) I appreciated it if you didn't

해석 A: 창문을 열어도 될까요?
B: 그러지 않으면 해요. 밖에 바람이 불거든요.

해설 would rather 뒤에 that이 생략돼 있으며 가정법 과거를 나타내는 과거동사가 온 (b)가 적절하다. (c)는 I'd 다음이 능동태가 되어야 하고, (d)는 아직 창문을 열지 않았는데 과거형 appreciated는 타당하지 않다.

어휘 appreciate 감상하다, 인정하다, 감사하다

10 유형 to부정사/ 과거분사

A: What does the boss have in mind?
B: The employer _____ as soon as possible and without blunders.
(a) wants the job to do
(b) wants that the job will be done
(c) wants that the job would be done
(d) wants the job done

해석 A: 사장님이 무슨 생각을 하고 계시지?
B: 사장님은 그 일이 가능한 한 빨리 아무 실수 없이 끝나길 바라셔.

해설 일이 이루어져야 하므로 수동형이 되어야 한다. 특히 want는 (b)나 (c)처럼 뒤에 that절을 취하지 않는다.

어휘 have ~ in mind 마음에 두다 blunder 실수

고난도 POINT 3 목적어와 목적격보어의 관계를 파악해야 한다.

일반적으로 want 뒤에 목적어가 오면 목적격보어로 to부정사가 온다고 알고 있다. 따라서 이 문제에서 **(a)**를 정답으로 고를 수 있다. 하지만 이처럼 목적어와 목적격보어가 나오는 경우에는 둘 사이의 관계를 정확히 파악해야 하는데, the job과 do의 관계는 수동이므로 수동형으로 써야 한다. 따라서 원래 wants the job to be done의 형태에서, 보통 to be는 생략하고 과거분사만 남겨서 wants the job done으로 쓴다.

---

11 유형 시제/ 태

A: This is not the present I _____.
B: Do you want it thrown away?

 (a) **have wanted**
 (b) have been wanting
 (c) am wanting
 (d) had want

[해석] A: 이건 내가 원하던 선물이 아니야!
B: 버릴 거니?

[해설] 전부터 원하고 있었던 선물에 대해 말하므로 과거에서 현재까지의 일을 표현하는 현재완료가 적합하다.

[어휘] throw away 버리다

---

12 유형 부사/ 분사

A: You are _____ with yourself. What happened?
B: I've won a lottery.

 (a) quite watching pleased
 (b) watching quite pleased
 (c) **quite looking pleased**
 (d) looking quite pleasing

[해석] A: 너 아주 즐거워 보이는 구나. 무슨 일이니?
B: 복권에 당첨됐어.

[해설] pleasing은 '기쁨을 주는,' pleased는 '기쁜'의 의미로 이 경우 상대가 기뻐 보인다는 의미이므로 pleased가 적합하다. 강조 의미의 부사 quite는 동사 앞에 사용한다.

[어휘] win a lottery 복권에 당첨되다

---

13 유형 대명사/ 시제

A: I'm having difficulty in running the foreign language institute.
B: When it comes to management, you had better ask _____ it these days.

 (a) one who used to manage
 (b) **those who have managed**
 (c) those who had been used to manage
 (d) them who would have managed

[해석] A: 외국어 학원을 운영하는 데 어려움을 겪고 있어.
B: 경영에 관한 문제라면, 요즘 학원을 운영하고 있는 사람들에게 물어보는 게 좋을 거야.

[해설] 요즘 운영하는 것이므로 현재완료형이 와야 한다. used to는 과거를 나타내므로 these days와 함께 쓰지 않는다.

[어휘] institute 기관, 연구소 management 경영

---

14 유형 분사/ 비교

A: It is incredible that you should paint the house yellow.
B: _____, I just spruced it up.

 (a) Being as dreary as
 (b) **It being as dreary as**
 (c) It been as dreary as
 (d) as dreary as

[해석] A: 네가 집을 노란색으로 칠하다니 믿을 수가 없어.
B: 집이 너무 단조로워서 멋을 좀 냈어.

[해설] 빈칸에 알맞은 의미가 되려면 As it was as dreary as ~가 되는데 이를 분사구문으로 바꾸면 주절의 주어와 다른 it은 남겨두고 was를 현재분사 형태로 바꿔 It being as dreary as~가 된다.

[어휘] dreary 단조로운 spruce up 멋을 내다

15 유형 복합관계형용사/대명사

A: Shall I take the red convertible or the white one?
B: It will look nice _____ you may take.
 (a) what the one
 (b) which one
 (c) whichever one
 (d) whatever the one

[해석] A: 빨간색 컨버터블로 할까, 흰색 컨버터블로 할까?
B: 어느 쪽을 선택하든 멋질 거야.

[해설] 선택지 중에서 고를 땐 which가 필요한데, B는 선택의 의향을 묻기보다는 어느 쪽을 선택해도 괜찮을 것이라는 뜻으로 말하고 있으므로 -ever가 붙은 형태인 복합관계형용사 whichever가 적합하다. 또한 막연한 어떤 것을 고르므로 대명사는 one이 적절하다.

[어휘] convertible 컨버터블(지붕을 열었다 닫았다 할 수 있는 승용차)

16 유형 비교/가정법

A: Are you sure of your memory of the accident?
B: Yes. I remember it as clearly _____ it happened yesterday.
 (a) therefore
 (b) as
 (c) so
 (d) as if

[해석] A: 그 사건에 대한 기억이 확실하니?
B: 응. 바로 어제 일어난 것처럼 분명하게 생각나.

[해설] 문맥상 '마치 ~와 같이'라는 뜻의 연결어가 들어가야 한다. 그래서 앞의 as ~ as와 뒤의 as if가 하나로 합쳐진 문장이라고 생각하면 된다. (b)는 '어제 일어난 일만큼이나'의 의미가 되어 실제로 어제 일이 일어났다는 뜻이 되므로 문맥상 자연스럽지 못하다.

17 유형 소유격 관계대명사

A: Where did the people from the east settle?
B: They ultimately went torward the plateau, _____ have supplied plentiful food from generation to generation.
 (a) where
 (b) in which
 (c) whose fertile lands
 (d) on which fertile lands

[해석] A: 동쪽에서 온 사람들은 어디에 정착했나요?
B: 그들은 결국 고원 쪽으로 갔는데, 그곳의 비옥한 땅은 대대손손 풍부한 먹거리를 제공해주었어요.

[해설] 빈칸 앞의 선행사가 the plateau인데 문맥상 그곳의 비옥한 땅이란 의미이므로 소유격 관계대명사가 나와야 한다. 따라서 (c)가 적절하다. (d)가 정답이 되려면 on which가 아니라 in which가 되어야 한다.

[어휘] plateau 고원 fertile 비옥한 plentiful 풍부한 generation 세대

18 유형 조동사

A: I wish that Mr. Smith would act nice to me all the time.
B: Well, I think that you _____ have made such mean comments about him before.
 (a) ought to
 (b) have got to
 (c) would not
 (d) should not

[해석] A: 나는 Smith씨가 언제나 나에게 잘 해주었으면 좋겠어.
B: 음, 내 생각엔 네가 전에 그에 관해서 그런 나쁜 말을 하지 말았어야 했다고 봐.

[해설] 문맥상 '하지 말았어야 했다'이므로 should not have p.p. 형태가 적합하다. (a)가 답이 되려면 반대의 의미가 들어가야 하므로 ought not to가 되어야 한다.

[어휘] mean 못된, 나쁜

19 유형 접속사 that

A: Do you happen to know about Java Man?
B: Certainly. I learned in the archaeology class. _____ Java Man, who lived before the early Ice Age, was the first mankind.

(a) **It is generally believed that**
(b) Generally believed what it is
(c) That is generally believed
(d) It is believed generally what

[해석] A: 너는 자바인에 대해 알고 있니?
B: 물론이지. 고고학 시간에 배웠어. 자바인은 초기 빙하시대 이전에 살았던 최초의 인류라고 일반적으로 알려져 있어.

[해설] 관계대명사 what 뒤에는 불완전한 문장이 나와야 하는데 빈칸 뒤의 내용이 완전한 문장을 이루고 있으므로 (d)는 정답이 될 수 없다. 접속사 that 이하의 내용을 가주어 it으로 받는 문장 구조가 어법상 적합하다.

20 유형 동사/시제

A: How did you learn to speak Arabic so well?
B: As a matter of fact, I _____ in a bakery with plenty of Arabian people. They taught me a lot.

(a) have working
(b) had been working
(c) **used to work**
(d) could have worked

[해석] A: 너는 어떻게 배웠기에 아랍어를 그렇게 잘 하니?
B: 사실 나는 빵집에서 많은 아랍 사람들과 일을 했었어. 그들이 많이 가르쳐 주었지.

[해설] A의 질문과 B의 두 번째 문장이 과거시제로 이루어져 있으며 문맥상 지나간 일을 말하므로 used to가 정답이다.

Part II Questions 21-40

21 유형 비교/부사

The Middle East country had _____ in its deposits as had been expected.

(a) three times as almost much oil
(b) much almost as oil three times
(c) as almost three times much oil
(d) **almost three times as much oil**

[해석] 그 중동 국가는 예상되었던 산유량의 거의 3배를 보유하고 있었다.

[해설] '~의 배'를 나타내는 배수사는 '배수사+as+원급+as'의 형태나 '배수사+비교급+than'의 형태로 쓴다. almost는 배수사를 수식하는 말이므로 three times 앞에 쓴다.

[어휘] deposits 매장량

22 유형 전치사/관계대명사

We might miss the plane, _____ we will have to pay an extra fee.

(a) in that situation
(b) **in which situation**
(c) of which situation
(d) of that situation

[해석] 우리는 비행기를 놓칠지도 몰라. 만약 그렇게 되면 추가비용을 내야 할 거야.

[해설] 문맥상 '그러한 경우에는'이라는 표현은 in that situation 또는 in the situation이다. 전치사 in 뒤에서 쉼표 앞의 절과 뒤의 절을 이어주며 앞의 내용을 받아주는 관계사가 필요하므로 (b) in which situation이 적절하다.

23 유형 비교

The higher the temperature of a molecule, _____.

(a) the more has it energy
(b) the more energy has it
(c) the more it has energy
(d) the more energy it has

해석 분자의 온도는 높아질수록 에너지가 더 많다.
해설 'the + 비교급 ~, the + 비교급 ~' 구문으로 more가 energy를 수식하므로 함께 오며, 주어, 동사의 순으로 쓴다.

24 유형 형용사/의문부사

To my surprise, no people around us are aware of _____ he was in the civil rights movement.

(a) how a momentous person
(b) how a person momentous
(c) how momentous person
(d) how momentous a person

해석 놀랍게도 우리 주위에 누구도 그가 시민운동에 있어서 얼마나 중요한 인물인지 모르고 있다.
해설 how+형용사+a+명사의 어순을 취한다.
어휘 momentous 중요한

25 유형 도치

Morrow did not go to school even a single day, _____ to send his own child to what they call a governmental institution.

(a) neither he means
(b) he does not mean
(c) he neither does mean
(d) nor does he mean

해석 Morrow는 단 하루도 학교에 가지 않았고, 소위 정부기관이라는 곳에 하나뿐인 자기 아이를 보낼 의도도 없다.
해설 문장을 연결하는 접속사가 필요한데 선택지에서 그런 역할을 하는 것은 nor이다. nor는 'and ~ not'의 의미로 부정의 의미를 띠므로 동사가 일반동사일 경우 뒤에 '조동사 + 주어 + 동사'의 어순으로 도치시켜 쓴다.
어휘 institution 기관

고난도 POINT 4 neither와 nor를 구별하라.

nor와 neither는 둘 다 '~도 그렇지 않다'는 부정의 의미이지만 쓰임에 차이가 있다. nor는 접속사로 쓰이며, neither는 부사로 쓰인다. 따라서 문제에서 요구하는 것에 접속사를 포함해야 한다면 nor가 적절하고 접속사가 이미 제시되어 있다면 neither가 적합하다.

26 유형 분사

Of all the major problems _____ contemporary people these days, those involved in environmental health will have the greatest effect on their way of life.

(a) being faced
(b) facing
(c) facing with
(d) having faced with

해석 요즘 현대인이 마주하고 있는 중요한 문제 중에서 환경건강과 관련된 것들이 우리의 삶에 가장 큰 영향을 미칠 것이다.
해설 face는 '직면하다, ~의 바로 앞에 놓여 있다'라는 의미로 쓸 땐 타동사로 쓰여 전치사를 사용하지 않고 직접 목적어가 뒤에 바로 나온다. 또한 문맥상 능동을 나타내므로 현재분사를 사용한다.
어휘 contemporary 현대의

고난도 POINT 5 분사 문제의 경우 단어의 쓰임을 명확히 알아야 한다.

앞뒤 문맥을 살펴 능동의 경우엔 현재분사를, 수동의 경우엔 과거분사 형태를 취한다. 이 문제에서 face는 '직면하다, 맞닥뜨리다'의 의미로 능동의 현재분사 형태가 맞으며 타동사이므로 전치사 없이 사용한다. 이처럼 현재분사를 쓸 것인지 과거분사를 쓸 것인지를 판단하기 위해서는 단어의 쓰임을 정확히 파악해야 한다.

27 유형 분사/조동사 should의 생략

The National Assembly has motioned that all foreign citizens _____ their embassy.
(a) living in South Korea registering
(b) live in South Korea be registered with
(c) live in the South Korea has registered
(d) living in South Korea register with

[해석] 국회는 한국에 살고 있는 모든 외국인들이 자국 대사관에 등록해야 한다는 것에 찬성했다.

[해설] motion은 일종의 '요구, 주장'을 나타내어 that절 뒤에 should가 필요하다. should가 생략되는 경우는 동사원형을 사용한다. 또 특히 register가 with와 결합해서 능동적 의미를 띔을 주의해야 한다.

[어휘] motion 손이나 몸짓으로 알리다, 지시하다, 말하다
embassy 대사관 register 등록하다

28 유형 접속사/시제/태

The renowned aviator told reporters _____ from seeking to cross the ocean by himself even though other people had failed.
(a) that he had it barely deterred
(b) who had it been barely deterred
(c) that he had barely been deterred
(d) about his having been barely deterred

[해석] 그 유명한 비행사는 비록 다른 사람들이 실패했지만 대양을 홀로 횡단하려는 시도를 단념하지 않았다고 기자들에게 말했다.

[해설] told의 목적어가 와야 하므로 명사절이 필요하다. 따라서 (b)와 (d)는 정답이 될 수 없다. 빈칸은 말하기 이전의 내용이므로 더과거 형태인 had p.p.가 사용된다. 비행사 자신이 대서양을 횡단하려는 의지가 방해받지 않은 것이므로 문맥상 수동형이 적합하다.

[어휘] renowned 유명한 aviator 비행사 barely 거의 ~않다
deter 단념시키다, 막다

29 유형 전치사/관계대명사

If, through laziness, you read at a slower rate than the rate _____ you are able, there might be great temptation for your mind to wander.
(a) which
(b) at which
(c) through which
(d) with which

[해석] 당신이 게을러서, 이해할 수 있는 속도보다 느리게 책을 읽는다면 정신이 방황할 만한 유혹이 많을 것이다.

[해설] '~한 속도로, ~한 비율로'를 나타낼 때 at the rate를 사용한다. 따라서 at which가 적절하다.

[어휘] laziness 게으름 temptation 유혹

30 유형 형용사/부사

I hope you submit your work _____ this afternoon. Otherwise, you will get an F for your grade.
(a) lately
(b) later
(c) more late
(d) the latest

[해석] 여러분의 과제를 오늘 오후 늦게라도 제출하기를 바랍니다. 그렇지 않으면 F 학점을 받을 것입니다.

[해설] later는 '더 늦게'의 의미보다는 '늦게라도'의 의미가 포함되어 있어 문맥상 적합하다. lately는 '최근에,' latest는 '최근'의 라는 의미이다.

31 유형 미래완료시제

By 2015, if all goes according to plan, 12 prestigious Western schools _____ branch campuses in a government-financed, 940-acre Global Education City.
(a) will open
(b) open
(c) will have opened
(d) will be opening

[해석] 2015년까지 모든 것이 계획대로 이루어진다면, 12개의 서구형 일류 학교들이 정부지원을 받는 940 에이커에 이르는 세계적 교육도시에 분교를 세울 것입니다.

[해설] By 2015라고 하는 미래의 시간이 제시되어 will have p.p. 형태의 미래완료시제가 적합하다.

[어휘] prestigious 일류의

고난도 POINT 6 미래완료를 써야 하는 경우를 알아두자.

미래완료는 미래의 특정 시점 이전에 일어난 일이 미래의 특정 시점에 완료되거나 지속된다는 것을 나타낼 때 쓰는 시제이다. 이를 알고 있었다면 이 문제에서도 정답을 쉽게 고를 수 있을 것이다. By 2015라는 미래의 특정 시점을 제시하고 있으므로 빈칸은 미래완료 시제가 적절하다. 이 외에도 by this time tomorrow, by that time, by tomorrow 등의 미래의 어떤 시점을 나타내는 어구와 함께 쓴다.

32 유형 문장의 형식/시제

_____ in history when significant progress was made within a relatively short span of time.
(a) Periods that
(b) Periods had been
(c) Throughout periods
(d) There had been periods

[해석] 상대적으로 짧은 시간 안에 역사상 중요한 진보가 이루어진 시기가 있었다.

[해설] 빈칸은 주어와 동사가 필요한 자리로 '~이 있다'의 의미가 필요하므로 there is 구문이 적합하다. 또한 when 이하의 시제로 볼 때 '있어 왔다'는 식이 되어야 하기에 과거완료가 타당하다.

[어휘] significant 중요한 throughout ~동안 내내

33 유형 최상급 강조

They have been offering plenty of useful Web services supplying us with access to _____ for research and development.
(a) online the very best resources
(b) the best very online resources
(c) the very best online resources
(d) online resources the best very

[해석] 그들은 연구 개발을 위한 최고의 온라인 자원에 대한 접근을 허용하는 쓸모 있는 웹상의 서비스를 많이 제공하고 있다.

[해설] 최상급의 강조는 the very를 최상급 앞에 쓴다.

34 유형 접속사/도치

In the course of his life, he learned that the robust person does not always win the race, _____ always a loser.
(a) never does the feeble person
(b) neither is the feeble person
(c) does not the feeble person
(d) nor is the feeble person

[해석] 그는 살아오는 과정에서 강한 사람이 경주에서 항상 이기는 것은 아니라는 것과 약한 사람이 항상 패배자가 되는 것은 아니라는 점을 배웠다.

[해설] 빈칸에는 문장을 연결하는 접속사가 필요하므로 nor가 적합하다. never, neither 등은 부사이므로 적절하지 않다. nor가 문장 앞에 오면 뒤에 주어와 동사가 도치된다.

[어휘] robust 억센, 강건한 feeble 연약한

35 유형 관계대명사/전치사

In the multi-cultural _____, it's safe not to worry about explaining the story of Passover because if people don't hear it from me, they'll hear it some other way.
(a) world I live
(b) world which I live
(c) world where I live in
(d) world which I live in

해석 내가 살고 있는 다문화 세계에서, 사람들이 나에게서 듣지 않는다 해도 다른 방법으로 듣게 될 것이기 때문에 유월절에 관한 이야기를 설명할 걱정은 하지 않아도 된다.

해설 선행사 world를 수식하는 관계대명사가 올 경우 뒤에 전치사가 필요하고 관계부사가 올 경우에는 전치사가 필요 없다. 즉, world which I live in은 world where I live로 쓸 수 있다.

36 유형 배수사 비교/대동사

Last year, Matt earned _____ who work for a large corporation.
(a) twice as much as his brother did
(b) twice more than his brother was
(c) twice as many as his brother was
(d) twice as more as his brother has done

해석 Matt는 대기업에 다니는 형보다 작년에 돈을 2배 더 많이 벌었다.

해설 배수 비교 문제로, 양을 나타내므로 much를 사용하고 earned를 대신 표현하는 것이므로 대동사 did가 적합하다.

37 유형 목적격 관계대명사

Jay Ron Philip, _____ one of the greatest composers in the world, wrote his music during the year known as the Gay 90s.
(a) who many people consider to be
(b) whose many people consider to be
(c) whom many people consider as
(d) what many people consider as

해석 많은 사람들이 세상에서 가장 위대한 작곡가 중 한 명이라고 여기는 Jay Ron Philip은 즐거운 90년대라고 알려진 시기에 그의 음악을 작곡했다.

해설 선행사가 사람이고 관계대명사가 목적격일 경우 whom을 쓴다. consider의 경우 consider A as B, consider A B, consider A to B 형태가 모두 가능하다.

38 유형 동명사 부정형/형용사 many

The Department of Fine Arts and Architecture has been criticized for _____ required courses scheduled for this semester.
(a) having not much
(b) not having much
(c) not having many
(d) having not many

해석 예술 및 건축학부는 이번 학기 동안 예정된 필수 과정이 많지 않다고 비판 받았다.

해설 준동사의 부정은 준동사 앞에 하는 것이므로 not having이 맞고, courses는 셀 수 있는 명사의 복수형이므로 many를 사용한다.

어휘 criticize 비판하다 required 필수적인

39 유형 비교+부사

The palaces in ancient China is so large that the rooms are _____ those of the similar era in other countries.
(a) four times nearly as large as
(b) as large four times as
(c) as four times nearly as
(d) nearly four times as large as

해석 고대 중국의 궁궐은 규모가 매우 커서 방의 크기가 비슷한 시대 다른 나라의 궁에 있는 방의 거의 네 배였다.

해설 배수사를 이용한 비교급은 '배수사+as+원급+as'의 형태나 '배수사+비교급+than'의 형태로 쓴다. nearly는 배수사를 수식하는 말이므로 four times 앞에 쓴다.

40 유형 부사

_____ the employees in the factory were making cars.
(a) Almost all of
(b) Most all of
(c) Most of all
(d) Almost the whole of

해석 공장의 거의 모든 직원들은 자동차를 만들고 있었다.

해설 almost는 부사이므로 수량을 나타내는 all 앞에 오지만 most는 한정 형용사로 오지 못한다. (b), (c)는 all을 빼야 한다. (d)의 almost는 the whole을 수식하지 못한다.

Part III Questions 41-45

41 유형 관계사

(a) A: Honey, what time is breakfast today?
(b) B: I suppose it will be fixed up at seven.
(c) A: Oh, I have a momentous meeting at nine in the morning, which I should be able to make it.
(d) B: I don't doubt that I will make breakfast by the time.

해석
(a) A: 여보, 오늘 아침식사 몇 시지?
(b) B: 내 생각엔 7시로 정해진 것 같은데.
(c) A: 아, 나 오늘 아침 9시에 중요한 약속이 있는데, 거기 꼭 가야 해.
(d) B: 그때까지는 확실히 아침 준비할 수 있을 거야.

해설 which는 목적격 관계대명사로 뒤에 불완전 문장이 와야 한다. 선행사 meeting을 가리키는 it이 빠져야 한다. be able to make it → be able to make

42 유형 접속사

(a) A: Are you going to heal me or what, Donald? I only ask, because I'll do it somewhere cleaner I'm going to bleed out.
(b) B: Of course. I'm sorry, I've been busy.
(c) A: Just do it. I've got places to be.
(d) B: Okay, okay. Let's see.

해석
(a) A: Donald, 치료해줄 거예요 말 거예요? 만약에 피가 날 거라면 좀 깨끗한 곳에서 하고 싶어서 묻는 거예요.
(b) B: 해줄게요. 미안해요, 좀 바빴어요.
(c) A: 어서 시작해요. 난 갈 곳이 있단 말이에요.
(d) B: 알았어요, 알았어. 자, 봅시다.

해설 (a)에서 because는 I only ask와 I'll do it somewhere cleaner를 연결해주고 있으므로 그 뒤에 나오는 I'm going to bleed out을 연결할 수 있는 접속사가 필요하다. 문맥상 if가 적절하다. I'm going to bleed out → if I'm going to bleed out

43 유형 이유를 나타내는 that's why 구문

(a) A: This is infuriating. I have been waiting for a taxi for over an hour.
(b) B: I heard that a traffic accident took place two hours ago.
(c) **A: Can I believe that? Then, that's because I couldn't catch a taxi.**
(d) B: Anyway you should get your rear in gear and not be late for the meeting.

[해석] (a) A: 이거 정말 열 받게 하는군. 1시간 넘게 택시를 기다리고 있어.
(b) B: 2시간 전에 교통사고가 있었다고 들었어.
(c) A: 그 말을 믿어도 될까? 그래서 내가 택시를 탈 수 없는 거구나.
(d) B: 어쨌든 서둘러서 모임에 늦지 않도록 해.

[해설] 택시가 오지 않는 것은 사고가 난 것 때문이고 그것이 원인이 되어서 결과적으로 택시를 탈 수 없는 것이다. that's why(그 이유 때문에, 그래서)는 앞에 제시된 원인에 대해 뒤에서 그 결과를 말할 때 쓰인다. that's because는 그 반대이다. that's because → that's why

[어휘] get your rear in gear 서두르다

44 유형 조동사 would

(a) **A: I like another glass of beer, please.**
(b) B: With one more glass, that will be ten beers. Aren't you going to have difficulty in making your way home tonight?
(c) A: I believe that beer is a kind of soft drink.
(d) B: You are not vulnerable to beer. What's the secret?

[해석] (a) A: 맥주 한 잔 더 주세요.
(b) B: 한 잔 더 하시면, 10잔째예요. 오늘밤 집에 가기 괜찮으시겠어요?
(c) A: 나는 맥주를 일종의 음료수라고 생각해요.
(d) B: 맥주에 약하지 않으시네요. 비결이 뭔가요?

[해설] I like는 일반적으로 '언제나 좋아하다'는 의미이다. 여기서는 한 잔 더 마시고 싶다는 의미이므로 '~하고 싶다'의 would like가 적절하다. I like → I'd like 혹은 I would like

45 유형 어순

(a) A: Do you think it's going to rain?
(b) B: Not for two hours. Perhaps later. How come?
(c) A: I am supposed to go on a hike with George. What do you think?
(d) **B: I imagine you had better call off it and go to the cinema.**

[해석] (a) A: 비가 내릴 것 같아?
(b) B: 2시간 동안은 아닐 걸. 아마 나중에 오겠지. 그런데 왜?
(c) A: George와 등산 가기로 했어. 어떻게 생각해?
(d) B: 취소하고 영화 보러 가는 게 나을 거야.

[해설] 대명사는 동사와 전치사로 이루어진 동사구에서 그 사이에 들어가야 한다. call off it → call it off

Part IV Questions 46-50

46 유형 관계사

(a) **What has Canada avoided the plagues that are afflicting everyone else?** (b) The short answer is a mixture of good policies and good luck. (c) The main reason for the country's economic resilience is that neither its financial system nor its housing market magnified the recession. (d) And for that regulators deserve a chunk of the credit.

해석 (a) 어떻게 캐나다는 그 밖의 다른 이들을 괴롭히고 있는 재앙을 피했을까? (b) 간단히 대답하면 좋은 정책과 행운이 조합된 것이다. (c) 캐나다의 경제적 유연성의 주된 이유는 금융시스템도 주택 시장도 경기 침체를 확대하지 않았다는 것이다. (d) 그리고 그러한 규제 장치가 있어서 상당한 신용도를 유지할 만한 것이다.

해설 (a)에서 What 뒤의 문장이 주어 Canada, 동사 has avoided, 목적어 plagues를 모두 갖춘 완전한 문장이므로 부사인 how가 적합하다. What → How

어휘 plagues 역병, 재앙 afflict 괴롭히다
resilience 유연성 magnify 확대하다
recession 침체, 후퇴 regulator 규제 장치

47 유형 동사

(a) Japanese carmaker Toyota's reputation is rapidly declining. **(b) The first warning signs of the problems were surfaced in 2007.** (c) Its North-American built trucks caused a string of accidents due to their defective gas pedals, but the concern tried to play them down. (d) It seems to forget the lesson that a stitch in time saves nine.

해석 (a) 일본 자동차 제조업체인 도요타의 명성이 빠르게 하락하고 있다. (b) 문제의 첫 번째 경고 조짐은 2007년에 떠올랐다. (c) 북미에서 제작된 트럭들이 결함 있는 가속 페달 때문에 연이은 교통사고를 일으켰지만 그 회사는 사고를 무시하려고 애썼다. (d) 도요타는 한 번의 수고가 아홉 번의 번거로움을 대신한다는 교훈을 잊은 것 같다.

해설 동사 surface는 자동사로서 수동형을 사용하지 않는다. were surfaced → surfaced

어휘 defective 결함 있는 concern 회사
play down 가볍게 보다

고난도 POINT 7 **Part III, IV는 동사에 유의하자.**

TEPS 문법의 Part III, IV를 어려워하는 수험자들이 많다. 하지만 기본 문법에서 출제되므로 먼저 동사부터 파악하여 공략하는 것이 중요하다. 주로 동사의 수 일치, 시제, 태와 관련된 문장구조의 기본적인 오류를 묻는 문제가 자주 출제되므로 동사 파악을 연습하도록 하자.

---

48 유형 동사/문장의 형식

(a) As a host of gardeners and farmers know, crossbreeding two wimpy specimens from time to time produces strong offspring. (b) That is an effect which has been known as hybrid vigor and it is common in plants. (c) It also can be found in some animals on the Earth. **(d) However, some speculate, it might be lacking European royalty.**

해석 (a) 많은 정원사와 농부들이 아는 것처럼, 2개의 약한 표본을 이종 교배하면 때때로 강한 자손을 생산해 내는 경우가 있다. (b) 이는 잡종 강세로 알려진 효과이며 식물에선 일반적으로 일어난다. (c) 지구상의 몇몇 동물에서도 찾아볼 수 있다. (d) 하지만 몇몇 사람은 유럽의 왕족에서는 이런 일이 희박한 것 같다고 생각한다.

해설 lack은 타동사로 쓰일 때 뒤에 전치사가 따라 나오지 않지만 lacking이라는 형용사 형태로 쓰일 경우 뒤에 전치사 in과 함께 사용된다. lacking → lacking in

어휘 a host of 많은 crossbreeding 이종 교배
wimpy 허약한 specimens 표본 offspring 후손
hybrid 잡종 vigor 활기 royalty 왕족

49 유형 동사/부사

(a) Corruption experts say that Bulgaria urgent needs protection for whistle-blowers if President Borisov is to stamp out rampant corruption. (b) Last November, a survey by the corruption-rating organization found that 82% of Bulgarians were reluctant to report corruption-related cases because they feared being targeted. (c) Bulgarians still have fresh memories of the old communist dictatorship. (d) That's why "the whistle-blower is all too often seen as a traitor or as being like a police informer."

[해석] (a) 부패 전문가들은 Borisov 대통령이 널리 퍼져 있는 부패를 뿌리 뽑을 계획이라면 불가리아는 내부 고발자를 위한 조치를 시급히 마련해야 한다고 말하고 있다. (b) 지난 11월에 행해진 부패를 평가하는 기관의 조사에서 불가리아 사람들의 82퍼센트가 그들이 목표물이 될까봐 두려워서 부패 관련 사건을 신고하는 것을 꺼려한다는 것을 알아냈다. (c) 불가리아 사람들은 여전히 옛날 공산주의 독재에 대한 생생한 기억을 갖고 있다. (d) 그래서 내부 고발자는 허다하게 반역자나 경찰의 내부 끄나풀로 여겨진다.

[해설] 첫줄에서 동사 needs 앞에는 형용사가 아닌 부사가 나와야 한다. 동사 앞에서 동사를 수식할 수 있는 품사는 부사이다. 형용사는 명사의 앞이나 뒤에 나와야 한다. urgent → urgently

[어휘] whistle-blower 내부고발자 rampant 널리 퍼진
a police informer 경찰에게 정보를 몰래 제공해주는 사람

50 유형 태+동사의 형식

(a) If the LDP seems at the end of the line, the bigger surprise is that it has been lasted so long. (b) It was born of the cold war, free of any ideology save anti-communism. (c) Its business was winning elections and dividing the spoils — and for decades it did that very efficiently. (d) But once communism had collapsed and economic growth had slowed down, the LDP had lost its purpose.

[해석] (a) 자민당이 한계점에 이른 것처럼 보인다면 더 놀라운 점은 자민당이 그렇게도 오랫동안 지속되었다는 점이다. (b) 자민당은 냉전의 소산물이었고 공산주의를 제외한 그 어떠한 이데올로기로부터 자유로웠다. (c) 자민당이 하는 일은 선거를 이기는 것이고 전리품을 나누는 것이었고 그들은 그 일을 수십 년 동안 효율적으로 수행온 것이다. (d) 하지만 공산주의가 붕괴되고 경제성장이 둔화되자 자민당은 목적을 잃었다.

[해설] 여기서 last는 '지속되다'의 의미이므로 수동형으로 쓰이지 않는다. has been lasted → has lasted

[어휘] LDP 일본 자민당(Liberal Democratic Party)
the end of the line 참을 수 있는 한계, 종점, 궁지
spoils 전리품

고난도 Actual Training 02

1. (d)	2. (a)	3. (b)	4. (c)	5. (d)	6. (b)	7. (a)	8. (d)	9. (c)	10. (c)
11. (d)	12. (b)	13. (d)	14. (d)	15. (b)	16. (b)	17. (c)	18. (d)	19. (c)	20. (d)
21. (b)	22. (c)	23. (c)	24. (d)	25. (c)	26. (d)	27. (c)	28. (a)	29. (d)	30. (d)
31. (d)	32. (c)	33. (d)	34. (a)	35. (d)	36. (b)	37. (c)	38. (d)	39. (d)	40. (c)
41. (d)	42. (d)	43. (d)	44. (b)	45. (d)	46. (c)	47. (c)	48. (c)	49. (b)	50. (d)

Part I Questions 1-20

1 유형 부대상황/분사

A: Do you mind my opening the door?
B: Well, it might get cold with the door _____.
(a) being opened
(b) opening
(c) to open
(d) open

해석
A: 문 열어도 될까?
B: 글쎄, 문을 열면 추울 것 같아.

해설 with+명사+보어 형태에서 보어로 가능한 것은 명사, 형용사, 현재분사, 과거분사, 전치사구 등이다. open은 형용사로 '열려 있는'의 의미를 나타낸다. (b)는 일부러 문을 연다는 뉘앙스로 해석되기에 문맥상 옳지 않다.

2 유형 부정사/태

A: Did you see the musical, the Phantom of the Opera?
B: No, but people say it is something _____.
(a) not to overlook
(b) not be overlooked
(c) not overlooked
(d) not overlooking

해석
A: 뮤지컬 "오페라의 유령" 봤니?
B: 아니, 하지만 사람들이 꼭 봐야 한다고 해.

해설 overlook은 '못 보고 넘어가다'란 의미로 문맥상 꼭 봐야 하는 것이므로 부정 표현이 와야 하고, something을 수식해주는 to부정사의 형용사 용법으로 써야 하므로 not to overlook의 형태가 되어야 한다.

3 유형 부정사

A: Didn't you forget _____ the door when you left?
B: Oh, my gosh. I'd better get back home and make sure.
(a) locking
(b) to lock
(c) being locked
(d) to be locked

해석
A: 외출할 때 문을 닫고 나가야 한다는 거 잊지 않았지?
B: 오, 이런. 집으로 돌아가서 확인해 보는 게 좋겠어.

해설 문을 잠가야 한다는 아직 일어나지 않은 미래의 일을 언급하고 있으므로 to부정사 형태가 나와야 한다.

어휘 lock 잠그다

고난도 POINT 8 자주 출제되는 forget을 알아두자.

forget은 동명사와 to부정사 모두 목적어로 취할 수 있는 동사이다. 하지만 의미에 차이가 있다. 먼저 동명사와 함께 쓰면, '과거에 ~했던 것을 잊다'의 의미가 되고, to부정사와 함께 쓰면 '미래에 ~할 것을 잊다'는 의미가 된다. remember 역시 같은 맥락에서 사용하므로 함께 알아두는 것이 좋다.

4 유형 접속사

A: While I was out for a moment, were there any telephone calls for me?
B: Not _____ I am aware of.
  (a) why
  (b) how
  (c) that
  (d) when

[해석] A: 내가 잠시 나간 사이에 전화 온 것이 있나요?
B: 제가 아는 바로는 없어요.

[해설] Not that I am aware of 자체가 '내가 알기로는 아니다'라는 뜻의 관용적인 표현으로 많이 쓰이며, 전치사 of의 목적어로 that이라는 대명사를 취한다.

[어휘] be aware of ~에 대해 알다

5 유형 시제

A: Is Elizabeth working overtime tonight too?
B: Yes, she is. She _____ the longest working week.
  (a) has
  (b) is
  (c) is being
  (d) has had

[해석] A: Elizabeth는 오늘밤에도 야근하고 있나요?
B: 네, 그래요. 그녀는 1주일 동안 근무시간이 가장 길었어요.

[해설] 1주일 동안이라는 시간이 제시되고 있으므로 현재완료형을 사용한다.

6 유형 간접의문문의 어순

A: What is the prospect of the deer diet?
B: Success in persuading the general public to accept deer as part of its diet hinges on _____ by the mass media.
  (a) how gives away information and recipes
  (b) how well information and recipes are given away
  (c) how information and recipes are given away well
  (d) how well information and recipes give away

[해석] A: 사슴 식단의 전망은 어떤가요?
B: 일반 대중을 설득해서 사슴을 식단의 일부로 받아들이도록 하는 데 성공하는 것은 정보와 요리법이 대중매체에 의해 얼마나 잘 배포되느냐에 달려 있죠.

[해설] 빈칸 앞에 on이 있는 것으로 보아 명사가 와야 하므로 명사절을 이끌면서 목적어 역할을 하는 간접의문문을 쓸 수 있다. 간접의문문은 '의문사+주어+동사'의 어순으로 쓴다. 대중매체에 의해 배포되는 것이므로 수동형으로 써야 하고 how가 well을 수식하므로 나란히 써야 하므로 (b)가 적절하다.

[어휘] hinge on ~에 달려 있다
give away 분배하다, 나누어주다

7 유형 관용어/동사의 명령형

A: Do you know the reason why John and Judy broke up?
B: _____ me. I'm not intrigued.
 (a) Search
 (b) Searches
 (c) To search
 (d) Searching

해석 A: John과 Judy가 왜 헤어졌는지 아니?
B: 모르겠어. 관심도 없어.

해설 Search me.는 '나를 뒤져봐.' 즉, '모르겠다.'라는 의미로 명령형의 형태로 써야 알맞다.

어휘 intrigued 관심 있는

8 유형 시제

A: I like your unique masks. How long have you been collecting them?
B: Since I _____ a child.
 (a) have been
 (b) had been
 (c) were
 (d) was

해석 A: 난 너의 독특한 가면들이 좋아. 얼마나 오랫동안 모은 거니?
B: 어렸을 때부터.

해설 현재완료와 어울려서 '~이래로'의 의미가 되려면 since 다음에 과거시제가 쓰여야 한다.

9 유형 시제

A: You are supposed to take it easy until you _____ your health.
B: It's easy for you to say in that you are single. In my case, I have a family to provide for.
 (a) will regain
 (b) will have regained
 (c) egain
 (d) gained

해석 A: 건강을 회복할 때까지 무리하면 안돼.
B: 넌 싱글이니까 그렇게 쉽게 말할 수 있는 거야. 난 부양해야 할 가족이 있어.

해설 시간, 조건의 부사절에서는 현재가 미래를 대신하므로 미래의 의미일지라도 현재형을 써야 한다.

어휘 in that ~라는 점에서, ~이므로

10 유형 분사/태

A: In case my infirm friend is unconscious after _____ down all of a sudden, what am I supposed to do?
B: You'd better call 911 Emergency Service.
 (a) being fallen
 (b) fallen
 (c) falling
 (d) felling

해석 A: 허약한 친구가 갑자기 쓰러져서 의식불명이 되면 무엇을 해야 하지?
B: 긴급구조대 911에 연락해야지.

해설 fall은 '떨어지다, 넘어지다'의 의미의 자동사, fell은 '~을 떨어뜨리다. 넘어뜨리다'의 의미의 타동사이다. 빈칸은 뒤에 목적어가 없으므로 자동사가 와야 하고 능동형으로 써야 하므로 (c)가 적절하다.

어휘 infirm 허약한

11 유형 문장의 형식/수 일치

A: Were you impressed with the Carpenter's performance yesterday?
B: I was touched to tears lots of times! Everything they sang _____ fantastic.
(a) to be
(b) being
(c) were
(d) was

해석 A: 어제 Carpenter의 공연에 감동 받았니?
B: 여러 번 눈물을 흘릴 만큼 감동받았어! 그들의 모든 노래는 환상적이었어.

해설 빈칸에 필요한 것은 동사이며 everything이 주어이므로 was가 적합하다.

12 유형 시제

A: The water in the river _____ during the night.
B: Don't you know the temperature dropped below zero?
(a) freeze
(b) froze
(c) has frozen
(d) had frozen

해석 A: 밤사이 강물이 얼었어.
B: 기온이 영하로 내려간 것 모르니?

해설 during the night으로 보아 과거시제가 적합하다.

고난도 POINT 9 전치사와 시제의 관계는 절대적이지 않다.

흔히 for는 숫자가 포함된 기간을 언급하여 완료시제와 함께 쓰이고 during은 그보다는 덜 구체적인 기간을 언급하여 과거시제와 함께 쓰인다고 알고 있다. 하지만 전치사 자체가 시제를 제한하지는 않는다. during 뒤에 나오는 기간이 분명히 과거라면 과거시제를 쓰고, 다른 문장과 비교해서 분명히 더 앞선 것을 나타내면 과거완료를 쓴다.

---

13 유형 동사의 보어

A: Do you think the government should continue subsidizing farmers?
B: I don't mean to sound highly _____ to farmers, but we need to draw the line somewhere.
(a) unsympathetically
(b) unsympathy
(c) unsympathize
(d) unsympathetic

해석 A: 정부가 계속해서 농부들에게 보조금을 지급해야 한다고 생각하나요?
B: 농부들에게 상당히 매정하게 들릴지 모르지만 어느정도는 선을 그어야 해요.

해설 sound는 2형식 동사로 뒤에 보어를 필요로 한다. 따라서 보어로 쓰이는 형용사가 나와야 한다.

어휘 subsidize 보조금을 지급하다 draw the line 선을 긋다 unsympathetic 인정 없는, 매정한

14 유형 비교/관계대명사

A: Is the attendance rate important?
B: I guess it is. Those who frequently play hooky are less likely to get high marks _____ on a regular basis.
  (a) as those who is attending
  (b) than those are attended
  (c) than which are attended
  (d) than those who are attending

해석 A: 출석률이 중요한가요?
B: 내 생각엔 그래요. 자주 학교를 빼먹는 사람들은 수업에 항상 출석하는 사람들보다 높은 점수를 받기가 어려워요.

해설 빈칸 앞의 less로 보아 뒤에 than이 나와야 하고 '~하는 사람들'은 those who로 표현한다.

어휘 play hooky 학교를 빼먹다
on a regular basis 정기적으로

15 유형 동사의 보어

A: Are you insinuating that I am _____?
B: No, I don't mean to offend you. It's a slip of tongue.
  (a) no cultured
  (b) not that cultured
  (c) none the culture
  (d) such that no culture

해석 A: 당신은 내가 그렇게 교양이 없다는 뜻으로 말하는 거야?
B: 아니, 네 기분 상하게 하려는 뜻은 없어. 말이 잘못 나왔어.

해설 빈칸은 보어 자리이므로 명사나 형용사가 적합하다. (a)에서 no는 형용사이므로 뒤에 명사가 와야 하고, (c)에서 none은 대명사이므로 뒤에 명사가 오지 않는다. 따라서 (b)가 적합하다. 여기서 that은 '그렇게, 그만큼'이란 뜻의 부사로 cultured를 수식한다.

어휘 insinuate 암시하다 cultured 교양 있는
a slip of tongue 말실수

16 유형 가정법

A: David is confident that he will win the race.
B: I'd be amazed if he _____, since the other participants are highly qualified.
  (a) wouldn't
  (b) could
  (c) will
  (d) didn't

해석 A: David는 자신이 경주에서 우승할 거라고 확신해.
B: 그가 우승할 수 있다면 놀랄 일이야. 다른 참가자들이 충분히 자격을 갖추고 있으니까.

해설 빈칸 앞의 I'd be로 보아 가정법 과거 문장임을 알 수 있다. 따라서 빈칸에는 과거동사가 적합하다. 문맥상 부정의 의미가 아니므로 (b)가 적절하다.

17 유형 전치사/부사

A: _____ the surface of the sun, the temperature is so high that nothing can survive.
B: You said it.
  (a) Nearby
  (b) Nearly
  (c) Near
  (d) Nearest

해석 A: 태양의 표면 근처에서는 온도가 너무 높아서 어떤 것도 살아남을 수 없어.
B: 맞는 말이야.

해설 빈칸 뒤에 the surface라는 명사가 나오는 것으로 보아 빈칸에는 전치사가 와야 한다. (a)는 형용사, (b)는 부사, (d)는 최상급 형태이므로 적합하지 않다.

어휘 proceed 진행하다

고난도 POINT 10 유사 어휘의 품사에 유념해야 한다.

near, nearby는 둘다 '가까운'이라는 의미가 있지만 그 쓰임이 다르다. near의 경우 형용사, 전치사 모두로 사용 가능하지만 nearby는 형용사로만 쓸 수 있다. 따라서 선택지에 유사 어휘가 나올 경우 문제에서 요구하는 품사를 먼저 파악한 후 정답을 찾는 것이 중요하다.

18 유형 동사/시제

A: What are you reading now?
B: It's about the story about the woodcutter. He _____ his axe to the tree, and began to chop.
(a) lied
(b) lain
(c) lay
(d) laid

해석 A: 뭐 읽고 있니?
B: 나무꾼에 관한 이야기야. 그가 나무에 도끼를 내려놓고 나무를 베기 시작했어.

해설 뒤에 명사가 나오므로 타동사 lay가 나와야 하며 문맥상 과거시제가 나와야 하므로 laid가 적합하다.

어휘 chop 찍어서 자르다

19 유형 문장의 형식

A: What all of us wish to know about is job security. Are you going to lay workers off?
B: Not at all, let me make this _____.
(a) clean
(b) clearly
(c) clear
(d) clearness

해석 A: 우리 모두가 알고 싶은 것은 직업의 안정성입니다. 노동자들을 정리해고할 건가요?
B: 아닙니다. 이점은 분명히 말씀드리지요.

해설 make는 5형식 동사로 목적어 다음에 목적격 보어를 취하는데, 목적격 보어에 동사원형이나 형용사가 온다. 따라서 (b)와 (d)는 적절하지 않으며 문맥상 '분명히 하다'라는 의미의 clear가 적합하다.

어휘 job security 직업 안정성
lay ~ off 일시해고하다, 정리해고하다

20 유형 전치사

A: How did your boss find a new employee?
B: He advertised _____ on the Internet.
(a) one
(b) to one
(c) on one
(d) for one

해석 A: 당신의 상관은 어떻게 새로운 직원을 구했나요?
B: 인터넷에 광고를 냈어요.

해설 I go to school.처럼 전치사 to 뒤에는 목적지나 목표물이 오는 경우가 많다. on은 '~위에, ~에 관한'의 뜻이므로 문맥상 적절하지 않다. for는 뒤에 명사가 올 경우 '~을 위해서'이므로 광고를 내서 직위에 알맞은 직원을 구한다는 의미에 부합한다.

Part II Questions 21-40

21 유형 자동사/타동사

It is crucial to remove _____ the way.
(a) whatever hurdle lays along
(b) whatever hurdles lie along
(c) whatever hurdles are lain along
(d) whatever hurdle is laid along

해석 길을 따라 놓여 있는 장애물이 어떤 것이라도 제거하는 것이 중요하다.

해설 뒤에 목적어가 없는 것으로 보아 자동사가 필요한 자리이다. lie는 '놓여 있다'는 의미의 자동사이므로 수동형으로 쓰지 않고, hurdle은 셀 수 있는 명사이므로 복수형을 사용한다.

22 유형 전치사/관계대명사

The newspaper is the source _____ the public derives its knowledge of the facts.
(a) on which
(b) by which
(c) from which
(d) to which

해석 신문은 일반 대중이 사실에 대한 지식을 얻는 근원이다.

해설 derive는 from과 함께 쓰여 '~에서 얻다'라는 의미를 갖는다. 따라서 빈칸 앞뒤 문장을 이어주는 관계대명사와 함께 from을 써야 한다.

어휘 derive 끌어내다, 얻다

23 유형 전치사/관계대명사

The manner _____ differs depending on who is present.
(a) in which young people address
(b) for which young people addressed
(c) in which young people are addressed
(d) with which young people are addressed

해석 젊은이들이 이야기하는 방식은 누가 있느냐에 따라 다르다.

해설 manner는 in the manner와 같이 전치사 in과 함께 쓴다. 따라서 관계대명사 앞에 in이 와야 하고 address는 '말을 걸다'라는 타동사로, 여기서는 목적어가 없으므로 수동형으로 써야 한다.

어휘 address 말을 걸다 depending on ~에 따라

24 유형 관계사/어순

James is able to do in _____ could take his employees lots of hours or even days.
(a) so short a time when
(b) such a short time that
(c) so short a time which
(d) such a short time what

해석 James는 그의 직원들이 오랜 시간 혹은 심지어 며칠 걸릴 수 있는 일을 매우 짧은 시간에 처리할 수 있다.

해설 do의 목적어이면서 could의 주어 역할을 하는 관계대명사가 필요하므로 what이 적합하며 such는 뒤에 '관사+형용사+명사'의 어순으로 쓴다.

고난도 POINT 11 관계대명사의 문제에서는 선행사 파악이 중요하다.

관계대명사에 관한 문제가 나올 경우, 먼저 선행사 여부를 파악해야 한다. 앞에 나오는 명사가 무조건 선행사라고 생각하면 자칫 오답을 고를 수 있다. 자주 출제되는 관계대명사 what의 경우에는 선행사를 포함하고 있기 때문에 앞에 선행사가 나오지 않는다. 위 문제에서 in such a short time은 부사구로 나온 것이며 time이 선행사에 해당하지 않으므로 정답을 (b)로 고르지 않도록 문맥을 잘 파악하여 선행사를 선택해야 한다.

---

25 유형 수동태/현재분사

The university reopened a couple of years ago for _____ five years when it got caught for committing admission crimes.
(a) after closing
(b) be closed after
(c) after being closed
(d) to be closed after

해석 그 대학교는 입시부정을 저지르다 들켜서 5년 동안 학교가 폐쇄된 후 몇 년 전에 다시 열었다.

해설 학교가 어떤 사정에 의해 폐쇄되었을 것이므로 수동형이 가능하고 after 뒤에 동사를 직접 사용하려면 ~ing형을 사용해야 한다.

26 유형 형용사/비교

The people who live in certain cities in Canada are _____ as English.
(a) to speak as likely French
(b) likely as to speak French
(c) likely to speak as French
(d) as likely to speak French

해석 캐나다의 몇몇 도시에 사는 사람들은 영어만큼 프랑스어를 말한다.

해설 'be likely + to부정사' 구문으로 likely to speak가 적절하고 likely는 형용사이므로 이를 수식해주는 부사 as가 likely 앞에 와야 한다.

어휘 be likely to부정사 ~할 것 같다

27 유형 전치사/관계사

A desert is referred to as a region _____ an average of less than ten inches of rain falls in a year.
(a) which had
(b) in which is
(c) in which
(d) in that

해석 사막은 1년에 평균적으로 10인치 미만의 비가 내리는 지역을 말한다.

해설 빈칸 뒤의 문장 성분이 완전하므로 '전치사+관계대명사'가 들어가야 한다.

28 유형 전치사/명사

The analyst was responsible _____.
(a) for their false stock picks
(b) as stock picks for their fault
(c) for stock picks their fault
(d) as their false stock picks

해석 그 분석가는 그들의 잘못된 주식 선택에 대해서 책임이 있다.

해설 여기서 picks는 '선택'이라는 의미의 명사이다. 따라서 '잘못된 주식 선택'이라는 의미가 되기 위해서는 false stock picks가 되어야 한다. 또한 responsible은 for와 함께 짝을 이루므로 (a)가 적절하다.

고난도 POINT 12 어휘의 품사를 정확히 숙지해야 한다.

위 문제에서와 같이 단어의 품사에 의해 정답이 좌우된다. 보통 알고 있는 pick은 동사로 '고르다, 뽑다'라는 의미이지만 이 문제에서 pick은 '선택, 선별'의 의미를 띠는 명사이다. 따라서 이를 먼저 파악해야만 적절한 어순인 false stock picks를 선택할 수 있다. 이처럼 어휘의 다양한 쓰임을 익혀 품사를 빨리 파악하는 것이 Part Ⅰ, Ⅱ의 문제를 푸는 중요한 지름길이 된다.

29 유형 분사/접속사

_____ by public opinion, the utmost care should be taken to preserve the purity of the public mind.
(a) As we were entirely governed
(b) We being governed entirely
(c) Governing as we are entirely
(d) Governed as we are entirely

해석 우리는 전적으로 여론의 지배를 받으므로, 대중들의 정신적 순결성을 보존하려면 매우 주의해야 한다.

해설 '분사+as+주어+동사'의 어순으로 분사를 강조한 구문이다. 문맥상 지배되는 것이므로 과거분사 governed가 적합하다. (a)는 과거시제라 시제가 맞지 않는다.

어휘 utmost 최고의

30 유형 전치사/관계대명사

After every presentation in this class will be an instant open discussion _____ comments and proposals.
(a) all students can make for which
(b) for which all students can make
(c) can make during which all students
(d) during which all students can make

해석 이 수업에서의 모든 발표 후에 전체 학생들이 논평과 제안을 할 수 있는 즉각적인 공개 토론이 있을 것이다.

해설 '전치사+관계대명사'가 나올 경우 뒤에 주어, 동사, 목적어 등을 갖춘 완전한 문장이 나와야 한다. for는 좀더 명확한 기간과 함께 쓰여 '~동안'을 나타내므로 여기서는 적절하지 않다.

고난도 POINT 13 관계대명사와 관계부사를 구분해야 한다.

관계대명사와 관계부사는 관계라는 말에서 알 수 있듯이 똑같이 앞 문장과 뒤 문장을 연결하는 접속사 역할을 하지만, 각각 대명사와 부사 역할을 한다는 차이가 있다. 따라서 '전치사+관계대명사' 경우 외에 일반적으로 관계대명사가 나올 경우에는 뒤의 문장 성분이 완전하지 않아야 하며 관계부사가 나올 경우에는 문장 성분이 완전하다. 또한 관계부사는 '전치사+관계대명사'로 바꿔 쓸 수 있다는 점에서 관계대명사와 다르다.

31 유형 관계대명사

The world is not all the time _____.
(a) when we want it
(b) what we want it to
(c) what we want to be
(d) what we want it to be

해석 세상은 항상 우리가 그러기를 바라는 대로 되지 않는다.

해설 선행사가 없으므로 관계대명사 what이 나와야 한다. 우리가 세상이 그러기를 바라는 것이므로 want 뒤에 목적어 it이 와야 하고 뒤에 나오는 to부정사는 앞에 나온 is를 의미하는 것이므로 be와 함께 써야 한다.

32 유형 시제

After years of dodging conviction and making the Government seem impotent, John _____ racketeering that includes murder.
(a) stood convicted with
(b) to standing convicted with
(c) stands convicted of
(d) standing convicted of

해석 수년간 법망을 피하고 정부를 무능하게 보이도록 만든 후에 John은 살인을 포함한 협박 혐의로 기소된 상태에 있다.

해설 빈칸에는 동사가 와야 한다. 과거에 악행을 저질렀으나 현재 살인을 포함한 혐의로 기소된 것이므로 현재형이 알맞다.

어휘 dodge 피하다 conviction 유죄 판결 impotent 무능한 racketeer 협박하다
stand convicted of ~로 유죄 판결을 받다

33 유형 도치

A few months ago _____ that U. S. forces stationed in the Middle East were releasing several thousand civilian Iraqis.
(a) had the announcement been
(b) the announcement was
(c) it was the announcement
(d) came the announcement

해석 몇 달 전에 중동에 주둔하는 미군이 몇천 명의 이라크인들을 석방했다는 발표가 있었다.

해설 부사구가 문장의 앞으로 나오는 경우는 뒤에 나오는 주절의 어순이 '동사+주어'의 순서로 도치된다.

어휘 station 주둔시키다 civilian 민간인

34 유형 관계대명사

The great ox, _____, survives on Ellesmere Island.

(a) once hunted almost to extinction
(b) hunted once almost to extinction
(c) almost once hunted to extinction
(d) hunted almost once to extinction

해석 한때 멸종될 정도로 사냥되었던 그 거대한 황소는 엘즈미어 섬에 살고 있다.

해설 빈칸은 문장 사이에 삽입되는 관계대명사절로 원래 which was once hunted almost to extinction이었는데, 주격 관계대명사 which와 뒤의 was를 생략한 형태이다.

35 유형 관계대명사

One of the best vegetable protein substitutes is the soybean _____ used to make imitation meat products.

(a) can be
(b) it can
(c) that can
(d) which can be

해석 가장 좋은 식물성 단백질 대체물 중의 하나는 유사한 육류 제품을 만드는 데 이용될 수 있는 콩이다.

해설 빈칸은 두 문장을 연결하면서 soybean을 설명하는 관계대명사가 와야 한다. soybean이 선행사이므로 which나 that이 적합하고 be used to 구문으로 '~하는 데 이용되다'라는 의미가 되어야 하므로 (d)가 적절하다.

어휘 protein 단백질 substitute 대체물

36 유형 동명사/부정사

I remember _____ frustrated at the time and as powerless as a very small fish in the sea.

(a) to feel
(b) feeling
(c) being felt
(d) to have felt

해석 나는 그 당시의 좌절감과 바다 속의 아주 작은 물고기 같은 무력감을 기억한다.

해설 remember 뒤에 to부정사가 오는 경우 미래를, 동명사가 오는 경우 과거의 일을 의미한다. 여기서는 at the time으로 보아 과거의 일임을 알 수 있다.

어휘 frustrate 좌절시키다

37 유형 시제/태

Back in the latter part of the 1960s, he wrote a report on smallpox vaccinations, saying that smallpox itself _____ in Europe since 1948.

(a) has not seen
(b) had not seen
(c) had not been seen
(d) has not been seen

해석 1960년대 말로 돌아가서, 그는 천연두가 1948년 이후로 발생하지 않았다는 내용의 천연두 예방 접종에 관한 보고서를 작성했다.

해설 그가 보고서를 쓴 것은 1960년대 말이고, 천연두가 나타나지 않은 것은 1948년이므로 과거완료가 적절하다. 문맥상 수동형이 적합하므로 (c)가 정답이다.

어휘 smallpox 천연두 vaccination 예방 접종

38 유형 접속사

_____, pioneers went on to areas still farther west, toward the Mississippi River.

(a) On account of the years passed
(b) For the years passed
(c) The years passed
(d) As years passed

해석 시간이 흐름에 따라, 개척자들은 미시시피 강을 향해 서쪽으로 훨씬 더 멀리 나아갔다.

해설 빈칸 뒤에 동사가 있고 선택지에도 모두 동사가 있으므로 접속사와 함께 써야 한다. (b)의 경우 접속사로서 for의 의미는 '~ 때문에'이므로 문맥상 어울리지 않아 (d)가 적합하다. (c)는 분사구문으로 볼 경우 능동의 의미가 되어야 하므로 과거분사가 적절하지 않다.

39 유형 형용사

The directors in the commission found the ill-prepared presentation _____.
(a) chaos and confusion
(b) chaotic and confused
(c) to chaos and to confuse
(d) chaotic and confusing

[해석] 위원회의 이사들은 제대로 준비가 안 된 그 발표를 매우 혼란스럽게 느꼈다.

[해설] find A B는 'A가 B임을 알다'라는 의미로 이때 B는 목적격 보어에 해당하여 형용사가 가능하다. 따라서 (a)는 적절하지 않다. 준비가 안 된 발표가 혼란스럽게 만든 것이므로 현재분사를 써야 한다.

[어휘] commission 위원회

40 유형 도치/조동사

Only after food has been dried or canned _____.
(a) that it could be stored for later use
(b) could be stored for later use
(c) could it be stored for later use
(d) it could be stored for later use

[해석] 식품은 건조되거나 통조림 상태가 된 후에만 나중에 사용하기 위해 저장될 수 있다.

[해설] 부정적 의미를 나타내는 부사(never, hardly, scarcely, rarely, no sooner, not until, not only)와 강조부사 only 등이 문두에 오면 주어와 동사가 도치된다.

Part Ⅲ Questions 41-45

41 유형 의문사

(a) A: If you don't mind, I'd like to see you one of these days.
(b) B: How about the day after tomorrow?
(c) A: Name the place and time, please.
(d) B: What does Wednesday at six in front of my office sound?

[해석]
(a) A: 괜찮으시다면 가까운 시일 내로 한번 뵙고 싶습니다.
(b) B: 내일 모레 어떠세요?
(c) A: 장소와 시간을 말해 주세요.
(d) B: 수요일에 제 사무실 앞에서 6시 어떠세요?

[해설] (d)는 How does it sound?에서 나온 표현으로, 동사 sound를 써서 '~이 어때?'라고 물을 경우 How로 시작해야 한다. sound는 자동사이므로 what과 함께 쓸 수 없다.
What does Wednesday → How does Wednesday

42 유형 형용사

(a) A: In your high school days, who did you have as your chemistry instructor?
(b) B: Mr. Kim. His class was terrible, I hated it so much.
(c) A: Oh, really? How come?
(d) B: He was biased. He would punish the students indiscriminate for no reason.

[해석]
(a) A: 고등학교 때 화학 선생님이 누구셨니?
(b) B: Kim 선생님이야. 그 수업은 끔찍해서 정말 싫었어.
(c) A: 오, 정말? 왜?
(d) B: 그 선생님은 편견이 있었거든. 아무런 이유 없이 학생들을 무차별하게 벌줬어.

[해설] punish를 수식하는 부사가 나와야 한다.
indiscriminate → indiscriminately

[어휘] biased 편견이 있는, 공평하지 않은
indiscriminate 무차별적인, 무분별한

43 유형 대명사/도치

(a) A: Good morning. May I help you?
(b) B: This camera delivered to me today doesn't work. I'd like to get a refund.
(c) A: I see. Would you give the receipt to me, please?
(d) B: Certainly. Here are you.

해설 (a) A: 안녕하세요. 도와드릴까요?
(b) B: 오늘 저에게 배송된 카메라가 작동하지 않아요. 환불받고 싶어요.
(c) A: 알겠습니다. 영수증을 주시겠어요?
(d) B: 물론이죠. 여기 있습니다.

해설 Here로 시작하는 문장에서는 보통 주어와 동사가 도치되어 'Here+동사+주어' 형태로 쓰이지만, 주어로 대명사가 나오면 'Here+주어+동사 형태'가 된다. Here are you. → Here you are.

44 유형 동사의 종류

(a) A: You look like a gifted person.
(b) B: I'm flattered, but I've been awarded to numberless prizes for my English composition.
(c) A: Oh, really? What is the secret to writing a good essay?
(d) B: All you have to do is practice.

해설 (a) A: 당신은 재능이 있는 사람 같군요.
(b) B: 과찬이에요. 그래도 영어 작문에서는 많은 상을 탔죠.
(c) A: 오, 그래요? 훌륭한 에세이를 쓰는 비결은 뭔가요?
(d) B: 연습하는 것뿐이죠.

해설 (b)에서 award는 수여동사로, 이 문장은 간접목적어 me가 주어로 쓰인 수동태 구문이다. 따라서 to가 빠져야 한다. awarded to → awarded

어휘 flatter 칭찬하다, 아첨하다 award 수여하다

45 유형 대명사

(a) A: Oh, no. I forgot to meet Bill at five. It's already half past five.
(b) B: Who is Bill? Anyway, call him right now and tell him about this situation.
(c) A: He's my business partner. The problem is that I lost his business card, so I don't know his phone number.
(d) B: Then just look him up on the Yellow Pages.

해설 (a) A: 오, 이런. 5시에 Bill을 만나기로 한 것을 깜박했어. 벌써 5시 반이야.
(b) B: Bill이 누구야? 어쨌든 그에게 당장 전화해서 이 상황에 대해 말해.
(c) A: 내 사업 파트너야. 문제는 그의 명함을 잃어버려서 전화번호를 모른다는 거야.
(d) B: 그러면 전화번호부에서 찾아봐.

해설 그를 전화번호부에서 찾는 것이 아니고 그의 전화번호를 찾는 것이므로 (d)에서 him을 it으로 고쳐야 한다. look him up → look it up

어휘 look up (사전 등에서) 단어를 찾다, 방문하다
Yellow Pages 전화번호부

Part IV Questions 46-50

46 유형 관계대명사

(a) Spain, like many European countries, provides protection for those with permanent jobs. (b) It led some employers to expand the use of temporary jobs, which provide fewer benefits. **(c) "Most of the job losses were recorded among workers on temporary jobs, many of them are youth," the study stated.** (d) For young people, those still in school are excluded from the base.

[해석] (a) 다른 많은 유럽 국가들처럼 스페인은 정규직에 있는 사람들을 위한 보호 장치를 제공한다. (b) 이로 인해 일부 고용주들은 수당을 더 적게 주는 임시직을 확대했다. (c) 대부분의 실업은 임시직 노동자들 사이에서 기록되었는데 이들 중 많은 사람들이 젊은이들이라고 연구 결과는 발표했다. (d) 젊은이의 경우 아직 재학 중인 학생들은 통계 근거에서 배제된다.

[해설] (c) 문장의 동사가 2개(were, are)이므로 연결되려면 접속사 역할을 하는 관계대명사가 필요하다. 선행사가 workers이고 전치사 of 뒤에 들어가는 것이므로 whom이 적합하다. many of them → many of whom

[어휘] a permanent job 정규직
a temporary job 임시직 benefits 수당, 혜택

47 유형 조동사 should

(a) Everyone has a preferred method for treating a hangover that includes Gatorade, greasy food, or a Bloody Mary. (b) In my experience, however, none of these work particularly well. **(c) So when a bartender recently recommended that I tried coconut water as a morning-after remedy, I was skeptical.** (d) However, since I'd been drinking everything else she'd put in front of me, I figured I'd give it a shot.

[해석] (a) 모든 사람은 게토레이, 기름진 음식, 블러디 메리 등 숙취를 해소하기 위해 선호하는 방법을 갖고 있다. (b) 그러나 내 경험으로는 이런 것들 중 어느 것도 특별히 효과가 있지 않다. (c) 그래서 최근에 한 바텐더가 숙취 제거용으로 코코넛 물을 먹어보라고 권했을 때 나는 별로 신통하게 여기지 않았다. (d) 그러나 그녀가 내 앞에 내놓았던 다른 것들을 다 마신 후에 나는 그것을 한 번 마셔보기로 생각했다.

[해설] 주절의 동사가 권유를 나타내는 recommend이므로 that 절 뒤의 동사는 should와 함께 쓴다. 따라서 동사원형이 와야 한다. that I tried → that I (should) try

[어휘] hangover 숙취 greasy 기름진
morning-after remedy 숙취해소책
skeptical 회의적인 give it a shot 시도하다

48 유형 관계사/대명사

(a) To my surprise, the little juice box seemed to work. (b) I didn't like the sweet taste at first, but I felt noticeably better within an hour. **(c) Coconut water, which it is extracted from fruit too young to have formed milk, is low in calories and has no fat and a lot less sugar than most juices.** (d) But its most momentous attribute, at least among barflies, is that it is referred to as an excellent hydrator.

[해석] (a) (나에겐) 놀랍게도 그 작은 주스 팩은 효과를 발휘하는 것 같았다. (b) 나는 처음에 그 달콤한 맛을 좋아하지 않았지만 한 시간 안에 눈에 띄게 나아지는 것을 느꼈다. (c) 코코넛 물은 우유를 만들기에는 덜 익은 열매에서 추출된 것으로 칼로리가 낮고 지방분이 없으며 대부분의 주스보다 당분이 훨씬 적다. (d) 그러나 적어도 술집 단골들 사이에서 그것이 갖는 가장 중요한 특성은 훌륭한 수분 공급원이라는 점이다.

[해설] (c)에서 which는 주격관계대명사로 and it의 의미이므로 다음에 나오는 it을 제거하여야 한다. which it is extracted → which is extracted

[어휘] noticeably 눈에 띄게 extract 뽑다
momentous 중요한 attribute 특성 barfly 술집단골
hydrator 수분 공급원

49 유형 전치사/관계대명사

(a) The proposal takes after one developed through a similar partnership in New Haven. **(b) It does away with the shoddy evaluation system which teachers are observed briefly in the classroom.** (c) Even the most ineffective ones regularly receive glowing ratings. (d) The new system would require more intensive monitoring and would finally take student performance into account.

[해석] (a) 그 제안은 뉴헤이븐에서 비슷한 공동 작업을 통해 개발된 것과 닮았다. (b) 그것은 교실에서 교사들을 단편적으로 관찰하는 엉터리 평가 제도를 폐지한다. (c) 가장 무능한 교사들조차도 찬사 일색의 평가를 정기적으로 받고 있다. (d) 그 새로운 시스템은 좀 더 강도 높은 감시체제를 요구할 것이고 결국에는 학생의 성취도를 고려할 것이다.

[해설] (b)에서 평가 '시스템에서'라는 의미이므로 in which 또는 under which가 적절하다. which → in[under] which

[어휘] shoddy 부정한, 엉터리의 ineffective 무능한 glowing 극찬하는

50 유형 명사

(a) You might think they would have learned their lesson by now. (b) At the end of 2005 Republicans in the House of Representatives passed a bill that cracked down on illegal immigration. (c) Instead, they did nothing to regularize the position of the 12 million or so people, mostly of Hispanic origin, who were living and working inside the United States without the proper papers. **(d) Additionally, the congressmen create no mechanism for allowing people from Mexico and other southern neighbors to work with temporary permissions.**

[해석] (a) 지금쯤 그들이 교훈을 얻었을 것이라고 여러분은 생각할 것이다. (b) 2005년 말에 하원의 공화당 의원들은 불법이민을 단속하는 법안을 통과시켰다. (c) 그 대신에 미국 내에서 적절한 서류 없이 살면서 일하고 있는 대략 1200만 가량의 히스패닉계 사람들의 지위를 적절하게 조정하는 일은 아무것도 하지 않았다. (d) 게다가 국회의원들은 멕시코와 다른 남부 지역에서 온 사람들이 일시적인 허가증을 가지고 일하는 것을 허용해주기 위한 어떤 방법도 만들지 않았다.

[해설] 문맥상 '일시적인 허가증'을 의미하는 것이므로 추상적 의미의 허락을 나타내는 permissions는 적합하지 않다. with temporary permissions → with temporary permit

[어휘] Republican 공화당원
House of Representatives 하원
pass a bill 법안을 통과시키다 crack down 단속하다
regularize 질서 있게 하다, 조정하다
Hispanic 라틴계통의

고난도 Actual Training 03

1. (b)	2. (c)	3. (b)	4. (b)	5. (c)	6. (d)	7. (b)	8. (c)	9. (b)	10. (b)
11. (c)	12. (b)	13. (c)	14. (c)	15. (d)	16. (c)	17. (c)	18. (c)	19. (c)	20. (b)
21. (c)	22. (c)	23. (c)	24. (d)	25. (d)	26. (a)	27. (a)	28. (b)	29. (c)	30. (d)
31. (c)	32. (d)	33. (c)	34. (c)	35. (a)	36. (b)	37. (d)	38. (c)	39. (c)	40. (d)
41. (c)	42. (c)	43. (a)	44. (c)	45. (a)	46. (c)	47. (c)	48. (b)	49. (b)	50. (c)

Part I Questions 1-20

1 유형 가정법

A: I'm going to be taking a year off next year.
B: Oh, really? _____ that.
 (a) I wished I will speak
 (b) I wish I could say
 (c) I wish I should have said
 (d) I wished I might speak

해석 A: 나는 내년에 1년 쉴 거야.
B: 정말? 나도 그럴 수 있으면 좋을 텐데.

해설 I wish 가정법으로, 현재에 대한 반대 사실을 이야기하고 있으므로 가정법 과거 형태가 되어야 한다. 문맥상 could가 적절하다.

고난도 POINT 14   가정법 문제의 핵심은 시제이다.

현재를 의미하지만 과거시제를 사용하는 것처럼 가정법에서 포인트는 시제에 따라서 동사의 형태가 달라진다는 점이다. '~할 수 있으면 좋을 텐데'와 같이 지금 현재 그렇게 할 수 없는 일에 대해 가정법을 쓸 때에는 과거동사가 와야 한다. 과거의 일에 대해 가정법을 쓸 때에는 과거완료가 온다.

2 유형 시제/부정사

A: What are you waiting for?
B: Michael _____ ring me at 2 o'clock in the afternoon. That was one hour ago.
 (a) is supposed to
 (b) has been supposed to
 (c) was supposed to
 (d) is supposing to

해석 A: 무얼 기다리고 있니?
B: Michael이 오후 2시에 나에게 전화하기로 되어 있었는데, 그게 한 시간 전이었어.

해설 '~하기로 되어 있다'는 be supposed to 구문을 사용하고 문맥상 과거의 내용이므로 (c)가 정답이다.

3 유형 분사

A: You know about Mr. Kim?
B: I know. He's a cool guy. _____ the blame, the dissident leader asked leniency for his party officials involved in fishy dealings.
(a) Stressed that he is willing to shoulder
(b) Stressing his will to shoulder
(c) To stress his willing to shoulder
(d) Stress to his willing shouldered

[해석] A: 너 Mr. Kim에 대해 아니?
B: 응. 그는 멋진 사람이야. 반체제 지도자인 그는 비난을 자신이 떠맡겠다는 의지를 강조하면서 수상한 거래에 연루된 자기 당 관리들에 대해 관대한 처분을 요청했어.

[해설] 빈칸 뒤에 주어와 동사가 있는 것으로 보아 빈칸은 접속사로 연결된 절이나 구가 와야 한다. (a), (b)는 분사구문으로 문맥상 지도자가 자신의 의지를 강조한다는 뜻이 되어야 하므로 수동형을 쓴 (a)는 맞지 않다. (c)는 willing을 willingness로 고칠 경우 정답이 될 수 있다.

[어휘] shoulder 떠맡다 dissident 반체제의, 반체제 인사 leniency 관대함 fishy 수상한

4 유형 관용 어법

A: I feel really restless because my grades for this semester will be announced tomorrow.
B: Why _____ now? If you had done your best, the grades would not be bad.
(a) worried
(b) worry
(c) concerns
(d) concern

[해석] A: 내일 이번 학기 성적이 공지될 거라서 너무 초조해.
B: 왜 지금 걱정해? 네가 최선을 다했으면 성적도 나쁘지 않을 거야.

[해설] 'why+동사원형' 구문으로 어떤 일이 불필요함을 나타낼 때 쓴다. '걱정하다, 불안해하다'의 의미로 worry가 적합하다. 이 의미로 concern을 쓰려면 수동형을 써야 한다.

[어휘] restless 불안한

5 유형 가정법

A: My father's car broke down again on the road. So he had it towed.
B: Well, I suppose that it's high time he _____ a new automobile.
(a) buy
(b) buys
(c) bought
(d) had bought

[해석] A: 아버지 차가 길에서 또 고장이 났어. 그래서 견인시키셨어.
B: 새로운 자동차를 구입하셔야 할 때가 된 것 같아.

[해설] 'it's high time (that) ~'은 가정법과거 구문으로 that 이하에 과거동사가 와야 한다.

[어휘] tow 견인하다 it is high time (that) (늦었지만) 이제는 ~할 때이다

고난도 POINT 15 빈칸 앞뒤에 초점을 두어야 한다.

이 문제의 핵심은 빈칸 앞에 나온 high time이다. it's high time이 가정법 구문이라는 것을 알고 있다면 정답을 쉽게 찾을 수 있다. 하지만 앞에 있는 suppose에 초점을 맞춰 it's high time을 놓치게 되면 자칫 오답을 고를 수 있다. 함정에 조심하도록 한다.

6 유형 도치/조동사 do

A: I cannot remember my father hugging me in my childhood, _____ sit on his knee.
B: If my memory serves me right, you were not alone.
(a) neither will I
(b) nor would I
(c) neither did I
(d) nor did I

해석 A: 나는 어린 시절에 아버지가 나를 안아 주셨던 것도, 그리고 아버지 무릎 위에 앉았던 것도 기억나지 않아.
B: 내 기억이 맞다면, 너는 혼자가 아니었어.

해설 하나의 문장에서 동사가 2개(remember, sit)이므로 접속사가 필요한데 선택지에서 이 역할을 하는 것은 nor이다. nor는 등위접속사로서 and ~ not의 의미이다. nor는 부정어이므로 뒤에 주어와 동사의 어순이 도치되며 동사가 일반동사이고 문맥상 지난 일을 말하므로 조동사 did가 주어 앞에 나와야 한다.

어휘 if my memory serves me right 내 기억이 옳다면

7 유형 시제

A: How was your trip to Thailand? Was it fantastic?
B: It was more intriguing than I believed it _____.
(a) will be
(b) would be
(c) had been
(d) had to be

해석 A: 태국 여행 어땠어? 좋았어?
B: 내가 생각했던 것보다 더 재미있었어.

해설 과거의 시점에서 본 미래 내용이므로 would가 나와야 한다.

어휘 intriguing 재미있는

8 유형 문장의 형식

A: What are the scientists studying?
B: They are currently studying _____ exist.
(a) the way which such rodents as hamsters
(b) how rodents such as hamsters
(c) in which such rodents as hamsters
(d) to the way in which such rodents as hamsters

해석 A: 그 과학자들이 무엇을 연구하고 있니?
B: 그들은 지금 햄스터 같은 설치류가 어떻게 생존하는지 연구하고 있어.

해설 studying의 목적어와 exist의 주어가 필요하므로 명사가 와야 한다. 따라서 (c)와 (d)는 적절하지 않다. (d)의 경우, to가 없다면 답이 될 수 있었을 것이다.

9 유형 관계대명사

A: What is it about Dennis _____ so compelling?
B: He's so cool.
(a) what you find
(b) that you find
(c) who you find
(d) who you finding

해석 A: Dennis는 어떤 점이 그렇게 매력적이지?
B: 그는 성격이 매우 좋아.

해설 it is ~ that 강조용법의 의문문 형태이다. 원래 You find something about Dennis so compelling.에서 something about Dennis를 강조하여 It is something about Dennis that you find so compelling.가 되고, 이것을 다시 something을 물어보는 의문문으로 바꾼 것이므로 빈칸엔 (b)가 적절하다.

어휘 compelling 매력적인, 설득력 있는

10 유형 접속사

A: How far had Brian and Hutch gone _____ they ran out of gas?
B: It was only a few miles.
  (a) while
  (b) when
  (c) long before
  (d) after

해석
A: Brian과 Hutch는 얼마나 가서 연료가 떨어졌지?
B: 불과 몇 마일 못 가서 였어.

해설 문맥상 연료가 떨어지기 전까지 달릴 수 있으므로 before나 when이 적합하다. long before는 '곧, 즉시'의 의미이므로 문맥상 적절하지 않다.

어휘 run out of gas 연료가 떨어지다

11 유형 도치

A: Do you believe that you'll pass the bar exam?
B: _____ my best, and I'll be an attorney some day.
  (a) Under no circumstance I will do
  (b) Under no circumstances will I do
  (c) Under any circumstances I will do
  (d) Under any circumstances should I do

해석
A: 네가 변호사 시험에 합격할 것이라고 믿고 있니?
B: 어떠한 상황에서도 나는 최선을 다할 것이고 그러면 언젠가는 변호사가 될 거야.

해설 어떤 상황에서도 최선을 다할 것이라는 의미이므로 any가 적합하다. 부사구가 문두에 오더라도 주어가 인칭대명사일 경우 주어 동사의 어순은 도치되지 않는다.

어휘 bar exam 변호사 시험 attorney 변호사

12 유형 부정사/시제

A: Oh, my gosh. It's too late. I've got to be leaving now. I enjoyed it very much. Thank you for your invitation.
B: Nice _____ you today. See you later.
  (a) to meet
  (b) to have met
  (c) to meeting
  (d) having met

해석
A: 오, 이런. 너무 늦었네. 지금 당장 가봐야겠어요. 아주 즐거웠어요. 초대해주셔서 고마웠습니다.
B: 오늘 만나서 즐거웠어요. 나중에 또 봐요.

해설 만나서 헤어질 때까지 즐거웠다는 내용이므로 현재완료형을 사용한다.

13 유형 한정사/명사

A: Is Amy also working tomorrow?
B: If my memory serves me right, she has _____ off.
  (a) every other days
  (b) every another day
  (c) every other day
  (d) every once in a while

해석
A: Amy는 내일 또 일하니?
B: 내 기억이 맞다면, 그녀는 이틀에 한 번 쉬어.

해설 '격일로'의 의미는 every other day로 쓴다. other는 보통 뒤에 복수명사가 오지만, every other의 경우 단수명사가 온다.

고난도 POINT 16 명사의 수 일치에 유의하자.

일반적으로 every와 each 다음에는 단수명사가, other 뒤에는 복수명사가 온다. 하지만 이 문제에서 나온 것처럼 every other day는 other 뒤에 day가 나오지만 단수로 쓴다. 이처럼 한정사와 명사의 문제가 나올 경우 단수로 써야 하는지, 복수로 써야 하는지 파악해야 한다.

14 유형 시제

A: Didn't you used to believe that your job is cut out for you?
B: Yes, but as time goes by, I feel sick and tired of it. And I _____ commuting at the moment.
(a) have hated
(b) have been hating
(c) am hating
(d) hated

[해석] A: 예전엔 네가 하는 일이 너에게 적합하다고 생각하지 않았니?
B: 그렇게 생각했지만, 시간이 지날수록 그 일에 싫증나는 데다 지금은 출퇴근하는 것이 너무 싫어.

[해설] at the moment는 '지금'을 의미하므로 현재나 현재진행형이 적합하다.

[어휘] cut out for ~에 딱 알맞은 commute 출퇴근하다

15 유형 관사/명사

A: What a good smell! It smells like orange.
B: Yes, I just cut _____.
(a) orange
(b) the orange
(c) many orange
(d) an orange

[해석] A: 좋은 냄새가 나네! 오렌지 같은 냄새가 나.
B: 응, 내가 막 오렌지를 잘랐어.

[해설] 오렌지는 셀 수 있으므로 관사를 사용한다. A는 막연하게 오렌지를 떠올리며 한 말이므로 관사를 쓰지 않았고, B의 말에서 구체적인 오렌지라는 대상이 처음 언급되므로 부정관사를 쓰는 것이 적절하다.

16 유형 동사/문장 형식

A: Good evening, Mr. Park. My name is David Lynn.
B: How do you do? Susan _____ a lot about you.
(a) had said to me
(b) has talked me
(c) has told me
(d) had spoken to me

[해석] A: 안녕하세요, Mr. Park. 내 이름은 David Lynn이에요.
B: 안녕하세요? Susan이 당신에 대해 이야기 많이 했어요.

[해설] say, speak, talk, tell은 모두 '말하다'의 의미를 가지지만 그 쓰임이 다르다. say는 뒤에 'something to someone' 의 형태로 오고 speak와 talk는 'with/to somebody about something'과 같이 쓰인다. tell은 'something, someone something, something+to부정사'와 같이 다양한 형태로 온다. 이 문제에서는 Susan이 상대방에 관한 이야기를 나에게 많이 해줬다는 의미이므로 (c)가 정답이다. (d)는 시제가 맞지 않다.

17 유형 관계대명사

A: Would you please explain to me what anarchism is?
B: Anarchism is a term describing a group of doctrines _____ significant uniting feature is the belief that government is both inimical and noxious.
(a) in that
(b) since
(c) whose
(d) and

[해석] A: 무정부주의가 무엇인지 설명해주시겠어요?
B: 무정부주의란 일련의 신조를 설명하는 용어인데 중요한 특징은 정부가 적대적이며 해롭다는 믿음입니다.

[해설] 빈칸은 앞뒤 문장을 연결해 주는 접속사 역할의 단어가 들어가야 한다. 하지만 빈칸 뒤 문장의 주어 feature가 가산 명사인데 관사가 없는 것으로 보아 앞 문장에 연결되는 내용임을 알 수 있다. 따라서 접속사 역할을 하면서 선행사 a group of doctines를 받는 관계대명사가 들어가야 한다. 관계대명사 자리 뒤에 명사가 있는 것으로 보아 소유격 whose가 적합하다.

[어휘] doctrine 신조, 주의 inimical 적대하는 noxious 유해한

18 유형 분사 구문/시제

A: What did you do after the hurricane had passed through?
B: The strong winds _____, we began to assess the damage.
(a) being abated
(b) abating
(c) having abated
(d) to abate

해석 A: 허리케인이 지나간 후에 어떻게 했습니까?
B: 강한 바람이 잦아들고 난 후에 우리는 피해 정도를 파악하기 시작했어요.

해설 뒤 문장과 주어가 달라 분사구문의 주어를 생략하지 않은 분사구문으로, 사건의 전후 관계로 보아 바람이 잦아든 것은 파악하기 전의 일이므로 완료형을 사용하는 것이 적합하다.

어휘 abate 줄어들다, 약해지다 assess 평가하다

19 유형 동사/전치사

A: What are the results of the archaeological excavations?
B: Excavations in several places on the east bank of the Euphrates River have disclosed an ancient community that _____ later reconstructions of the city of Babylon.
(a) had laid beneath
(b) had lay beneath
(c) had been lying under
(d) had been laying under

해석 A: 그 고고학 발굴의 결과는 무엇인가요?
B: 유프라테스 강의 동쪽 강둑에 있는 몇몇 장소에서 이루어진 발굴로 이후 복원된 바빌론시 아래에 있는 고대 공동체를 발견했습니다.

해설 lie는 lie-lay-lain-lying의 형태로 '~에 눕다, ~에 놓여 있다, ~한 상태에 있다'는 의미를 띠며 뒤에 전치사가 온다. lay는 lay-laid-laid-laying의 형태로 '~을 눕히다, ~을 놓다'는 의미를 띠며 뒤에 목적어가 온다.

어휘 later 나중의 excavation 발굴 reconstruction (옛 건물 등의) 재현물, 복원물

20 유형 관용 표현

A: Boy, rumor _____ he will be fired for his scandal.
B: Serves him right. He has not managed well.
(a) has that
(b) has it that
(c) that has
(d) that it has

해석 A: 아, 그가 추문으로 해임될 것이라는 소문이 있던데.
B: 그럴 만해. 그는 잘 관리하지 못했어.

해설 rumor has it that이라고 하면 '~라는 소문이 있다'는 의미이다. it은 일종의 진목적어 가목적어 구문으로, 그 어순을 잘 기억해 둬야 한다.

어휘 serve a person right 인과응보다

고난도 POINT 17 숙어가 문법 시험에 출제될 경우 어순을 주의한다.

위에 나온 'rumor has it that~'과 같이, 숙어는 익숙해진 말을 일컫는다. 이는 기존의 문법이나 어휘의 의미와는 다른 것을 조합하여 새로운 의미가 생겨난 것이므로 문법 시험에 출제될 경우 주로 어순을 묻는 유형이 많다. 따라서 정확한 숙어의 의미와 함께 어순을 잘 기억하도록 한다.

Part II Questions 21-40

21 유형 시제/태

Mr. White, the former General and the incumbent Secretary of Defence, _____ embezzlement and fraud.
(a) charged with
(b) had been charged of
(c) has been charged with
(d) is being charging of

해석 전 육군 장군이자 현 국방부 장관인 Mr. White는 횡령과 사기 혐의로 기소되었다.
해설 charge는 전치사 with와 어울려 쓰이고, of는 accuse와 어울려 쓰인다. 문맥상 Mr. White가 어떤 혐의로 기소된 것이므로 수동형이 와야 한다.
어휘 embezzlement 횡령 fraud 사기

22 유형 비교

The more stress you are under, _____ develop cancer.
(a) the likely you are more to
(b) the more you likely are to
(c) the more likely you are to
(d) the likely more you are to

해석 당신이 스트레스가 많으면 많을수록 암에 걸리기 쉽습니다.
해설 'the+비교급+주어+동사, the+비교급+주어+동사'는 '~하면 할수록 더욱더 ~하다'는 의미를 갖는다.
어휘 develop (병)에 걸리다

23 유형 비교/전치사

The ban-on-crude-oil-import policy would push petroleum prices in the country _____ the world level.
(a) almost up to ten times
(b) up to ten times almost
(c) up to almost ten times
(d) almost ten times up to

해석 원유 수입 금지 정책은 나라의 석유 값을 세계 수준의 거의 10배 정도까지 오르게 할 것이다.
해설 '거의 10배'가 하나의 의미 단위가 되며 그 앞에 up to를 쓴다.
어휘 crude oil 원유 petroleum 석유

24 유형 관계대명사/수 일치

Of all the things edible, flour is the one _____ food for more people than any of the other grain crops in America.
(a) it provides
(b) that providing
(c) provides
(d) that provides

해석 먹을 수 있는 것들 중에서 밀가루는 미국에서 다른 어떤 곡물보다도 더 많이 사람들에게 음식을 제공하는 것이다.
해설 선행사 the one을 빈칸 뒤의 문장이 설명해 주고 있으므로 주격관계대명사와 동사가 나오는 (d)가 적합하다.
어휘 edible 먹을 수 있는

25 유형 관계대명사/태

Much of _____ about the behavior of porpoises has come from observations made at Sea World in Florida.

(a) which said
(b) which is said
(c) what said
(d) what is said

[해석] 돌고래의 행동에 관해 이야기 중 상당수는 플로리다의 씨월드에서 이루어진 관찰에서 나왔다.

[해설] of의 목적어로 명사가 나와야 하는데 선행사가 없으므로 관계대명사 what이 적절하고 문맥상 수동이므로 is said가 적절하다.

[어휘] porpoise 돌고래

26 유형 문장의 형식

Certain fish eggs include droplets of oil, _____ to float on the surface of the water.

(a) allowing them
(b) allows them
(c) they are allowed
(d) this allows them

[해석] 어떤 물고기 알은 물의 표면 위에 떠 있을 수 있도록 해주는 기름 방울을 포함한다.

[해설] include라는 동사가 나왔으므로 접속사 없이 쓴 (c), (d)는 적합하지 않다. 'allow+목적어+to부정사'의 형태에 맞춰 분사구문으로 쓴 (a)가 적절하다.

[어휘] droplet 작은 방울

27 유형 복합 관계대명사

No one knows exactly how big China's Internet police force is these days, although estimates run as high as 40,000. But _____, its sophistication is less than ever.

(a) whatever its scale
(b) however it's scale is
(c) however its scale
(d) whatever it's scale is

[해석] 비록 4만 정도로 추정되지만 중국의 인터넷 경찰력이 요즘 얼마나 큰지 누구도 정확히 알지 못한다. 하지만 그 규모가 얼마가 되든지 간에 정교함은 전보다 덜하다.

[해설] '그것의 규모가 얼마가 되든지'를 영어로 나타내면 its scale is what~ 형태가 된다. is 뒤는 보어 자리이므로 부사인 however가 올 수 없다. 이를 복합 관계대명사 형태로 앞으로 이동시키면 whatever its scale is가 되고 여기서 be동사는 생략할 수 있다.

고난도 POINT 18 however와 whatever를 구별해야 한다.

however와 whatever는 둘 다 양보구문을 만들지 만 쓰임이 다르다. however는 뒤에 형용사나 부사가 오고 whatever는 형용사나 부사가 오지 않는다. 따라서 위 문제에서는 빈칸의 ever 자리 뒤에 its scale이라는, 형용사나 부사가 아닌 명사가 왔으므로 whatever가 적절하다.

28 유형 수사/명사

The sports complex was built just _____ from my office.

(a) five mile away
(b) five miles away
(c) on five miles away
(d) in five mile away

[해석] 그 스포츠 종합단지는 내 사무실에서 딱 5마일 떨어져서 지어졌다.

[해설] 수사가 단위를 나타내는 명사와 함께 쓰일 때는 '수사+단위명사+형용사/부사' 형태로 쓴다. 이때 단위명사는 수사에 맞춰 단수 또는 복수형을 취한다.

[어휘] complex 종합단지

29 유형 동사/전치사

Elizabeth's grandfather, Henry Tudor, became King Henry VII of England in 1485. He _____ his son Henry VIII in 1509.
(a) was succeeded in
(b) was succeeded to
(c) was succeeded by
(d) succeeded to

해석 Elizabeth의 할아버지인 Henry Tudor는 1485년에 영국의 Henry 7세가 되었다. 그는 1509년에 아들 Henry 8세에게 국왕의 자리를 물려주었다.

해설 여기서 succeed는 '~의 뒤를 잇다'라는 의미의 타동사로 그가 아들에게 자리를 물려준 것이므로 수동형으로 써야 한다. 자동사 succeed가 to와 함께 쓰면 '~를 물려받다'라는 의미가 되므로 (d)는 적절하지 않다.

30 유형 관계대명사

It is not a religion _____ tenets almost everyone would think inordinate.
(a) which
(b) what
(c) that
(d) whose

해석 거의 모든 사람이 생각하기에 교의가 지나치다고 여겨지는 것은 종교가 아니다.

해설 빈칸에 알맞은 관계대명사를 넣을 때 관계대명사의 선행사가 있는 경우는 what이 제외된다. 문맥상 '종교의 교의'라는 의미가 되어야 하므로 소유격 관계대명사가 필요하다.

어휘 tenet 교의, 신조 inordinate 지나친, 과도한

31 유형 형용사+명사

Some children like to read _____ during their spare time.
(a) that kinds of book
(b) that kinds of book
(c) that kind of book
(d) those kind of books

해석 몇몇 아이들은 여가 시간에 그런 종류의 책들을 읽는 것을 좋아한다.

해설 'kind of+명사'의 경우, this kind, these kinds처럼 kind 앞에 붙는 지시사에 따라 kind의 단수와 복수가 정해진다. book은 셀 수 있는 명사이므로 앞에 온 지시사 that에 맞게 단수형으로 써야 한다. (a), (b), (d)의 경우 that kinds, those kind로 문법에 맞지 않다.

32 유형 접속사

_____ the off-shore drillers had located the oil field, they prepared its development.
(a) Until
(b) If
(c) What
(d) Once

해석 해저 유전 시추공들이 유전을 찾자, 유전에 대한 개발을 준비했다.

해설 앞부분의 시제가 과거완료이고 뒷부분이 과거인 것으로 보아 앞부분의 일이 먼저 일어났음을 알 수 있다. 따라서 이를 나타내는 once가 문맥상 적절하다.

어휘 off-shore 앞바다의 driller 시추공, 착암공 oil field 유전

33 유형 간접의문문

The Consumer Price Index has been listing _____.
(a) how much costs every car
(b) how much does every car cost
(c) how much every car costs
(d) how much are every car cost

해석 소비자 물가지수는 모든 차가 얼마인지의 목록을 작성해왔다.

해설 list는 타동사로 뒤에 목적어가 필요하다. 선택지에 나온 것처럼 의문문이 목적어가 될 경우 간접의문문으로 쓰고 '의문사+주어+동사'의 어순을 취한다.

34 유형 문장의 형식

According to the research, _____ is essential for the development of robust bones and teeth.

(a) the calcium
(b) that calcium
(c) calcium
(d) though calcium

[해석] 연구에 따르면 칼슘은 강한 뼈와 치아 발달을 위해 필수적이다.

[해설] 빈칸에 필요한 것은 주어가 될 수 있는 명사가 나와야 한다. (b)와 (d)는 that, though와 같은 접속사가 나와서 적절하지 않다. 또한 calcium의 일반적이고 보편적인 성질을 나타내는 것이므로 the와 함께 쓰지 않는다.

35 유형 전치사/관계대명사

_____ people use social space reflects their social relationships and their ethnic identities.

(a) The way in which
(b) It is the way
(c) Which is the way
(d) Which way is

[해석] 사람들이 사회적 공간을 이용하는 방법이 사회적 관계와 그들의 민족적 정체성을 반영한다.

[해설] 동사가 use, reflects 두 개가 있으므로 접속사가 필요하다. 관계대명사 which가 접속사 역할을 하는 The way in which가 올바르다.

36 유형 동사의 형식/분사

Congressmen eager to promote a piece of legislation no doubt _____ whenever their bill languishes in committee.

(a) seeming to feel thwarted
(b) seem to feel thwarted
(c) seems to feel thwarting
(d) seems to feel thwarted

[해석] 법안 통과를 간절히 바라는 국회의원들은 그들의 법안이 위원회에서 제대로 통과되지 않을 때마다 좌절감을 느끼는 것 같다.

[해설] 주어가 Congressmen으로 복수형이므로 동사는 seem이 되고, 좌절시키는 것이 아니라 좌절을 느끼는 것이므로 수동형 thwarted를 쓴다.

[어휘] Congressman 국회의원 legislation 법안 thwart 좌절시키다 languish (의안 등이) 무산되다, 유보되다

37 유형 접속사

Grounded on the assumption that light is made up of color, the post-impressionists came to the conclusion _____ not really black.

(a) was shadows that
(b) which was that shadows
(c) that was shadows
(d) that shadows were

[해석] 빛이 색으로 구성되어 있다는 가정에 근거하여, 후기 인상파 화가들은 그림자가 사실은 검은색이 아니라는 결론에 도달했다.

[해설] the conclusion에 관한 내용이 나와야 하므로 동격의 that 구문을 사용한다. 동격의 that 구문은 뒤에 완전한 문장이 나오므로 (d)가 적절하다. 이처럼 동격의 that은 the conclusion, the idea, the fact 등의 단어 뒤에 많이 쓰인다.

고난도 POINT 19 접속사 that과 관계사 that을 구별하자.

동일하게 명사 뒤에 쓰이는 that이지만 접속사일 수도 있고 관계대명사일 수도 있다. 이 문제에서처럼 앞에 conclusion이라는 일종의 동격 제시어구 뒤에서 that이 접속사로 쓰일 경우 that 이하 구문은 conclusion의 내용이 된다. 또한 동격의 that일 경우에는 뒤에 완전한 문장이 온다는 점이 관계대명사 that과 다르다.

38 유형 접속사/도치

Even though one of his ships ended up in succeeding in sailing all the way back to his motherland past the Cape of Good Hope, Magellan himself never completed the first circumnavigation of the globe, and _____.

(a) nor did most of his crew too
(b) neither most of his crew did
(c) neither did most of his crew
(d) nor most of his crew did also

[해석] 비록 자신의 배 중 하나가 희망봉을 지나 조국으로 돌아오는 항해에 성공했지만 Magellan 자신은 그의 첫 세계 일주를 결코 완수하지 못했고, 그의 선원들 대부분도 그러했다.

[해설] nor는 접속사로서 and not의 의미이다. 빈칸 앞에 있는 and로 보아 여기서 nor는 적절하지 않다. 부정문에서 '~도 역시 그렇지 않다'란 표현은 'neither+조동사(be 동사)+주어'로 나타낸다.

39 유형 조동사/시제

If the cosmos is getting larger, in the past it _____ at the moment.

(a) must be smaller than it is
(b) should have been smaller than it is
(c) must have been smaller than it is
(d) would have been smaller than it is

[해석] 우주가 점점 커지고 있다면 과거에 그것은 지금보다 더 작았음에 틀림없다.

[해설] 빈칸에는 강한 추측의 의미를 나타내는 말이 와야 하는데 과거를 이야기하고 있으므로 must have been이 적절하다.

40 유형 문장의 형식

_____ that gold was found around San Francisco and that the California Gold Rush began, making many people in the U.S. migrate to the West.

(a) Since 1848
(b) What in 1848
(c) In 1848 that it was
(d) It was in 1848

[해석] 황금이 샌프란시스코에서 발견되고 캘리포니아 골드러시가 시작되어 미국의 많은 사람들이 서부로 이주했던 때는 바로 1848년이었다.

[해설] that절이 and로 양쪽에 연결되어 있고 that절의 내용이 모두 완전하므로 강조 용법의 It was ~ that 구문에 관한 문제이다.

Part III Questions 41-45

41 유형 문장의 형식

(a) A: Would you back up your car a little, please?
(b) B: I see. I'll do it at once.
(c) A: Look at who's here! Is that you, Edward?
(d) B: Yeah, it's me. It's been a long time since I saw you last.

[해석]
(a) A: 차 좀 뒤로 후진해 주실래요?
(b) B: 알겠습니다. 당장 해드릴게요.
(c) A: 아니, 이게 누구야! 너 Edward지?
(d) B: 그래, 나야. 지난번에 본 뒤로 오랜만이다.

[해설] look 뒤에 절이 오면 전치사 at을 쓰지 않는다. Look at who's → Look who's

[어휘] back up (차를) 후진하다

42 유형 동사

(a) A: I was wondering what your nationality is.
(b) B: I'm from Colombia which is located in South America.
(c) **A: What takes you to this country?**
(d) B: I came here to study the Korean language.

해설 (a) A: 당신의 국적이 궁금합니다.
(b) B: 저는 남미에 있는 콜롬비아에서 왔습니다.
(c) A: 우리나라엔 어떻게 해서 오시게 되었어요?
(d) B: 한국어 공부하러 왔어요.

해설 직역하면 '무엇이 당신을 이곳으로 오게 했니?'의 의미이다. 이와 같은 상황에서는 보통 come의 의미를 나타내는 bring을 사용한다. takes → brings

43 유형 동사/분사

(a) **A: I'd like to have this prescription fill, please.**
(b) B: I'll handle it right now.
(c) A: Could you also give me something for a pimple?
(d) B: Apply this ointment. It will work.

해설 (a) A: 저는 이 처방전대로 조제 받고 싶습니다.
(b) B: 지금 바로 처리해 드리겠습니다.
(c) A: 그리고 여드름 약도 좀 주실래요?
(d) B: 이 연고를 발라보세요. 효과가 있을 거예요.

해설 (a)에서 have는 사역동사로 쓰여 뒤에 목적어와 목적격 보어를 취한다. 목적어와 목적격 보어의 관계가 능동일 경우 목적격 보어는 원형부정사가 오고, 수동일 경우 과거분사가 온다. 여기서 this prescription과 fill의 관계는 수동이므로 과거분사가 되어야 한다. have this prescription fill → have this prescription filled

44 유형 시제

(a) A: Hello. Could you put me through to Howard?
(b) B: I'm sorry, but he is not in right now.
(c) **A: Would you have him call me when he will get back?**
(d) B: Does he have your phone number?

해설 (a) A: 안녕하세요. Howard 좀 연결해 주실래요?
(b) B: 죄송합니다만 지금 자리에 없는데요.
(c) A: 돌아오면 제게 전화 해달라고 해주시겠어요?
(d) B: 그가 선생님 전화번호를 알고 있나요?

해설 시간, 조건의 부사절에선 현재시제가 미래시제 대신 사용되므로 (c)의 when절의 동사는 현재형으로 써야 한다. will get → gets

어휘 put ~ through 연결하다

45 유형 동사

(a) **A: Is anybody awaiting on you?**
(b) B: No. I want a short-sleeved shirt in white, large size.
(c) A: I believe we don't have any in stock.
(d) B: Can you check and get me one next weekend?

해설 (a) A: 저희 직원이 손님을 도와 드렸나요?
(b) B: 아니요. 저는 하얀색, 큰 걸로 소매가 짧은 스커트를 원합니다.
(c) A: 제가 알기론 재고가 없는데요.
(d) B: 확인해보시고 다음 주말에 제가 하나 살 수 있을까요?

해설 await는 타동사로 뒤에 on과 함께 쓰지 않는다. 문맥상 '시중들다'를 나타내는 wait on이 적절하다. 같은 의미로 Are you being served?가 쓰인다. awaiting → waiting

어휘 await 기다리다, 맞아들이다
short-sleeved 소매가 짧은 stock 재고

Part IV Questions 46-50

46 유형 의문형용사

(a) Holding teachers responsible for student performance is now all the rage. (b) So, let's make a simple thought experiment in the sports world. **(c) Imagine an amateur baseball league in which team owners dictate whose bats players use.** (d) The owners seek to single out the utmost, but the research on bats is so poor, they might choose the worst.

[해석] (a) 선생님들에게 학생들의 성취도에 대해 책임지게 하는 것이 지금 대유행이다. (b) 자, 백악관으로부터 정치권에 이르기까지 단순한 생각 실험을 해 보자. (c) 팀의 구단주가 선수들이 어떤 방망이를 사용해야 하는지 지시하는 아마추어 야구 리그를 상상해보라. (d) 구단주는 최상의 것을 고르기 위해 노력하지만 방망이에 대한 연구가 너무 부실해서 그들은 최악의 것을 고를 수도 있다.

[해설] (c)에서 문맥상 bats 앞에는 '어떤, 어느'의 의미를 지닌 형용사 역할의 의문사가 필요하므로 which가 정답이다.
whose bats → which bats

[어휘] single out 선택하다

47 유형 동사

A tree trunk shattering in the wind can sound very much like a lightning strike. (a) I braced for the worst when I heard that sound the other day while lying in bed at home. (b) My thought was the tree was about to crash down, pounding my garden into rubble but thankfully, that did not happen. **(c) When I pulled back the shade, I found that the wind had wrenched off a massive branch and lowered it deftly into the neighbor's yard with no real property damage to speak.** (d) A sharp-eyed tree surgeon would have pointed at it and have it condemned.

[해석] 바람에 부서지는 나무줄기 소리가 마치 번개 치는 소리처럼 들린다. (a) 나는 일전에 집에서 침대에 누워 있다가 그 소리를 들었을 때 최악의 경우를 대비했다. (b) 내 생각에는 나무가 곧 부러져서 정원을 덮쳐 조각낼 것 같았는데 감사하게도 그런 일은 일어나지 않았다. (c) 내가 차양을 잡아당겼을 때 이야기할 만한 큰 재산 피해 없이 바람이 거대한 나뭇가지를 끊어 이웃집 마당으로 교묘하게 늘어뜨려 놓은 것을 발견했다. (d) 예리한 눈의 나무 외과의사가 있었더라면 그것을 지적하고 배상을 받았을 것이다.

[해설] speak는 외국어를 말하는 경우를 빼고는 1형식 동사로 사용되며 전치사가 뒤에 나와서 speak of, speak to의 형태로 사용된다. 본문에서는 문맥상 speak of가 되어야 한다.
to speak → to speak of

[어휘] shatter 박살내다 brace for 준비하다
crash down 부딪치다 pound 두드리다
rubble 잡석, 깨진 돌조각
pull back 잡아당기다, 철수하다
wrench off 힘으로 잡아 빼다 deftly 빠르게, 기술 있게
indemnify 배상하다

48 유형 전치사/관계대명사

(a) According to statistics recently released by the Bureau of Statistics, people aged 65 or older now account for more than 20% of the population in each of 30 rural cities. **(b) This is a fresh reminder of the rapid pace on which the nation's population is going gray.** (c) The lowest fertility rate in the world makes the whole thing seem horrible. (d) But productive solutions are unlikely as long as we view this problem with horror.

해석 (a) 최근에 통계청에서 발표한 통계에 따르면 65세 이상의 노인들이 지금 30개 시골 도시에서 인구의 20퍼센트 이상을 차지한다고 한다. (b) 이것은 나라의 인구가 고령화되는 속도가 빨라지고 있음을 새롭게 상기시킨다. (c) 세계에서 가장 낮은 출산율이 모든 상황을 끔찍하게 만드는 것 같다. (d) 그러나 우리가 이 문제를 두렵게 바라본다면 생산적인 해결책은 나올 것 같지 않다.

해설 (b)에서 pace는 전치사 at과 어울려 쓴다. pace on which → pace at which

어휘 statistics 통계 자료 release 발표하다, 내놓다
go gray 노령화되다 productive 결실 있는

49 유형 분사/태

(a) In one of the most heated general elections ever, the British Conservative Party won over the ruling Labor Party. **(b) But the Conservatives failed to win a majority, forcing to form a coalition government.** (c) As a result, it left British politics in flux for some time. (d) After the voting tally came out, leaders of political parties insisted on a major say in the formation of the next government.

해석 (a) 지금까지 가장 열띤 총선 중의 하나에서 보수당이 집권 여당인 노동당을 이겼다. (b) 그러나 보수당은 다수표를 얻는 데 실패했고 어쩔 수 없이 연립정부를 형성했다. (c) 그 결과로 한동안 영국 정계가 요동쳤다. (d) 투표결과가 집계되고 나서 정당의 지도자들은 다음 정부의 형태에 대해 중요한 발언권을 주장했다.

해설 (b)에서 force는 '강요하다'는 의미이지만 여기서는 문맥상 수동형으로 써야 하므로 being forced to가 적합하다. 이때 being은 생략 가능하다. forcing to → (being) forced to

어휘 general elections 총선 Conservative Party 보수당
ruling 정권을 잡은 Labor Party 노동당
a coalition government 연립정부 flux 변화, 불안정
tally 총 집계, 기록

50 유형 문장의 형식/형용사

(a) Probation is a device to deter future crimes in imposing penalties on crimes committed in the past. (b) But it was managed in the same way as other penalties. **(c) So the Constitution Court find it unconstitutionally for raising the hazard of double jeopardy and excessive penalty.** (d) I am not comfortable with the idea of reinstating probation.

해석 (a) 집행유예는 과거에 저지른 범죄에 대해 형벌을 가하여 미래의 범죄를 막기 위한 장치이다. (b) 그러나 그것은 다른 형벌과 같은 방법으로 운영되었다. (c) 그래서 헌법재판소는 이중 위험과 지나친 형벌의 위험성을 제기하므로 그것을 헌법에 위반된다고 했다. (d) 나는 집행유예를 원상태로 회복시킨다는 생각에 대해 마음이 불편하다.

해설 (c)에서 find는 find A B로 쓰여 'A를 B라고 생각하다'의 의미를 나타낸다. B는 보어로서 명사나 형용사가 되어야 한다. it unconstitutionally → it unconstitutional

어휘 probation 집행유예 reinstate 원상태로 복귀시키다

고난도 Actual Training 04

1. (b)	2. (c)	3. (c)	4. (d)	5. (c)	6. (c)	7. (c)	8. (c)	9. (b)	10. (c)
11. (c)	12. (d)	13. (d)	14. (c)	15. (c)	16. (c)	17. (d)	18. (b)	19. (d)	20. (a)
21. (d)	22. (c)	23. (d)	24. (a)	25. (d)	26. (a)	27. (d)	28. (a)	29. (c)	30. (d)
31. (b)	32. (a)	33. (d)	34. (d)	35. (c)	36. (b)	37. (c)	38. (c)	39. (d)	40. (b)
41. (a)	42. (b)	43. (a)	44. (d)	45. (c)	46. (d)	47. (b)	48. (b)	49. (d)	50. (d)

Part I Questions 1-20

1 유형 시제

A: Is it possible for your dream to come true?
B: Certainly, the time will surely come when my dream _____ true.
(a) comes
(b) will come
(c) will have come
(d) coming

해석
A: 너의 꿈이 이루어지는 것이 가능할까?
B: 물론이지, 내 꿈이 실현될 날이 반드시 올 거야.

해설 when 이하가 the time을 꾸미는 형용사절로 쓰이고 미래를 나타내므로 will을 사용해야 한다.

고난도 POINT 20 when이 나오는 명사절과 부사절을 구별하라.

when절이 나올 경우 무조건 미래시제를 현재시제가 대신하지는 않는다. when절은 부사절 외에 명사절이나 형용사절로도 쓰일 수 있으므로 문장 내에서 절의 역할을 파악하여 시제를 결정하는 것이 중요하다. 시간을 나타내는 부사절의 경우 현재시제가 미래시제를 대신하지만 절 자체가 목적어나 주어의 역할을 하는 명사절의 경우 미래시제를 그대로 쓴다.

2 유형 조동사/동사의 형식

A: I'm surprised to hear that the actor died of lung cancer.
B: The doctor insisted that he _____. The actor ought to have followed his advice.
(a) had not smoked
(b) should not have smoked
(c) not smoke
(d) did not smoke

해석
A: 나는 그 배우가 폐암으로 죽었다는 소식을 듣고 깜짝 놀랐어.
B: 주치의가 그 사람에게 담배를 피우지 말라고 주장했어. 그는 의사의 충고를 따랐어야 했는데.

해설 insist처럼 요구, 주장, 명령, 제안의 동사가 나오면 that절 뒤에서는 내용상 의무의 조동사 should가 나오고 생략된다 하더라도 그 뒤의 동사는 원형을 쓴다. 따라서 문맥상 The doctor insisted that he should not smoke. 가 되어야 하는데, should는 생략할 수 있으므로 he not smoke가 정답이 된다.

44

3 유형 가정법

A: I was so angry that I took the boss by the collar.
B: You went too far. _____ your shoes, I would not have done that.
 (a) I had been in
 (b) I should have been on
 (c) Had I been in
 (d) Were I with

[해석] A: 난 너무 화가 나서 상사의 멱살을 잡았어.
B: 너무 심했어. 내가 네 입장이었다면 그렇게 하지 않았을 거야.

[해설] 주절의 would have done으로 보아 가정법 과거완료 문장임을 알 수 있다. 따라서 If I had been in your shoes가 되어야 하는데 if를 생략하여 Had I been in your shoes로 썼다.

[어휘] take A by the collar A의 멱살을 잡다

4 유형 가정법/시제

A: Do you remember of our boarding school days?
B: Sure. I wish we _____ to get to know one another better in the time we had.
 (a) will be able
 (b) would have been able
 (c) were able
 (d) had been able

[해석] A: 우리가 기숙학교 다니던 시절 기억하니?
B: 물론이지. 우리가 함께 했던 시절에 좀 더 서로를 잘 알고 지냈으면 좋았을 텐데.

[해설] I wish 가정법 구문으로 in the time we had에서 과거에 대한 내용임을 알 수 있다. 따라서 가정법 과거완료를 써야 한다.

5 유형 형용사/명사

A: What is the merit of Glacier National Park?
B: Extensive forests, _____, abundant wildlife, and beautiful waterfalls are among the attractions of Glacier National Park.
 (a) it has spectacular mountain scenery
 (b) the mountain scenery is spectacular
 (c) spectacular mountain scenery
 (d) and the spectacular scenery of the mountains

[해석] A: 글레이셔 국립공원의 장점은 무엇입니까?
B: 광대한 삼림, 눈이 휘둥그레질 정도의 산악 풍경, 풍부한 야생동물, 아름다운 폭포 등이 글레이셔 국립공원의 매력들입니다.

[해설] '형용사+명사' 형태가 접속사 and에 의해 병렬로 연결되고 있다.

6 유형 분사구문

A: Jason, what did you do yesterday?
B: _____ snowy, I went out to make a snowman with my son.
 (a) Being
 (b) As being
 (c) It being
 (d) Having been

[해석] A: Jason, 너 어제 뭐했니?
B: 눈이 내려서, 밖에 나가서 우리 아들과 눈사람을 만들었어.

[해설] 문맥상 빈칸은 이유를 말하는 내용이므로 As it was snowy가 되는데 이때 주절의 주어 I와 종속절 As의 주어가 다르므로 it을 그대로 남겨두어야 한다.

7 유형 수량형용사/명사

A: Bob, how's your lawsuit going?
B: Since I have _____, I am confident that I will win the case.
(a) many evidence
(b) a number of evidences
(c) much evidence
(d) the number of evidence

해석 A: Bob, 소송 어떻게 되어가니?
B: 내가 증거를 충분히 가지고 있어서 승소할 자신 있어.

해설 evidence는 불가산명사이므로 복수형으로 쓸 수 없고, much와 함께 쓴다.

어휘 lawsuit 소송 win the case 승소하다

8 유형 부사/도치

A: Do you happen to know about the South Korean miners and nurses who were sent to West Germany in the 1960s?
B: Of course. _____ substantial money, back home, but they saved earnings as well.
(a) Not merely were they remitting
(b) Not only they were remitting
(c) Not only did they remit
(d) Not merely they remit

해석 A: 혹시 1960년대에 서독으로 파견되었던 한국의 광부와 간호사들에 대해 알고 있니?
B: 물론이지. 그들은 고국으로 상당한 돈을 송금했을 뿐 아니라 수입을 저축하기도 했어.

해설 Not only가 문장 앞에 올 경우 주어와 동사의 위치가 도치된다. 동사가 일반동사일 경우 do(does/did)가 주어 앞에 온다.

어휘 remit 보내다

9 유형 관계대명사

A: Will my dream come true?
B: If you try your best, you can _____.
(a) do who you want
(b) be whoever you want to be
(c) be anyone whoever you want to be
(d) do anything whatever you want to

해석 A: 내 꿈이 실현될까?
B: 최선을 다해 노력하면 뭐든 네가 원하는 사람이 될 수 있어.

해설 빈칸 앞에 선행사가 없으므로 (a)는 적절하지 않고, 선행사가 필요 없는 복합관계사가 와야 한다. 따라서 선행사가 나온 (c), (d) 역시 정답이 될 수 없다.

10 유형 부사/도치

A: Do you help him?
B: He is not poor, _____ need I help.
(a) but
(b) and
(c) nor
(d) neither

해석 A: 그를 도울 거니?
B: 그는 가난하지도 않고, 내가 도와줄 필요도 없어.

해설 nor는 'and ~ not'의 부정적인 의미를 지니고 있는 등위접속사이며 nor 뒤에는 '동사+주어'의 어순으로 도치가 된다. neither는 'not ~ either'와 같은 의미의 부정 부사이다. 여기서 need는 조동사로 쓰였다.

11 유형 부정사

A: As I told you, I urge you _____ for your health.
B: Thank you for your advice, but that's easier said than done.
   (a) to have worked out on a regular basis
   (b) walking out on a regular basis
   (c) to work out on a regular basis
   (d) on a regular basis to walk out

해석
A: 내가 말했듯이 네 건강을 위해서 규칙적으로 운동을 했으면 해.
B: 충고 고마워, 하지만 말이 쉽지.

해설
urge는 '촉구하다'라는 의미로 뒤에 목적어와 to부정사인 목적격 보어를 취하는 동사인데, 상대에게 어떠한 행동을 하도록 촉구한다는 것은 앞으로 있을 미래에 일어날 일을 말하는 것이므로 단순부정사인 to+동사원형이 적합하다. 완료부정사인 to+have p.p. 형태가 되면 촉구하기 이전의 일에 대해서 말하는 것이 된다.

어휘
on a regular basis 정규적으로, 규칙적으로

12 유형 간접의문문

A: How much do they cost?
B: I don't know how _____.
   (a) much cost these shoes
   (b) do these shoes cost
   (c) does these shoes cost
   (d) much these shoes cost

해석
A: 그거 얼마나 하니?
B: 난 이 신발 값이 얼마나 되는지 몰라.

해설
간접의문문은 '의문사+주어+동사'의 어순이다. 정도를 나타내는 의문사 how 다음에는 보통 형용사나 부사가 온다.

13 유형 한정사/형용사

A: Elizabeth is naughty. It wouldn't be easy to deal with her at the party.
B: Don't forget. Elizabeth is going to be accompanied _____ seniors.
   (a) with three other
   (b) with other three
   (c) by other three
   (d) by three other

해석
A: Elizabeth는 장난이 심해. 파티에서 그녀를 말리기는 쉽지 않겠어.
B: 잊지 마. Elizabeth는 다른 선배 세 명과 함께 갈 거야.

해설
여기서 other는 형용사에 가까운 한정사로 수사보다 뒤에 위치한다. 뒤에 이어지는 일반형용사는 '지시+수량+대소+성질/상태+신구+색깔+소속+재료'의 순으로 쓴다. accompany는 수동형이 되는 경우 전치사 by가 따라 나온다.

14 유형 비교/부사

A: Are you going to the Art Center to see Rossini's opera?
B: No, the price of the tickets is _____ high for me.
   (a) too far
   (b) so much
   (c) far too
   (d) too much

해석
A: 예술회관에서 하는 Rossini의 오페라를 보러 갈 거니?
B: 아니, 티켓 가격이 너무 비싸.

해설
형용사를 강조할 때 형용사 앞에 much too를 사용할 수 있고 much 대신 far를 사용해도 된다. (b)와 (d)에 나오는 much는 원급인 high를 수식할 수 없다.

15 유형 관사

A: _____ fantastic magician, Mike always works hard to create a new trick.
B: I agree, he is trying to be beyond man's ability.
(a) Which
(b) Because
(c) A
(d) Also

해석 A: 끝내주는 마술사인 Mike는 항상 새로운 기술을 연마하기 위해서 열심히 해.
B: 맞아, 그는 인간의 능력을 뛰어넘으려는 것 같아.

해설 여러 직종 중에서 마술사라는 하나의 직종을 나타내므로 magician 앞에 부정관사가 와야 적합하다. Mike는 magician과 동격으로 magician을 한정할 수 있는 요소가 필요하므로 (a), (b), (d)는 적절하지 않다.

16 유형 태/전치사

A: In this shop, _____ credit card?
B: No, only cash is available.
(a) has the item covered in
(b) is the item covered with
(c) is the item covered by
(d) does the item cover to

해석 A: 이 가게에서 신용카드로 결제가 되나요?
B: 아니요. 현금만 가능합니다.

해설 the item이 상점에서 파는 물건이므로 수동태로 써야 하고 결제수단으로서의 기능을 의미하므로 수단의 전치사 by가 필요하다. covered with는 '~로 덮여 있다'라는 의미일 때 쓴다.

17 유형 비교

A: What do you think about the renowned novel?
B: The more I read, _____.
(a) the better I got bored
(b) the more I got boring
(c) the worse boring I got
(d) the more bored I got

해석 A: 그 유명한 소설에 대해 어떻게 생각하니?
B: 읽으면 읽을수록 점점 더 지루해져.

해설 'the+비교급 ~, the+비교급 ~'은 '~하면 할수록 더욱 더 ~하다'는 의미이다.

18 유형 수사/형용사

A: How long will you stay at Jane's house?
B: I will stay at her house for _____.
(a) a few days more
(b) three more days
(c) more three days
(d) more a few days

해석 A: 얼마 동안 Jane의 집에 머무를 거니?
B: 3일 더 머물러 있을 거야.

해설 수량 형용사 three는 대소를 나타내는 형용사 more보다 앞에 나온다.

19 유형 관사/전치사

A: Do you by chance know the woman who is smiling?
B: She is the new United States of America _____. She is going to address the audience.
(a) the Ambassador in South Korea
(b) the Ambassador at the South Korea
(c) Ambassador on the South Korea
(d) Ambassador to South Korea

해석 A: 혹시 미소 짓고 있는 여인이 누구인지 아나요?
B: 그녀는 새로 부임한 한국 주재 미국 대사예요. 그녀는 청중들에게 연설할 거예요.

해설 빈칸은 앞에 나오는 the new United States of America와 연결되는 명사가 들어가야 하며 그 앞에 관사가 올 수 없다. 또한 어느 나라에 주재하는 대사를 말할 때는 전치사 to를 사용한다.

어휘 ambassador 대사

20 유형 형용사

A: Do you know how many people are starving around the world?
B: Yes, I do. _____ ten million people in the world are in peril of starvation.

(a) An estimated
(b) The estimated
(c) Estimated
(d) Estimating

[해석] A: 전 세계에서 얼마나 많은 사람들이 굶고 있는지 아니?
B: 응, 알아. 대략 천만 명의 사람들이 굶어 죽을 위기에 처해 있어.

[해설] estimated는 '대략의, 추측의'란 의미를 나타내는 형용사로 쓰인다. 따라서 앞에 관사 an과 함께 쓴다.

[어휘] peril 위험 starvation 기아, 굶주림

Part II Questions 21-40

21 유형 전치사/관사

Gerry Brown is considered by most art critics _____ greatest landscape painter in the United States of America.
(a) to be
(b) as he was the
(c) that he was the
(d) as the

[해석] Gerry Brown은 미국에서 가장 위대한 풍경 화가로 대부분의 비평가들에게 인정받고 있다.

[해설] consider가 '~을 ~로 여기다, 생각하다'의 의미일 때 consider A as B 형태로 쓴다. 빈칸 뒤에 최상급 형용사가 있으므로 the가 와야 한다.

22 유형 분사/부사

As predicted by American historian Arthur Schlesinger, the 1980s were supposed to be followed by something _____: giving all for the cause.
(a) close resembles its 1960s
(b) closely resembled the 1960s
(c) closely resembling the 1960s
(d) close to resemble its 1960s

[해석] 미국 역사학자 Arthur Schlesinger가 예언한 바와 마찬가지로, 1980년대는 1960년대와 상당히 닮은 어떤 것, 즉 명분을 위해서는 무엇이라도 바치려는 풍조가 이어질 것으로 예상되었다.

[해설] 빈칸은 동사가 나올 자리가 아니므로 (a), (b)는 제외되고 to부정사는 미래 의미를 나타내므로 적절하지 않다. 그리고 연대를 달할 때는 숫자 앞에 the를 붙인다.

23 유형 접속사/형용사

An ostrich's egg is such an efficient structure for protecting the embryo inside _____ not easy to break.
(a) as is
(b) that
(c) and is
(d) that it is

[해석] 타조 알은 안쪽의 배아를 보호하기 위해 효율적으로 만들어져 있어서 깨뜨리기가 쉽지 않다.

[해설] 'such a+형용사+명사+that+주어+동사' 구문이다.

24 유형 문장의 형식

_____, Richard Johnson is also well renowned for his prolific biography of well known politicians.

(a) A prominent American novelist
(b) He is a prominent American novelist
(c) A prominent American novelist who is
(d) Despite a prominent American novelist

해석	저명한 미국의 소설가인 Richard Johnson은 잘 알려진 정치가들의 전기를 많이 쓴 것으로도 유명하다.
해설	Richard Johnson과 동격을 이루는 말이 들어가야 한다. (b), (c)는 접속사로 연결되지 않았으므로 적절하지 않으며 (d)는 문맥상 의미가 맞지 않다.
어휘	prolific 다작의, 다산의

25 유형 관계사/부사

In contemporary politics it is as momentous to define _____ as it is to define what you are. This is especially true in a country as congenitally moderate as the U.S.

(a) who you are not
(b) who you are not
(c) what you are nor
(d) what you are not

해석	현대 정치에서는 자신이 어떤 존재라고 규정하는 것과 마찬가지로 어떤 존재가 아니라고 규정하는 것도 중요하다. 이것은 특히 미국 같은 선천적으로 정치적으로 온건한 나라에서 사실이다.
해설	as ~ as 구문이다. what you are와 대조되는 부정의 의미가 나와야 하므로 what you are not이 적합하다.
어휘	momentous 중요한 congenitally 선천적으로

26 유형 관계대명사

So as to grow vegetables properly, farmers have to know _____.

(a) what each vegetable requires
(b) that each vegetable requires
(c) whether each vegetable's requirements are
(d) that is required by each vegetable

| 해석 | 채소를 적절히 재배하려면 농부들은 각각의 채소가 필요로 하는 것을 알아야 한다. |
| 해설 | know의 목적어 자리이므로 명사가 와야 한다. 따라서 선행사를 포함한 관계대명사 what을 쓴 (a)가 적절하다. |

27 유형 전치사/관사

James was so altruistic in youth that he used to strip the very coat from his back and donate it to unwashed vagrants, along with _____ country home.

(a) keys of its
(b) keys on its
(c) the keys in his
(d) the keys to his

해석	James는 젊은 시절 매우 이타적이어서 입고 있던 자기 코트를 바로 벗어서 세수도 하지 않은 부랑자들에게 주고 시골에 있는 자기 집 열쇠까지 넘겨주었다.
해설	일반적인 열쇠가 아니고 James의 시골집 열쇠를 지칭하므로 정관사 the와 함께 쓰고, '~의 비결, ~의 열쇠'를 나타낼 때 key 뒤에 전치사 to를 사용한다.
어휘	altruistic 이타적인 vagrant 부랑자

28 유형 비교

There was _____ of the burglar than the fingerprint on the gun.

(a) no clearer evidence
(b) no most clear evidence
(c) no more clear evidences
(d) not the clearest evidences

| 해석 | 총 위의 지문보다 그 강도에 대한 더 분명한 증거는 없었다. |
| 해설 | 빈칸 뒤의 than으로 보아 비교급 구문이며 1음절의 짧은 단어이므로 clearer가 적절하다. evidence는 불가산명사이므로 evidences 형태로 쓰지 않는다. |

29 유형 분사/문장의 형식

_____, concentrate on your test that was given by your instructor.

(a) For being seated
(b) When to seat
(c) **While seated**
(d) During seating

[해석] 자리에 앉아있는 동안 강사가 출제한 시험에 집중하세요.

[해설] seat는 3형식 타동사이므로 목적어를 취하거나 목적어가 없는 경우 수동태로 쓴다. 원래는 While you are seated인데, 주어와 be동사가 생략되고 seated만 남았다.

고난도 POINT 21 전치사와 접속사를 구분해야 한다.

위 문제의 선택지에 나온 for, while, during은 의미는 동일하지만 품사가 달라 쓰임이 다르다. 우선 while은 접속사로 뒤에 주어와 동사로 이루어진 절이 온다. 위 문제의 경우 while you are seated 형태가 될 수 있다. 그런데 주어와 be동사가 생략되어 while seated처럼 접속사 뒤에 분사가 바로 나오는 경우가 많으므로 전치사와 혼동하지 않도록 주의한다. for와 during은 전치사로 뒤에 명사가 온다. 하지만 for는 뒤에 숫자가 포함된 기간이, during은 특정 기간을 나타내는 명사가 온다는 점에 차이가 있다. 이처럼 각각의 품사와 쓰임을 숙지하고 있다면 정답을 쉽게 고를 수 있을 것이다.

30 유형 관계사/수 일치

Five years after the September 11 attacks, books _____ of the shocking events are beginning to be published.

(a) deepen greatly that our comprehension
(b) deepening great our comprehension
(c) that greatly deepens our comprehension
(d) **that greatly deepen our comprehension**

[해석] 911 테러가 발생하고 5년 후, 그 충격적인 사건에 대한 우리의 이해를 심화시켜 주는 책들이 출판되기 시작하고 있다.

[해설] books를 선행사로 받으면서 뒤에 동사 deepen의 주어 역할을 할 수 있는 주격 관계대명사 that이 쓰인 (d)가 정답이다. (b)는 great가 greatly였다면 정답이 될 수 있고 (c)는 동사가 단수형으로 오답이다.

31 유형 분사

Once America was the great exporter of trends — not just fads, like multiple earrings, but whole new life-styles _____ characteristic garments and substances of choice.

(a) involved
(b) **involving**
(c) involved in
(d) to involve

[해석] 한때 미국은 유행의 대수출국이었다. 여러 개의 귀걸이를 하는 것 같은 단지 일시적 유행만이 아니라 특징적인 의복과 엄선해서 고른 물건들을 포함한 완전히 새로운 생활양식을 수출했다.

[해설] new life-styles의 내용이 characteristic garments를 포함하므로 능동형을 써야 한다.

[어휘] fad 일시적 유행 garment 의복

32 유형 비교

Delivery time from the sender to the receiver is _____ a few seconds, even from one country to another.

(a) **no more than**
(b) no fewer than
(c) as much as
(d) no less than

[해석] 보내는 사람으로부터 받는 사람에게 가는 데 걸리는 배달 시간은 한 나라에서 다른 나라로 갈 때도 단지 몇 초에 불과하다.

[해설] no more than = as little as = only 단지
no fewer than = as many as = ~만큼 많은 [수]
no less than = as much as = ~만큼 많은 [양]

33 유형 부정사/태

In the early 19th century one of the prestigious schools, the University of Michigan became the first state university _____ by a commission elected by the voters of the state.

(a) to have managed
(b) it was managed
(c) having managed
(d) to be managed

해석 19세기 초에 명문 학교 중 하나인 미시간 대학은 그 주의 투표자들에 의해 선출된 위원회가 운영하는 첫 번째 주립 대학이 되었다.

해설 빈칸 뒤의 by로 보아 수동태가 들어가야 하며, 그 당시를 기준으로 미래에 일어나는 일이므로 to부정사 형태가 적절하다.

34 유형 문장의 형식/태/시제

Nowadays there are about 5.3 million university graduates in India who are out of work, _____ behind by the increasingly strict demands of the tech-driven economy.

(a) leave
(b) be left
(c) having left
(d) having been left

해석 요즘 인도에는 기술 주도 경제의 점점 더 엄격해지는 요구에 뒤처져서 실직 중인 약 530만 명의 대학 졸업생이 있다.

해설 빈칸 앞에 '주어+동사' 형태가 나온 것으로 보아 뒷부분은 접속사가 있거나 분사구문 형태가 와야 한다. 문맥상 '남겨지다, 뒤처지게 되다'의 의미이므로 수동형인 having been left가 적절하다.

어휘 out of work 실직 중인

고난도 POINT 22 분사의 태는 목적어 여부로 결정된다.

과거분사와 현재분사의 구별은 TEPS 고난이도 문제에서 자주 출제되는 중요한 유형이다. 목적어의 여부로 두 분사를 구별하는 것이 가장 쉬운 방법이다. 뒤에 목적어가 나오면 현재분사, 목적어가 없으면 과거분사가 나온다는 점을 숙지한다면 정답을 쉽게 고를 수 있다.

35 유형 접속사

The two capitalists made out that _____ they divorced themselves from communists, they became at risk of losing not just their souls but their political viability.

(a) if
(b) even though
(c) unless
(d) since

해석 그 두 명의 자본주의자는 스스로를 공산주의자들로부터 분리시키지 않으면 자신들의 영혼뿐만 아니라 정치적 생존력까지도 상실할 위험성이 있다는 것을 이해했다.

해설 문맥상 '~하지 않으면'이란 의미가 필요하므로 unless가 적합하다.

어휘 make out 이해하다, 인식하다 viability 생존력

36 유형 관사/수 일치

One of George Bernard Shaw's _____, Pygmalion, was related to the story that formed the rudiment for the musical 'My Fair Lady.'

(a) most famous work
(b) most famous works
(c) the most famous work
(d) the most famous works

해석 George Bernard Shaw의 가장 유명한 작품 중 하나인 '피그말리온'은 뮤지컬 '마이 페어 레이디'의 기초를 이루는 이야기와 관련되어 있었다.

해설 소유격 앞과 뒤에는 정관사 the가 붙지 않으며 one of 뒤에는 복수명사가 와야 한다.

어휘 rudiment 기본, 기초

37 유형 the+형용사

_____ not fully supported by the local government in Liverpool county.

(a) Homeless are
(b) Homeless is
(c) The homeless are
(d) The homeless is

해석 노숙자들은 리버풀 카운티의 지방정부에 의해 충분히 지원받지 못한다.

해설 '정관사 the+형용사'는 보통명사의 복수 의미로, 뒤에 복수동사와 함께 쓴다. 빈칸은 주어 자리이고 homeless는 형용사이므로 (a), (b)처럼 쓸 수 없다.

38 유형 문장의 형식/대명사

Art attempts to take something invisible, something spiritual, and _____: art shows people images of the people.

(a) making it possible
(b) make them possible
(c) make it visible
(d) take it visible

해석 예술은 보이지 않는 영적인 것을 취해서 보이는 것으로 만드는 것이다. 예술은 사람들에게 그 사람들의 이미지를 보여주는 것이다.

해설 make는 뒤에 '목적어+목적격 보어'의 형태를 취한다. 문맥상 something invisible과 반대되는 내용 즉, 그 어떤 것을 보이는 것으로 만드는 것이므로 something을 받는 대명사 it을 목적어로 하고 visible을 목적격 보어로 나타낼 수 있다.

39 유형 문장의 형식/태

The first _____ during the last period of the dinosaurs' reign.

(a) flowers are plants appearing
(b) plants have flowers appeared
(c) plants flowers were appeared
(d) flowering plants appeared

해석 최초의 꽃이 피는 식물이 공룡 시대의 마지막 시기에 나타났다.

해설 flowering plants가 내용상 하나의 단어로 주어가 되며, appear는 자동사이므로 수동태로 쓰지 않는다.

어휘 flowering plants 꽃이 피는 식물

40 유형 명사

_____ of his childhood home in Anchorage, Alaska, supplied the inspiration for one of his most popular novels.

(a) Remembering
(b) Memories
(c) It was the memories
(d) He remembered

해석 알래스카 앵커리지에 있는 그의 어린 시절 고향에 대한 추억이 그의 가장 인기 있는 소설 중 하나에 대한 영감을 제공해 주었다.

해설 supplied가 이 문장의 동사이므로 (c), (d)는 답이 될 수 없고 (a)는 뒤에 목적어가 와야 하므로 적절하지 않다.

어휘 inspiration 영감

Part III Questions 41-45

41 유형 부사

(a) A: This office is getting too smaller for our growing business.
(b) B: You're telling me. We need to consider moving somewhere.
(c) A: Precisely, but what place do you have in mind?
(d) B: Yeah, I've already talked to a real estate agent.

해석
(a) A: 늘어나는 일거리로 이 사무실이 너무 좁아지고 있어요.
(b) B: 맞아요. 우리는 다른 곳으로 이사 가는 걸 생각해야 해요.
(c) A: 맞는 말이지만, 생각하고 있는 장소는 있나요?
(d) B: 네, 부동산 업자에게 이미 이야기해 두었어요.

해설 too는 원급을 수식하는 부사이다. getting too smaller → getting too small

42 유형 동사

(a) A: I'm sorry for the loss of your employer. Does anybody know the reason why he killed himself?
(b) B: In his suicide note he mentioned about too many blunders he had made in his life.
(c) A: All of us make errors, but I suppose that we don't have to punish ourselves by resorting to extreme measures.
(d) B: I see eye to eye. I wish he had made out that.

해석
(a) A: 사장님이 돌아가셔서 유감이에요. 그가 자살한 이유를 아는 사람이 있나요?
(b) B: 유서에서 살면서 너무 많은 실수를 저질렀다고 했대요.
(c) A: 우리 모두 실수를 하지만, 극단적인 방법을 써서 스스로 벌할 필요는 없다고 생각해요.
(d) B: 나도 그렇게 생각해요. 사장님이 그것을 이해했으면 좋았을 텐데요.

해설 mention은 전치사 없이 사용하는 타동사이다. mention about → mention

어휘 blunder 실수 resort to ~에 의존하다, ~을 쓰다
see eye to eye 공감하다, 의견이 일치하다

43 유형 관사

(a) A: Do you have the time to talk with me?
(b) B: Yes, I do. Why do you want to have a talk?
(c) A: I got two complimentary tickets.
(d) B: Really? You made my day.

해석
(a) A: 나와 이야기할 시간 있어?
(b) B: 응. 왜 그러는데?
(c) A: 공짜 콘서트 표가 생겼어.
(d) B: 정말? 덕분에 정말 기뻐.

해설 '~할 시간이 있니?'라고 물을 때는 'Do you have time to ~?'를 쓴다. have the time → have time

어휘 complimentary ticket 공짜표

고난도 **POINT 23** 명사와 관사의 관계를 알아두자.

이 문제에서 나온 time은 추상적이고 넓은 의미의 '시간'이라는 의미로 불가산명사로 쓰인다. 하지만 시각, 특별한 한 때, 시기, 구체적인 시간을 나타낼 때는 형용사의 수식을 받아 가산명사화 되어 부정관사나 정관사와 함께 쓸 수 있다. (a)에서 사용된 Do you have the time?은 관용적으로 많이 쓰는 표현으로 '지금 몇 시예요?'라는 의미로 여기서 time은 '(시계에 나타나는) 시각'을 나타내어 가산명사로 쓰였다. 하지만 문제에서 요구하는 것은 일반적인 의미의 '시간 있어요?'라는 말로 추상명사가 쓰여야 하므로 정관사와 함께 쓰지 않는다.

44 유형 동명사

(a) A: I'm considering purchasing a vehicle.
(b) B: How come? You are right down the street from your company.
(c) A: Some day I may need one.
(d) **B: There seems no point on having a car if you don't actually need it.**

해석
(a) A: 차를 한 대 살 생각이야.
(b) B: 왜? 너 회사 코앞에 살잖아.
(c) A: 언젠가는 한 대 필요할 거 같아.
(d) B: 정말로 필요하지 않으면 살 이유가 없는 것 같아.

해설 '~할 이유가 없다'라는 의미로 There is no point를 많이 쓰는데 뒤에 동명사가 나온다. 전치사 on은 필요 없다. on having → having

어휘 vehicle 자동차

45 유형 형용사

(a) A: I'm too busy to do this. Could you help me with my assignments?
(b) B: I will try to do as much as I can.
(c) **A: I am confident that you are adopt at everything.**
(d) B: Don't overestimate me.

해석
(a) A: 난 너무 바빠서 이걸 할 수 없어. 내 숙제 좀 도와줄래?
(b) B: 내가 할 수 있는 한 최선을 다할게.
(c) A: 나는 네가 매사에 능숙하다고 확신해.
(d) B: 너무 과대평가하지 마.

해설 혼동되는 동사 adopt와 형용사 adept를 구별해야 한다. 문맥상 '모든 것에 능숙하다'는 의미가 와야 하므로 adept가 적합하다. adopt → adept

어휘 be confident that ~을 확신하다 adept 능숙한

Part IV Questions 46-50

46 유형 관계대명사

(a) Despite the often heated national debate, the majority of Americans are still in favor of the death penalty. (b) According to a recent study, approximately 65 percent of Americans still think that the death penalty looks appropriate for crimes such as first-degree murder. (c) More than 80 percent of Americans wanted the death penalty given to Timothy McVeigh. **(d) It is the man killed hundreds in the Oklahoma City bombing.**

해석
(a) 종종 발생하는 열띤 국가적 논쟁에도 불구하고, 미국인의 대다수는 여전히 사형 제도에 찬성하고 있다. (b) 최근 조사에 다르면 미국인의 약 65퍼센트가 여전히 사형 제도가 일급 살인과 같은 범죄에는 적절한 것처럼 보인다고 생각한다. (c) 80퍼센트가 넘는 미국인은 Timothy McVeigh에게 사형이 내려지기를 원했다. (d) 그는 오클라호마시 폭탄사고로 수백 명을 죽인 장본인이다.

해설 (d) 한 문장에 동사가 2개(is, killed)이고 접속사가 없으므로 관계대명사를 사용한 who killed가 올바른 표현이다. the man killed → the man who killed

어휘 first-degree murder 일급 살인

47 유형 조동사 should

(a) In the house of a well-to-do Italian, nine o'clock at night finds the larder as bare as though the place were uninhabited. **(b) Provision is bought only in the exact quantity needed.** (c) The refuse of the well-heeled man's kitchen is carefully stored by the cooks. (d) One of their main jobs is selling the leftover to dealers in "second-hand" food.

[해석] (a) 이탈리아의 한 부유한 가정에서 밤 9시에는 식품저장고가 마치 그곳에 사람이 살지 않은 것처럼 텅 빈다. (b) 식량은 정확하게 필요한 양만 구입된다. (c) 부유한 사람의 부엌에서 나오는 찌꺼기는 요리사가 주의하여 저장한다. (d) 그들의 중요한 일 중 하나는 남은 음식을 '중고' 음식으로 상인들에게 파는 것이다.

[해설] provision이 '양식, 식량'의 의미로 쓰일 때는 복수형으로 써야 한다. Provision is → Provisions are

[어휘] well-to-do 부유한(= well-heeled) larder 식품저장고 bare 텅 빈 uninhabited 사람이 살지 않는 refuse 찌꺼기, 쓰레기 second-hand 중고의

48 유형 의문사

(a) It is nothing new that young people face difficulties finding jobs. **(b) You don't have to look at jobless numbers to see how youth unemployment is widespread, because there are so many unemployed young people around us.** (c) Official statistics show that youth unemployment is over 8%. (d) Some analysts put the number of people out of work at 4 million.

[해석] (a) 젊은이들이 일자리를 얻는 데 어려움을 겪고 있는 것은 어제 오늘 일이 아니다. (b) 우리 주위에 일자리가 없는 젊은이들이 너무나도 많이 있기 때문에 청년 실업이 얼마나 널리 퍼져 있는지를 알아보기 위해 실업자 수를 들여다 볼 필요는 없다. (c) 공식통계로는 청년실업이 8퍼센트를 넘어섰다고 한다. (d) 몇몇 분석가들은 실업자 수를 400만 정도로 보고 있다.

[해설] 정도를 나타내는 how로 시작하는 문장의 경우 형용사나 부사가 how 뒤에 함께 사용된다. how youth unemployment is widespread → how widespread youth unemployment is

49 유형 대명사

(a) Japan Inc. shrugged when Samsung Electronics surpassed Sony in operating profits for the first time in 2001. (b) But in retrospect, that was a prelude to what was later known as the Japanese disease. (c) Japan Airlines, Japan's national air carrier, which declared bankruptcy, still flies jets despite falling demand. **(d) Sony finds it lagging behind Samsung and Apple more often than it would like.**

[해석] (a) 2001년에 삼성전자가 소니의 영업 이익을 처음으로 앞섰을 때 일본 기업계는 무시해 버렸다. (b) 그러나 돌이켜보면 그것은 나중에 일본 병으로 알려진 것의 서막이었다. (c) 일본의 국적항공사인 일본항공은 파산을 선언했는데 수요가 하락하고 있음에도 불구하고 여전히 운항하고 있다. (d) 소니는 스스로 원하는 것보다 더 자주 삼성과 애플사에 뒤처지고 있다는 것을 알고 있다.

[해설] (d)에서 문맥상 소니 자신이 알게 된 것이므로 재귀대명사 형태로 써야 한다. finds it → finds itself

[어휘] Japan Inc. 정계와 밀착된 일본 재계를 빗대어 부르는 말 shrug 무시하다 surpass 초과하다 operating profits 영업 이익 prelude 서막, 전조 lagging 뒤처진, 더딘

50 유형 일치

(a) South Korea's recent nuclear plant deal with the United Arab Emirates is so astounding that few Japanese want to bring up the topic. (b) Not long ago, many Japanese thought Japan was leaving South Korea in the dust in high tech while the gap in general-purpose technologies has narrowed. (c) But now they think otherwise. **(d) Japanese officials say that nuclear reactor by South Korea highly competitive both in price and technology.**

[해석] (a) 최근 한국의 아랍 에미리트 연합국과의 핵발전소 거래는 너무 놀라워서 그 주제를 제기하고 싶어 하는 일본인은 거의 없다. (b) 얼마 전만 해도 많은 일본 사람들은 한국이 일반적인 기술의 차이는 좁혀졌지만 높은 수준의 기술에서는 일본이 한참 앞서 있다고 생각했다. (c) 그러나 지금 그들은 다르게 생각한다. (d) 한국의 원자로는 가격에서나 기술에서 모두 매우 경쟁력이 있다고 일본 관리들은 말하고 있다.

[해설] (d)에서 가격과 기술 모두에서 경쟁력이 있다는 것이므로 전치사의 위치가 both 앞으로 가야 한다. both in price and technology → in both price and technology

[어휘] astounding 놀라움을 주는
bring up (문제 등을) 제기하다
leave ~ in the dust ~를 크게 앞지르다
general-purpose 일반적인, 다목적의

고난도 Actual Training 05

1. (d)	2. (b)	3. (c)	4. (a)	5. (d)	6. (b)	7. (b)	8. (a)	9. (c)	10. (d)
11. (b)	12. (c)	13. (b)	14. (d)	15. (a)	16. (d)	17. (c)	18. (b)	19. (c)	20. (a)
21. (d)	22. (b)	23. (b)	24. (a)	25. (b)	26. (c)	27. (d)	28. (c)	29. (a)	30. (b)
31. (a)	32. (c)	33. (a)	34. (c)	35. (d)	36. (a)	37. (c)	38. (d)	39. (b)	40. (a)
41. (c)	42. (c)	43. (d)	44. (c)	45. (c)	46. (a)	47. (c)	48. (a)	49. (c)	50. (a)

Part I Questions 1-20

1 유형 접속사

A: Do you think I need a diet?
B: Well, _____ you are exercising every day, it is probably not necessary.

(a) although
(b) despite
(c) supposed
(d) providing

해석
A: 내가 다이어트를 해야 한다고 생각하니?
B: 네가 매일 운동을 하고 있다면, 필요하지 않을 것 같아.

해설 빈칸 뒤에 주어와 동사가 있으므로 접속사가 와야 한다. 문맥상 providing이 적절하다.

고난도 POINT 24 다양한 접속사를 알아야 한다.

일반적으로 접속사 문제는 선택지 모두 다른 뜻의 접속사가 제시되므로 접속사를 다양하게 알고 있어야 한다. 자주 출제되는 when이나 if, unless, although, since, because, as 외에도 이 문제에서 나온 providing(~한다면, ~라면)이나 supposing, on the condition that, given that, now that 등 많이 쓰이지 않는 접속사들도 함께 알아두는 것이 좋다.

2 유형 시제

A: What's happening here?
B: Don't disturb yourself. I _____ it under control.

(a) had had
(b) have
(c) have been
(d) am having

해석
A: 여기 무슨 일이야?
B: 걱정 마. 내가 잘 관리하고 있어.

해설 질문이 현재진행형이지만 (d)를 고르지 않도록 조심해야 한다. 진행형은 진행중인 동작에 대한 것이다. 이 문제는 잘 관리하고 있는 '상태'를 나타내는 것이므로 여기서 have는 진행형을 쓰지 않고 현재시제를 사용한다.

3 유형 도치

A: When did the criminal begin to open his mouth?
B: Only after they got him a lawyer _____.
   (a) started to talk he
   (b) he started to talk
   (c) did he start to talk
   (d) he did start to talk

해석
A: 범인이 언제 입을 열었습니까?
B: 변호사를 선임해주고 나서야 말하기 시작했어요.

해설
부사인 only가 이끄는 절이 문장의 앞에 나올 때 주절에 있는 주어와 동사가 도치된다. 이때 조동사나 be동사가 아닌 일반동사일 경우 조동사 do(does/did)를 주어 앞에 내세우므로 did he start to talk로 써야 한다.

4 유형 복합관계대명사

A: Should I wear the first jacket or the second?
B: _____ feels more comfortable.
   (a) Whichever
   (b) That
   (c) Which
   (d) What

해석
A: 첫 번째 재킷을 입을까요, 두 번째 것을 입을까요?
B: 어느 것이든 편한 걸로 입으세요.

해설
선행사 jacket을 포함하는 관계대명사를 써야 하는데, 문맥상 선택의 의미를 담고 있는 whichever가 적절하다.

5 유형 조동사

A: Did your boss acknowledge your new business suggestion?
B: No, he _____ see it my way.
   (a) mightn't
   (b) shouldn't
   (c) mustn't
   (d) wouldn't

해석
A: 네 상사가 새로운 비즈니스 품목을 인정했니?
B: 아니, 그는 나처럼 생각하려고 들지 않았어.

해설
강한 의지, 고집을 나타내는 조동사 would의 부정형 wouldn't가 적당하다.

고난도 POINT 25 조동사의 의미를 알아두자.

조동사 관련 문제는 접속사와 마찬가지로 선택지에 여러 조동사가 제시되고 문맥에 맞게 골라야 한다. 이 문제 역시 선택지마다에서 의미가 모두 다른 조동사가 제시되었다. 우선 might는 추측을, should와 must는 의무를, would는 주어의 강한 의지, 고집을 나타낸다. 여기서는 주어인 he의 고집을 나타내는 것이므로 wouldn't가 적절하다. 이 외에 가능성을 나타내는 can, 의무를 나타내는 ought to, 과거를 나타내는 used to가 자주 쓰인다.

6 유형 비교

A: What do you think of Mr. Park as a doctor?
B: He is _____ I've met.
   (a) as a competent doctor as
   (b) as competent a doctor as
   (c) most competent doctor that
   (d) a very competent doctor

해석
A: Mr. Park을 의사로서 어떻게 생각해?
B: 그는 내가 만난 사람들 중 가장 능력 있는 의사야.

해설
문맥상 최상급의 의미가 와야 한다. 'the+최상급' 또는 'as ~ ever+과거동사' 구문으로 최상급을 나타낼 수 있다. '~만큼 ~한'의 의미인 as ~ as 구문의 경우 'as+형용사+관사+명사+as'의 어순으로 쓴다. (c)는 the가 있어야 한다.

7 유형 동사의 부정문

A: The tickets to the World Cup have sold out. Will we never get to see the match now?
B: No, I _____.
(a) suppose we'll not so
(b) don't suppose we will
(c) suppose we will
(d) don't think it not suppose

해석
A: 월드컵 입장권이 매진됐어. 그 경기는 이제 절대 못 보는 걸까?
B: 그래, 아마 못 볼 거야.

해설 No로 대답했으므로 경기를 못 본다는 말에 동의 표현이 나와야 한다. 단 suppose, think 등의 동사가 들어가는 부정문은 I suppose we won't가 아니라 I don't suppose we will과 같이 suppose, think 부분에 부정을 표현한다.

8 유형 전치사/동명사

A: You look really into this project.
B: Do you think so? Our department _____ the highest sales ever.
(a) is devoted to recording
(b) is devoted to record
(c) is devoting to record
(d) is devoting to be recorded

해석
A: 너 이 프로젝트에 정말 열심인 것 같아.
B: 그런 것 같니? 우리 부서에서 사상 최고의 판매실적을 기록할 거야.

해설 devote는 be devoted to -ing 또는 devote ~ to -ing의 형태로 쓰는 동사이다. 여기서 to는 전치사로, 뒤에 동명사가 와야 한다. (c), (d)는 is devoting itself to recording이 될 경우 정답이 될 수 있다.

> 고난도 **POINT 26** to가 전치사로 쓰이는 관용 표현을 알아두자.
>
> to는 방향을 나타내는 전치사로 뒤에 명사나 동명사가 온다. 간혹 to부정사와 혼동하여 동사원형을 쓸 수 있으므로 특정 동사와 함께 자주 쓰이는 전치사 to의 관용 표현을 알아야 한다. 자주 쓰이는 관용 표현으로는 이 문제에 나온 be devoted to와 be attributed to(~의 탓으로 돌리다), contribute to(~에 기여하다), look forward to(~을 기대하다), object to(~에 반대하다), be used to(~에 익숙하다) 등이 있다.

9 유형 가정법/태

A: Why didn't you tell me you were going to watch a movie?
B: I _____ you if you had been willing to pay attention to me.
(a) had told
(b) was telling
(c) would have told
(d) would have been told

해석
A: 영화 보러 간다고 왜 나한테 말 안했어?
B: 네가 나에게 주의를 기울였다면 너한테 말했을 거야.

해설 if you had been willing to를 통해 가정법 과거완료 문장임을 알 수 있다. 빈칸에는 조동사 과거형 +have p.p. 형태이며 능동형을 쓴 (c)가 적절하다.

10 유형 조동사/문장의 형식

A: Should I apply for the internship at Citibank?
B: It _____.
(a) will try not to cost you
(b) will try to cost you not
(c) won't cost to try you
(d) won't cost you to try

해석
A: 시티은행에 인턴으로 지원해야 할까?
B: 해본다고 돈 드는 건 아니잖아.

해설 내용상 시도해서 돈 드는 일이 아니라는 말이 되어야 하므로 to try가 진주어가 되고 won't cost가 가주어 It 뒤에 이어져야 한다.

11 유형 의문사

A: Sunny, _____?
B: Barack Obama. I believe he is an eloquent speaker.
(a) you vote for whom
(b) for whom did you vote
(c) for whom you vote
(d) whom did you vote

[해석] A: Sunny, 누구한테 투표했어?
B: Barack Obama에게 투표했어. 그는 언변이 뛰어난 사람 같아.

[해설] 누구에게 투표를 했냐는 질문이 되기 위해서는 vote for에서 for의 목적어로 의문사 whom이 와야 한다. 전치사가 의문사 앞에 와서 for whom did you vote?의 표현도 가능하므로 정답은 (b)이다.

[어휘] eloquent 언변이 뛰어난

12 유형 조동사

A: Do you think you were right to dump her?
B: No, I _____.
(a) shouldn't have never
(b) shouldn't
(c) shouldn't have
(d) shouldn't have been done

[해석] A: 네가 그녀를 찬 게 옳았다고 생각해?
B: 아니, 그러지 않았어야 했어.

[해설] 그가 여자를 찬 게 were로 봐서는 과거이다. 과거의 일에 대한 아쉬움을 나타낼 때는 should have p.p.를 쓰는데 dump의 반복을 피하기 위해 조동사만 쓴 (c)가 정답이다.

[어휘] dump (애인을) 차다

> **고난도 POINT 27** 영어 생략의 범위를 알아두자.
>
> 영어는 같은 단어의 반복을 피하여 적절하게 생략한다. 이 문제에서도 원래 B의 대답은 'No, I shouldn't have done.'이라고 쓰는 것이 맞지만 조동사 뒤에 대동사 do를 쓰지 않고 생략하는 것이 일반적이므로 'No, I shouldn't have.'가 적절한 답이다. 이와 같은 예는 to부정사에서도 마찬가지이다. 'Would you like to have some coffee?'라는 물음에 'Yes, I'd like to.'라고 대답하는 것처럼 to부정사를 완전히 다 쓰지 않고 대동사 do를 생략하는 것이 일반적이다.

13 유형 접속사

A: Have you ever experienced doing something you didn't want to?
B: Luckily no, _____ so upset.
(a) or would I be
(b) or I would be
(c) nor would I be
(d) nor I would be

[해석] A: 하기 싫은 일을 하게 된 경험이 있니?
B: 다행히도 없어, 안 그랬으면 아주 속상했을 거야.

[해설] Luckily로 보아 다행히 없다는 의미이지만 뒤에 upset이 나오므로 빈칸에는 '그렇지 않다면'이란 뜻이 들어가야 한다. 따라서 or가 오고 부정어가 아니므로 도치시키지 않는다.

14 유형 조동사

A: Who left the door open?
B: Sorry, I _____ have left it open.
(a) will
(b) should
(c) need
(d) must

[해석] A: 누가 문 열어놨어?
B: 미안해, 내가 그랬나봐.

[해설] 과거 일에 대한 추측을 나타내므로 must have p.p.가 적합하다.

15 유형 형용사

A: If you have any doubts on the veracity of this report, please contact me.
B: Thanks, but I'm certain _____.
   (a) of it
   (b) that it is
   (c) of that
   (d) to have it

해석 A: 이 보고서의 진실성에 대해 의문이 들면 연락하세요.
B: 알겠어요, 하지만 전 이게 사실이라고 확신해요.
해설 I'm certain 다음에 that절이나 of 전치사구가 나와야 한다. 그러므로 of 전치사구인 of it이 답이다.

16 유형 동사

A: Did she decide to take the better position?
B: No, but I'd hoped _____.
   (a) her to taking it
   (b) she takes it
   (c) her to take it
   (d) that she would take it

해석 A: 그녀가 더 나은 자리를 맡기로 결정했나요?
B: 아니오, 하지만 난 그녀가 그러기를 바랐어요.
해설 hope는 to부정사와 that절을 목적어로 쓴다. 'hope+목적어+to부정사' 형태는 쓰지 않는다.

17 유형 부정사

A: Do you remember we _____ soccer after school?
B: Yes. I miss those days.
   (a) are used to playing
   (b) used to playing
   (c) used to play
   (d) are used to play

해석 A: 우리가 방과 후에 축구했던 거 기억나?
B: 응, 그때가 그리워.
해설 be used to -ing는 '~하는 데 익숙하다'는 의미이고, 'used to+동사원형'은 '~하곤 했다'는 의미이다.

18 유형 관계대명사 what의 관용 표현

A: How was the party?
B: It was a disaster. _____, it rained all day.
   (a) Which is more
   (b) What is worse
   (c) Which is worse
   (d) That is more

해석 A: 파티는 어땠어?
B: 엉망이었어. 더구나, 하루 종일 비가 왔어.
해설 부정적 의미의 '더구나, 설상가상으로'는 what is worse로 표현한다.

19 유형 조동사/시제

A: What are you going to do if you win the Lotto?
B: I have never thought about it, but I _____ around the world.
   (a) would travel
   (b) would have traveled
   (c) might travel
   (d) might have traveled

해석 A: 로또에 당첨되면 뭘 할 거야?
B: 생각 안 해봤는데, 세계 일주를 할까봐.
해설 한 번도 생각해보지 않았으므로 막연한 추측을 나타내는 might가 적절하다. would는 주어의 의지를 나타내므로 문맥상 적합하지 않다. might have traveled는 과거에 대한 추측이므로 미래를 나타내는 빈칸과는 어울리지 않는다.

20 유형 가정법/형용사

A: Are you interested in buying this building?
B: I wish I had _____ more money in my bank account.

(a) a little
(b) a few
(c) few
(d) little

해석 A: 이 건물을 사는 데 관심 있니?
B: 내 은행 계좌에 돈이 조금만 더 있으면 좋겠는데.

해설 money는 셀 수 없는 명사이므로 '조금 더'를 나타내는 표현으로 a little이 와야 한다. little은 '거의 없다'는 부정의 뜻을 나타낸다.

고난도 POINT 28 가산명사와 불가산명사의 수량형용사를 구분해야 한다.

여러 가지 종류의 수량형용사가 있지만 같이 쓰는 가산명사와 불가산명사에 따라 구분해 사용해야 한다. 이 문제에 나온 것처럼 a little, little은 불가산명사와 쓰는 수량형용사이고 이 외에 much, a small amount of(적은 양의), quite a little(많은), only a little(적은), a good deal of(많은) 등이 있다. 가산명사와 쓰는 수량형용사로는 a few, few, a number of(많은), many, a good many(많은), only a few(적은), quite a few(많은) 등이 있다. 이 외에 a lot of, lots of, plenty of는 가산명사와 불가산명사 모두에 쓸 수 있으므로 함께 알아두자.

Part II Questions 21-40

21 유형 명사/관사

In Israel, _____ of workers are women.

(a) a estimated 40 percents
(b) an estimated 40 percents
(c) a estimated 40 percent
(d) an estimated 40 percent

해석 이스라엘에서 근로자 중 약 40퍼센트가 여성이다.

해설 percent는 항상 단수형으로만 쓰이고 estimated는 앞에 부정관사 an을 동반한다.

22 유형 관사

_____ aren't fond of peanuts since all of them have allergies to them.

(a) Jefferson family
(b) The Jefferson family
(c) The Jeffersons family
(d) Jeffersons families

해석 Jefferson씨 가족은 모두 땅콩 알레르기가 있어서 땅콩을 싫어한다.

해설 한 가족을 지칭하여 나타낼 경우 정관사 the와 함께 쓴다. the Jefferson family 혹은 the Jeffersons로 쓴다.

23 유형 시제

He _____ a graduate of Seoul National University and worked for Samsung before coming to Nokia.

(a) was
(b) is
(c) has been
(d) had been

해석 그는 서울대학교 졸업생으로 노키아에 들어오기 전에 삼성에서 일했다.

해설 그가 서울대 졸업생이라는 사실은 변하지 않으므로 현재시제를 써야 한다.

24 유형 전치사

George is a best-performing salesman _____ Mercedes-Benz.

(a) for
(b) in
(c) at
(d) into

해석 George는 메르세데스 벤츠에서 가장 실적이 좋은 판매원이다.

해설 어떤 회사나 단체, 팀에 소속되어 있는지 말할 때 전치사 for를 사용한다.

25 유형 분사/태

Once _____, the semiconductor chips are assembled in all sorts of electrical devices.

(a) to produce
(b) produced
(c) were produced
(d) they have produced

해석 일단 반도체가 만들어지면 각종 전자제품에 조립된다.

해설 once가 접속사로 쓰인 형태이다. 원래 once they are produced인데 they are가 생략되었다.

고난도 POINT 29 주어와 be동사 생략에 유의하자.

종속절의 주어가 주절의 주어와 일치할 경우, 종속절의 주어와 be동사는 생략이 가능하여 접속사와 분사만 쓰는 경우가 많다. 이 점을 알고 있었다면 이 문제에서 (a)와 (c)를 정답에서 제외할 수 있다. 그리고 분사는 뒤의 목적어 여부에 따라서 태가 결정된다. 이 문제에서는 생략된 종속절의 주어가 the semiconductor chips이고 빈칸 뒤에 목적어가 없으므로 수동으로 쓰여서 원래 Once they are produced였는데, 생략되어 Once produced가 된 것이다.

26 유형 접속사

_____ fishing continues to threaten fish's survival significantly, their greatest virtual threat is habitat loss caused by water contamination.

(a) Unless
(b) Since
(c) While
(d) Because

해석 어업이 계속해서 어류의 생존을 상당히 위협하기는 하지만 사실상 이들에게 가장 큰 위협은 수질오염에 의한 서식지 소실이다.

해설 앞뒤 문장을 이어주는 접속사를 찾아야 한다. 문맥상 '~라고는 해도, ~이지만'을 나타내는 While이 적절하다.

어휘 fishing 어업

27 유형 형용사

It was Marilyn Monroe's sexiness, combined with her excellent acting performance, which made her _____ presence.

(a) such renowned a on-screen
(b) renowned such an on-screen
(c) on-screen renowned such a
(d) such a renowned on-screen

해석 Marilyn Monroe를 영화계에서 유명인사로 만든 것은 바로 훌륭한 연기력과 결합된 그녀의 섹시함이었다.

해설 'such+a(n)+형용사+명사'의 어순을 알고 있어야 한다. 문맥상 '영화계에서 유명한 존재'라는 말이 되어야 한다.

28 유형 비교

John can barely change the fluorescent light, _____ repair a chair.

(a) yet
(b) furthermore
(c) much less
(d) even so

해석: John은 부서진 의자를 수리하는 것은 고사하고 형광등도 간신히 교체한다.

해설: barely는 '거의~않다, 간신히 ~하다'라는 뜻으로 부정적인 의미를 띤다. much less는 부정문 뒤에서 더 심한 것을 말할 때 '~는 말할 것도 없다'라는 뜻의 표현이다. even so나 yet은 절이 와야 한다.

어휘: fluorescent light 형광등 even so 그렇다 하더라도

29 유형 부사/형용사

_____ without passing the Highest Civil Service Examination.

(a) Not a single judge can be appointed
(b) Can a single judge not be appointed
(c) A single judge can be appointed
(d) No single judge cannot be appointed

해석: 사법고시를 통과하지 않으면 어떤 판사도 임명될 수 없다.

해설: '하나도 ~아니다'라는 뜻으로 'no+명사, not a+명사, not any+명사'의 형태가 사용된다. without이 부정을 뜻하므로 (a)가 적절하다. (d)는 이중부정이라 적절하지 않다.

어휘: Highest Civil Service Examination 사법고시

30 유형 전치사

Classifying people _____ similar consumer behavior may help marketing research companies to establish their strategies.

(a) to
(b) with
(c) for
(d) within

해석: 유사한 소비 행태를 가진 사람들을 분류하는 것은 마케팅 연구 회사들이 전략을 세우는 데 도움이 될 것이다.

해설: 문맥상 '유사한 소비행태를 가진 사람'이 주어가 되기 때문에 '~를 가진'의 뜻이 있는 전치사 with가 적합하다.

어휘: consumer behavior 소비행태

31 유형 수 일치/명사

A number of _____ of the North and South poles have begun to minimize environmental pollution.

(a) countries in the regions
(b) countries in the region
(c) country in the regions
(d) country in the region

해석: 남극과 북극 지역에 있는 많은 나라들은 환경오염을 최소화하기 시작했다.

해설: a number of는 복수를 나타내므로 countries를 쓰고 북극과 남극이라는 두 지역이므로 regions를 써야 한다.

32 유형 문장의 형식

Calculus, _____ refined and mathematical symbolic system, can reduce complicated problems to simple terms.

(a) it is a
(b) that it is a
(c) a
(d) is a

해석: 세련되고 수학적인 상징체계인 미적분학은 복잡한 문제들을 단순한 용어로 줄일 수 있다.

해설: 콤마와 콤마 사이에 들어갈 수 있는 것은 관계대명사+동사, 관계대명사와 동사 없이 주어와 동격관계를 이루기 위한 관사 a나 an, 앞의 주어를 수식하는 과거분사나 현재분사 등이다.

33 유형 도치

Scarcely _____ his room when his girlfriend came into his room.

(a) had he cleaned up
(b) did he clean up
(c) he did clean up
(d) he had cleaned up

[해석] 그가 방을 치우자마자 여자 친구가 들어왔다.

[해설] Scarcely ~ when은 '~하자마자 ~하다'로 앞에 일어난 일이 뒤에 일어난 일보다 먼저 일어났으므로 한 시제 앞서서 쓴다. 또한 scarcely는 부정을 나타내므로 주어와 동사가 도치된다.

34 유형 관계부사

Ever since the 1930s, archaeologists have believed that the Tigris and Euphrates valley in ancient Mesopotamia (now Iraq) was the 'cradle of civilization,' _____ around 8000 B.C., people first settled in villages to cultivate wild grain and domesticate animals.

(a) which
(b) when
(c) where
(d) with which

[해석] 1930년대 이래로 줄곧 고고학자들은 고대 메소포타미아(지금의 이라크)에 있는 티그리스와 유프라테스 계곡을 '문명의 발상지'라고 믿어왔는데, 그곳에서 기원전 8000년경 사람들은 처음으로 마을에 정착해서 야생의 곡식을 재배하고 동물들을 길들였다.

[해설] 선행사가 cradle of civilization으로 장소를 나타내고 뒷 문장이 완전하므로 빈칸은 관계부사 where나 '전치사+관계대명사'가 와야 한다.

[어휘] cultivate 경작하다 domesticate 사육하다, 길들이다

고난도 POINT 30 삽입된 말에 유의하자.

이 문제에서처럼 빈칸 뒤에 있는 around 8000 B.C.라는 말로 혼동을 주어 빈칸의 역할이 무엇인지 금방 파악할 수 없도록 하는 유형이다. around 8000 B.C.가 삽입되지 않았다면 빈칸 앞의 cradle과 뒷문장이 완전하다는 것으로 관계부사 where 위치라는 것을 쉽게 파악할 수 있다. 이처럼 TEPS 고난도 문제에서는 삽입된 말로 함정을 만들고 있으므로 구조 파악에 유의해야 한다.

35 유형 전치사/관계대명사

The value of money was determined by the value of the material _____ it was made, such as silver and gold.

(a) by which
(b) of which
(c) what
(d) from which

[해석] 돈의 가치는 은이나 금과 같이 재료가 되는 물질의 가치에 의해 결정됐다.

[해설] 원래 the value of the material was made from silver and gold이었으므로 빈칸엔 from which가 적절하다.

36 유형 수 일치/명사

The professor gave an assignment to students to write _____.

(a) a paper of three pages
(b) a three pages paper
(c) a paper of three page
(d) a three paper pages

[해석] 교수는 학생들에게 세 장의 리포트를 쓰는 과제를 내주었다.

[해설] 세 장 분량은 three pages가 되며 리포트는 셀 수 있으므로 관사와 함께 쓴다. 두 개의 명사는 of로 연결하면 된다.

37 유형 문장의 형식

In the 2nd half of the 18th century, Andrew Webster opened the Wilderness Trail and made _____ the first settlements in the rural countryside.
(a) possibly it was
(b) as possible
(c) possible
(d) it possible

해석 18세기 후반에 Andrew Webster는 윌더니스 트레일을 개통하여 시골지역에서 최초의 정착지가 생겨날 수 있게 했다.

해설 5형식 문장에서 make 이하의 목적어가 to부정사가 아닌 명사구인 경우는 가목적어 it을 사용하지 않는다. 원래 made the first settlements in the rural countryside possible에서 목적어가 길어 위치를 바꾼 경우이다.

38 유형 명사/수 일치

_____ given a bonus to commemorate the 50th anniversary.
(a) All personnels was
(b) All personnels were
(c) All personnel was
(d) All personnel were

해석 50주년을 기념하기 위해 모든 직원들에게 보너스가 지급되었다.

해설 personnel은 집합명사로 복수형으로 쓰지 않지만 의미 때문에 동사는 복수형을 쓴다.

어휘 personnel 총 인원, 전 직원

39 유형 문장의 형식

_____ is how international students can do so well in courses given in a foreign language.
(a) That I find interesting
(b) What I find interesting
(c) Why I find interesting
(d) What I find it interesting

해석 내가 재미있다고 생각하는 것은 어떻게 유학생들이 외국어로 하는 수업에서 그렇게 잘해낼 수 있는지이다.

해설 주어 자리이므로 명사가 와야 한다. 따라서 선행사를 포함한 관계대명사 what을 쓰는 것이 적절하다. (d)의 경우 관계대명사가 왔는데 뒤의 문장이 완전하므로 적절하지 않다.

40 유형 태/분사

_____ about the reason why he attempted to steal the money, the criminal answered he hasn't paid his rent for several months.
(a) When inquired
(b) When inquiring
(c) Having inquired
(d) Having inquiring

해석 돈을 훔치려 한 이유에 대해 질문을 받았을 때 범인은 몇 달 동안 집세를 내지 못해서였다고 대답했다.

해설 문장의 주어 the criminal과 inquire의 관계가 수동이므로 원래 When the criminal was inquired about the reason이었으나 주어와 be동사가 생략된 형태가 맞다.

Part Ⅲ Questions 41-45

41 유형 의문사

(a) A: What do you think of the technical trainer?
(b) B: He's obviously very knowledgeable, but I don't think he knows how to communicate with us very well.
(c) A: Oh, really? How do you say that?
(d) B: I can't understand the jargons he uses.

해석 (a) A: 그 기술 교육관에 대해 어떻게 생각해요?
(b) B: 그는 정말 박식하지만 우리와 의사소통하는 법을 잘 모르는 것 같아요.
(c) A: 아, 그래요? 왜 그렇게 생각해요?
(d) B: 그가 사용하는 전문용어를 이해할 수가 없어요.

해설 문맥상 보면 '왜 그렇게 생각해요?'라는 말이 와야 한다. How do you say that? → What makes you say that? 또는 Why do you think like that?

어휘 jargon 전문용어

42 유형 시제

(a) A: Did you meet her? How was it?
(b) B: It was really good. We had dinner and afterwards walked around the park.
(c) A: Really? You must be happy. You wanted to meet her for a long time.
(d) B: I guess I am a lucky man.

해석 (a) A: 그녀를 만났니? 어땠어?
(b) B: 정말 좋았어. 저녁도 먹고 나중에 공원 산책도 했어.
(c) A: 진짜? 행복했겠네. 오랫동안 그녀를 만나고 싶어 했잖아.
(d) B: 내 생각에 난 운이 좋은 것 같아.

해설 for a long time은 과거부터 현재까지 이어지는 것이므로 현재완료와 함께 쓴다. wanted → have wanted

43 유형 수 일치

(a) A: What do you want for dinner tonight?
(b) B: I've been craving noodles.
(c) A: Noodles? Thai or Chinese?
(d) B: Both sounds good. Which do you prefer?

해석 (a) A: 오늘 저녁 뭐 먹을래?
(b) B: 국수가 정말 먹고 싶었어.
(c) A: 국수? 태국식 아니면 중국식?
(d) B: 둘 다 좋은데. 넌 어느 쪽이 더 좋니?

해설 both가 주어이므로 복수동사가 와야 한다. sounds → sound

어휘 crave 원하다, 갈망하다

44 유형 전치사/문장의 형식

(a) A: I'm hungry now. When are we going to eat?
(b) B: Oh, I didn't know it was time to eat dinner. I reserved a restaurant.
(c) A: Really? What name is under the reservation?
(d) B: My father's name, James Park.

해석 (a) A: 배고프다. 우리 언제 밥 먹어?
(b) B: 밥 먹을 시간이 되었는지 몰랐네. 식당을 예약해 놨어.
(c) A: 진짜? 누구 이름으로 되어 있어?
(d) B: James Park, 아버지 성함이야.

해설 예약자 이름을 말할 때 'under+이름'을 쓴다. 따라서 '누구의 이름으로 예약이 되어 있니?'의 의문문은 What name is the reservation under? 혹은 Under what name is the reservation?으로 써야 한다.

45 유형 관사/명사

(a) A: Can you be a more careful driver?
(b) B: Well, I am trying to drive smoothly.
(c) **A: Are you? I think you are making sudden stop at every traffic light.**
(d) B: Sorry, I will be more cautious.

[해석]
(a) A: 좀 더 조심스럽게 운전할 수 없니?
(b) B: 글쎄, 난 부드럽게 운전하려고 노력하고 있는데.
(c) A: 너가? 신호등마다 급정거하는 것 같은데.
(d) B: 미안해. 좀 더 조심할게.

[해설] '급정거하다'는 make a sudden stop으로 쓴다. 여기에서 stop은 가산명사이므로 부정관사를 붙인다. making sudden stop → making a sudden stop

Part IV Questions 46-50

46 유형 수사

(a) **Arabic ranks six in the world's league table of languages, with an estimated 186 million native speakers.** (b) It belongs to the Semitic group of languages which also includes Hebrew and Amharic, the main language of Ethiopia. (c) There are many Arabic dialects. (d) Classical Arabic — the language of the Qur'an — was originally the dialect of Mecca which is now in Saudi Arabia.

[해석]
(a) 아랍어는 약 1억 8600만 명의 모국어 사용자가 있으며 세계 언어 성적표에서 6위를 차지한다. (b) 아랍어는 히브리어와 에티오피아의 주요 언어인 암하라어도 포함되는 셈 어족에 속한다. (c) 아랍어에는 방언이 많다. (d) 코란의 언어인 고전 아랍어는 원래 지금의 사우디아라비아에 있는 메카의 방언이었다.

[해설] (a)에서 여섯 번째라는 의미의 서수로 표현되어야 한다. ranks six → ranks sixth

[어휘] estimated 어림잡은 dialect 방언

47 유형 접속사

(a) The third most popular buzzword, right after downsizing and outsourcing, is teamwork. (b) "Easy," you say, "I've been playing on teams for years." **(c) You might be surprised, therefore, to find out that what it takes to win on the sports field might not be the same as what's required to field a winning team at work.** (d) Take this quiz to see how suited you are to being an effective team member.

[해석]
(a) 구조조정과 아웃소싱에 이어 세 번째로 인기 있는 문구는 팀워크이다. (b) "그야 쉽지, 난 몇 년째 팀으로 일하고 있는걸."하고 당신은 말할 것이다. (c) 하지만 스포츠 경기에서 이길 때 필요한 것과 직장에서 우수한 팀을 배치할 때 필요한 것이 다를 수 있다는 사실을 알면 놀랄지도 모른다. (d) 이 퀴즈를 통해 당신이 유능한 팀원이 되기에 얼마나 적합한지 점검해보라.

[해설] (b)에서 팀웍크가 쉽다고 생각하지만 (c)에서는 스포츠 경기와 직장에서의 상황이 not be the same하다는 반대되는 내용이 나온다. 따라서 전환의 접속부사가 와야 한다. therefore → however

[어휘] buzzword 선전 문구 downsizing 인원축소 outsourcing 아웃소싱, 외부조달 field 경기에 참가시키다, 배치하다

48 유형 태/전치사

(a) Animal behavior can be explained how they act to preserve their genes in the population. (b) It can be used to explain why a lioness will nurse not only her own young, but the young of her close genetic relatives in the pride. (c) It can also be used to explain why a new dominant male lion will kill cubs in the pride that do not belong to him. (d) Killing the cubs causes the nursing females to come into heat faster, thereby giving the male lion an opportunity to get his genes into the population much faster.

[해석] (a) 동물의 행동은 자신의 유전자를 개체군에 보존하기 위해 행동하는 양식을 보면 알 수 있다. (b) 이것은 왜 사자 무리에서 암사자가 자신의 새끼뿐 아니라 유전적으로 가까운 친척들의 새끼들까지 돌보는지 설명하는 데 사용될 수 있다. (c) 또한 왜 주도권을 새로 잡은 수사자가 사자 무리 중에서 자기 핏줄이 아닌 다른 새끼들을 죽이는지 설명하는 데 사용될 수 있다. (d) 새끼들을 죽이면 젖을 먹이던 암사자는 좀 더 빨리 교미할 수 있게 되고, 따라서 수사자에게 자신의 유전자를 개체군에 남길 기회를 훨씬 빨리 제공하게 된다.

[해설] '~에 의해 설명되다'는 be explained by로 쓴다. (a)에서는 유전자를 개체군에 보존하기 위해 행동하는 양식이 동물의 행동을 설명해준다고 하고 있다. can be explained → can be explained by

[어휘] lioness 암사자 nurse 젖먹이다 pride 사자 무리 dominant 지배적인 heat 발정, 교미기

49 유형 수 일치

(a) One traditional icon of St. Patrick's Day is the shamrock. (b) This stems from an Irish tale that tells how St. Patrick used the three-leafed shamrock to explain the Trinity. (c) He used it in his sermons to represent how the Father, the Son, and the Holy Spirit could all exist as separate element of the same entity. (d) Though originally a catholic holy day, St. Patrick's Day has evolved into more of a secular holiday.

[해석] (a) 성 패트릭의 날의 전통적 상징은 클로버이다. (b) 이는 성 패트릭이 삼위일체를 설명하기 위해 세 잎 클로버를 어떻게 이용했는지를 말해 주는 아일랜드 설화에서 기원한다. (c) 성부와 성자와 성령이 같은 존재이면서도 각각의 다른 요소로 존재할 수 있는지를 보여주기 위해 성 패트릭은 설교할 때 세잎 클로버를 이용했다. (d) 성 패트릭의 날은 원래는 가톨릭의 축일이었지만 세속적인 축일로 발전하였다.

[해설] (c)에서 separate는 '분리된'이라는 뜻이므로 두 개 이상의 요소를 나타낸다. separate element → separate elements

[어휘] shamrock 클로버 stem from ~로부터 기원하다 the Trinity 삼위 일체 entity 실재, 존재, 본체 holy day 축일 secular 세속적인, 비종교적인

50 유형 분사

(a) We have changed our name to Allstream Inc., from AT&T Canada, signaled our new status as a fully independent leading communication solutions. (b) The name, Allstream, embodies how we deliver leading communication solutions by demonstrating collaboration, responsiveness and flexiblity with all stakeholders. (c) Shortly, you will receive detailed information about our new brand and the benefits Allstream can bring to your business. (d) If you have any questions, please feel free to contact me anytime.

[해석] (a) 완전히 독립적인 주요 통신사로서의 자사의 새로운 입지를 나타내고자, 이름을 AT&T 캐나다에서 Allstream 주식회사로 변경하였습니다. (b) Allstream이라는 이름은 모든 투자자들에게 협동력, 응답 능력, 융통성을 보여줌으로써 당사가 어떻게 선도적인 통신 솔루션을 제공하는지를 구현한 것입니다. (c) 곧, 귀하는 당사의 새 브랜드와 Allstream에서 귀하의 비즈니스에 제공하게 될 혜택에 대한 자세한 정보를 받게 될 것입니다. (d) 문의가 있으시면 언제라도 저에게 연락 주시기 바랍니다.

[해설] (a)에서 signaled는 뒤에 our new status라는 목적어를 취하므로 능동형이 되어야 한다. signaled → signaling

[어휘] embody 구체적으로 표현하다, 구현하다 stakeholder 투자자

고난도 Actual Training 06

1. (d)	2. (a)	3. (a)	4. (b)	5. (d)	6. (b)	7. (d)	8. (a)	9. (b)	10. (b)
11. (b)	12. (c)	13. (c)	14. (a)	15. (d)	16. (a)	17. (d)	18. (c)	19. (d)	20. (a)
21. (c)	22. (d)	23. (b)	24. (d)	25. (b)	26. (b)	27. (a)	28. (c)	29. (a)	30. (c)
31. (a)	32. (b)	33. (b)	34. (d)	35. (a)	36. (c)	37. (b)	38. (b)	39. (a)	40. (a)
41. (b)	42. (b)	43. (d)	44. (b)	45. (b)	46. (d)	47. (d)	48. (a)	49. (d)	50. (b)

Part I Questions 1-20

1 유형 전치사/문장의 형식

A: What is the characteristics of the Roman conquest of the Greeks?
B: The experts say that it is marked by _____.
  (a) Roman plunder of works on a massive scale of art
  (b) a massive scale of Roman art works on plunder
  (c) art works of Roman scale on a massive plunder
  (d) Roman plunder of art works on a massive scale

해석 A: 로마제국의 그리스 정복의 특징은 무엇이니?
B: 전문가들은 로마가 대규모로 예술작품을 약탈한 것이 특징이라고 말해.

해설 Romans plundered art works on a massive scale. 은 문장인데 이것을 전치사 by의 목적어로 넣기 위하여 명사 구조로 만들 수 있다. 그러면 Roman plunder(명사) of(목적 표시의 of) art works on a massive scale이 된다.

2 유형 동사

A: Why does he look so tender with her?
B: Didn't you know? He _____ her last month.
  (a) married
  (b) got married with
  (c) married to
  (d) got married

해석 A: 저 남자는 여자랑 왜 저렇게 다정해 보이니?
B: 몰랐어? 지난달에 결혼했잖아.

해설 타동사 marry는 전치사를 수반하지 않으므로 (a)가 적절하다. (b)는 with를 to로 바꾸면 정답이 될 수 있다.

3 유형 어순

A: Are you two relatives?
B: Yes. Mom says he is _____ from me.
  (a) many times removed
  (b) many times moved me
  (c) removed many times
  (d) moved many times

해석 A: 너희 둘이 친척이니?
B: 응. 엄마가 그러는데 그는 나에게 몇 촌쯤이래.

해설 여기서의 time은 시간의 의미보다는 특히 복수로 쓰여서 친척 관계의 촌수를 나타낸다. 특히 친척 사이의 관계가 멀어지는 경우에는 removed를 쓴다는 것도 주의해야 한다. 배수사는 수식하는 말 바로 앞에 쓰므로 (c)는 적절하지 않다.

어휘 removed (혈연 관계가) ~촌인

4 유형 명사/소유격

A: What's the most famous tourist site in this country?
B: _____ was built hundreds of years ago and it attracts so many tourists.
  (a) The Queen Castle of England's
  (b) The Queen of England's Castle
  (c) The Queen of England Castle's
  (d) The Queen Castle of England

[해석] A: 이 지역에서 가장 유명한 관광명소는 어디니?
B: 영국 여왕의 성은 수백 년 전에 지어졌는데 수많은 관광객들을 모으고 있어.

[해설] 의미상 'the Queen of England'는 한 단어로 그 뒤에 소유격을 쓴다.

5 유형 접속사

A: I have recovered quickly from the injury _____ my mother has nursed me devotedly.
B: That's good news.
  (a) in case
  (b) what if
  (c) unless
  (d) now that

[해석] A: 어머니가 극진히 간호해 주셔서 부상에서 빨리 회복됐어요.
B: 좋은 소식이네요.

[해설] 선택지로 보아 적합한 접속사를 고르는 문제이다. 빈칸 앞뒤의 내용이 원인과 결과로 이어지고 있으므로 '~이므로, ~이기 때문에'를 의미하는 now that이 적절하다.

6 유형 동사의 강조

A: Why didn't you confirm the meeting schedule to me?
B: I _____. Check your voice mail.
  (a) do confirm
  (b) did confirm
  (c) confirm
  (d) had confirmed

[해석] A: 왜 회의 일정을 나에게 확인시켜주지 않았니?
B: 했어. 음성 사서함을 확인해봐.

[해설] A가 과거시제로 물었으므로 대답 역시 과거시제가 적합하다. 여기서는 동사 앞에 did를 써서 동사의 의미를 강조했다.

7 유형 문장의 형식

A: Who _____ broke into the office?
B: I have nothing to do with this incident.
  (a) was it
  (b) have done it that
  (c) did it that
  (d) was it that

[해석] A: 누가 사무실에 들어왔지?
B: 저는 이 사건과 관련 없어요.

[해설] It ~ that 강조구문의 의문문 형태이다. 원래 문장은 It was who that broke into the office.인데 의문문으로 바뀌어 Who was it that broke into the office?가 된 것이다.

고난도 POINT 31 같은 유형의 문제도 묻는 것에 따라 다르게 출제된다.

it ~ that 강조구문은 이를 응용한 의문문 형태가 자주 출제된다. 위에서처럼 원래 Who broke the window?에서 Who를 강조하여 의문문으로 만든 형태도 있고, 원래 What does he want?에서 What을 강조하여 What is it that he wants?와 같이 만든 경우도 있다. 이처럼 강조구문이 나올 때에는 의문사나 간접의문문과 결합하여 출제되는 경우가 많으므로 예문을 통해 학습해 두는 것이 중요하다.

8 유형 접속사

A: Is it true Sam's new book has become a best seller?
B: Yes, _____ that the publishing company has asked him to write a book again.
   (a) his book was so famous
   (b) famous was his book so
   (c) his book was famous so
   (d) so famous his book was

[해석] A: Sam의 신간이 베스트셀러가 된 게 사실이야?
B: 응, 그의 책이 너무 유명해져서 출판사에서 책을 한 권 더 쓰라고 했대.

[해설] so ~ that과 so that은 의미에 차이가 있다. so ~ that은 '너무 ~해서 ~하다'이고 so that은 '~하도록, ~하기 위해서'이다. 이 문제에서 요구하는 것은 너무 유명해져서 출판사에서 또 다른 책을 요구한 것이므로 so ~ that이 적합하다.

9 유형 조동사

A: Why did they call him down for not coming?
B: They believe he _____ met Jennifer, his talkative girlfriend; otherwise, he should be here by now.
   (a) could have
   (b) must have
   (c) would have
   (d) should have

[해석] A: 어째서 그들은 그가 오지 않는다고 불평이지?
B: 그가 수다쟁이 여자친구 Jennifer를 만난 게 틀림없다고, 그렇지 않다면 지금쯤 여기 와 있어야 한다고 생각하니까.

[해설] 문맥상 과거 사실에 대한 강한 추측이 적절하다.

[어휘] call down 비난하다, 헐뜯다 talkative 수다스러운

10 유형 명사/관사

A: Can you break this $1 bill into smaller money?
B: I am extremely sorry but I don't think I have _____.
   (a) the enough changes
   (b) enough change
   (c) an enough coin
   (d) enough coin

[해석] A: 이 1달러짜리 지폐를 잔돈으로 바꿔주실 수 있나요?
B: 정말 죄송하지만 잔돈이 없는 것 같아요.

[해설] change는 '잔돈'으로 쓰일 때 s가 붙지 않는다. 1달러짜리 지폐를 바꾸는 것이기 때문에 coins도 가능하다.

11 유형 대명사

A: Let's finish playing hide and seek. It's time to go. Where are you?
B: _____!
   (a) Here am I
   (b) Here I am
   (c) Here is me
   (d) Here me is

[해석] A: 숨바꼭질 그만하자. 가야 할 시간이야. 어디 있니?
B: 여기 있어!

[해설] here가 앞에 나오면 뒤에는 원래 'Here+동사+주어'의 순서로서 도치 또는 후치되지만 주어가 대명사인 경우에는 'Here+주어+동사'의 순서로 쓴다.

고난도 POINT 32 대명사가 출제되는 중요한 두 가지 유형을 알아야 한다.

대명사는 명사와 비슷하게 주어와 목적어 역할을 할 수 있지만, 명사와 다른 용법으로 출제되는 두 유형이 있다. 첫 번째가 위의 문제에 출제된 유형이다. Here comes the bus.처럼 Here가 문장 앞에 나올 경우 뒤에 나오는 주어와 동사는 도치되지만 주어가 대명사일 경우에는 Here you are.처럼 도치되지 않는다. 두 번째로 put on과 같이 '동사+부사' 형태의 동사가 대명사 목적어를 취할 경우, put on it이라 쓰지 않고 반드시 put in on이라 쓴다는 것이다. 대명사 영역에서 자주 출제되는 유형이므로 유의하도록 하자.

12 유형 가정법/도치

A: I am sorry to say he only has a few days left.
B: It might not have got to this stage, _____ diagnosed a little earlier.
 (a) if he were
 (b) if he has been
 (c) had he been
 (d) had he

[해석] A: 이런 말 하게 돼서 유감이지만 그는 살 날이 며칠 남지 않았어요.
B: 만약 조금 더 일찍 진단을 받았더라면 이렇게까지 되지는 않았을 텐데요.

[해설] might not have p.p.로 보아 가정법 과거완료 구문임을 알 수 있다. 따라서 뒤에 나오는 if절의 동사는 had p.p.를 써야 하고 if를 생략했을 경우 도치되어 had가 앞에 나온다. 진단을 받는 것이므로 수동태로 쓴다.

13 유형 동명사

A: How are your new part-time workers doing in their job?
B: I am considering the possibility _____ the job myself.
 (a) doing
 (b) do
 (c) of doing
 (d) to do

[해석] A: 새로 고용한 아르바이트생들은 일을 잘하고 있니?
B: 내가 직접 일을 할까 고려하고 있는 중이야.

[해설] '~할 가능성'이라는 의미의 possibility를 수식할 경우, of -ing의 형태를 취한다.

14 유형 대명사

A: How is the business going?
B: Not so good. Actually, I don't see _____ any worse.
 (a) how anything could get
 (b) how something could get
 (c) something could get how
 (d) anything could get how

[해석] A: 회사 형편이 어때?
B: 좋지 않아. 솔직히 말해서 최악이야.

[해설] I don't see how anything could get any worse.는 상황이 좋지 않을 때 쓰는 관용적 표현이다. 직역하면 어떤 것이 어떻게 더 나빠질지 모르겠다는 의미로서, 대책이 서지 않는다는 의미가 된다. 특히 상황에 따른 anything과 something의 의미 차이를 잘 생각해서 문제를 풀어야 한다.

> **고난도 POINT 33** any와 some의 차이를 유의해야 한다.
> any는 조금이라도 변화가 있을 때 써서 any better라고 하면 조금이라도 좋아진 것을 나타낸다. 반면, some은 어느 정도 상당한 변화가 있을 때 사용한다. 또한 Anyone can do it.에서처럼 any는 '전부'라는 의미도 있다는 점에서 차이가 있다.

15 유형 시제

A: What's wrong with her?
B: She _____ since she fought with her boyfriend.
 (a) had been upset ever
 (b) ever has been upset
 (c) was being upset ever
 (d) has been upset ever

[해석] A: 저 여자애 왜 저래요?
B: 남자 친구랑 싸우고 나서부터 시무룩해져 있어요.

[해설] since는 과거의 한 시점 이래로 계속된다는 뜻이므로 앞에 나오는 절은 현재완료 시제를 쓴다. ever는 완료시제와 함께 쓸 때 ever since의 형태로 쓴다.

16 유형 대명사

A: Look, the sky over Korea, especially in autumn is very, very blue.
B: _____.
 (a) So it is
 (b) It is so
 (c) So is it
 (d) Me, either

[해석] A: 봐, 한국의 하늘은 특히 가을에 매우 파래.
B: 정말 그러네.

[해설] 동조나 동감의 표현을 나타낼 때는 so를 사용하는데, 두 가지 표현이 있다. 'So+주어+동사'는 '정말 그렇다'라는 의미이고 'So+동사+주어'는 '나도 그래'와 같은 의미이다. 여기서는 하늘이 파랗다는 데 단순 공감을 표현하고 있으므로 (a)가 적절하다.

17 유형 수 일치/명사

A: I like the jeans in this clothing store.
B: _____ way too high.
 (a) These pairs of jeans values
 (b) This pair of jeans value
 (c) This pairs of jeans values
 (d) These pairs of jeans value

[해석] A: 나는 이 옷가게의 청바지가 맘에 들어.
B: 이런 청바지는 값이 많이 나가.

[해설] 청바지를 세는 단위인 pair는 앞에 붙는 지시사에 따라 형태가 달라지고 뒤에 오는 동사 또한 pair에 따라 단수, 복수가 결정된다. this pair of jeans values 혹은 these pairs of jeans value와 같은 형태로 쓴다.

[어휘] way 훨씬, 매우

18 유형 관사/명사

A: Is there _____ for me to fit in?
B: Sure, I think you are the last one.
 (a) a space
 (b) the space
 (c) space
 (d) spaces

[해석] A: 내가 들어갈 자리가 있니?
B: 물론이지, 네가 마지막인 것 같아.

[해설] space가 막연한 '공간'을 의미할 때는 불가산명사이므로 복수형으로 쓰지 않고 관사를 함께 쓰지 않는다.

19 유형 수동태/전치사

A: Beijing is trying to be _____ one of the cities to take charge.
B: I think it must be.
 (a) chosen for
 (b) choosing
 (c) chose
 (d) chosen as

[해석] A: 베이징은 그 일을 책임질 도시 중의 하나로 선정되려고 애쓰고 있어.
B: 내 생각으로는 틀림없이 될 것 같은데.

[해설] 선정되는 것이므로 수동태가 와야 하고 베이징과 도시 중의 하나는 동격이기에 자격을 나타내는 전치사 as가 들어가야 한다.

고난도 POINT 34 전치사의 쓰임을 알아야 한다.

동일한 전치사가 여러 가지 의미로 사용되기 때문에 각 전치사의 대표적인 쓰임은 숙지해야 한다. 위 문제에서처럼 전치사의 의미로 정답을 골라야 할 때는 특히 중요하다. as는 be known as처럼 '~로서'라는 의미로 자격을 나타내거나 '~처럼'이라는 뜻으로 쓰인다. 위 문제의 경우 빈칸 뒤에 나오는 one of the cities~가 하나의 자격을 나타내므로 (a) chosen for가 아닌 (d) chosen as가 적합하다.

20 유형 형용사

A: Maybe some kind of an electrical storm or something is coming?
B: That _____. The sky's just as blue as anything.

(a) doesn't seem likely
(b) seems to be likely
(c) seems like
(d) is to seem likely

해석 A: 심한 뇌우 같은 것이 생길 것 같지 않니?
B: 그런 것 같지 않은데. 하늘이 더할 나위 없이 맑잖아.

해설 B가 A의 말에 동의하고 있지 않으므로 부정적 의미의 어구가 와야 한다. likely는 '~할 것 같은'이란 형용사로 seem의 보어로 쓰였다.

어휘 electrical storm 심한 뇌우

Part II Questions 21-40

21 유형 부정사

_____, she curbed almost all of the unnecessary spending.
(a) To satisfy making ends
(b) Made ends meet
(c) To make ends meet
(d) Satisfying ends meet

해석 생계를 위해 그녀는 거의 모든 불필요한 지출을 줄였다.

해설 make ends meet는 관용표현으로 '생계를 맞추다'를 뜻한다. 목적의 의미를 띠는 to 부정사를 써서 문장 앞에서 동사 curb를 수식한다.

어휘 curb 억제하다

22 유형 접속사

Clark didn't register for the class, _____.
(a) being afraid and worried taking a martial art class
(b) being for fear to taking a martial art class and being worried
(c) being fearful to taking a martial art class and tired
(d) for he was afraid and worried to take a martial art class

해석 Clark는 무술 수업을 받는 것이 두렵고 걱정되어서 그 수업에 등록하지 않았다.

해설 for는 이유를 나타내는 접속사로 쓰인다. afraid나 for fear, fearful 뒤에 동명사를 쓰려면 동명사 앞에 전치사 of가 와야 한다.

23 유형 명사

Whether he accepts our offer or not is _____.
(a) a matter of tasting
(b) a matter of taste
(c) a tasting matter of
(d) a taste of matter

해석 그가 우리의 제의를 받아들이는 것은 취향의 문제이다.

해설 taste는 명사로 쓰여 '기호, 취향'을 나타낸다. 따라서 '선택의 문제'를 표현하려면 a matter of taste라고 쓴다.

24 유형 시제

Today, we _____ the seriousness of air pollution.
(a) are discussed
(b) will discuss about
(c) discussed about
(d) will be discussing

[해석] 오늘은 대기오염의 심각성에 대해 논의할 것입니다.
[해설] discuss는 타동사로 뒤에 about과 함께 쓰이지 않는다. 또한 오늘이지만 잠시 후에 논의가 진행될 것이니 미래시제가 적합하다.

25 유형 병렬 구조

During the first year that she and I were neighbors, our conversations turned frequently to two points of poetry: the power of exciting the sympathy of the reader by a faithful adherence to the truth of nature, and the power _____ of novelty through imagination.
(a) to give the interest
(b) of giving the interest
(c) to give interest
(d) of giving interest

[해석] 그녀와 내가 이웃으로 지낸 첫 해 동안 우리의 대화는 자주 시에 관한 두 가지 관점, 즉 자연의 진실에 대해 충실히 집착하여 독자의 공감을 불러일으키는 힘과 상상력을 통해 색다른 경험에 대한 흥미를 제공하는 힘으로 모아졌다.
[해설] and를 중심으로 the power of가 병렬로 연결되어야 한다. 정답은 (b) 아니면 (d)가 되는데, of novelty라는 수식어가 있기에 interest 앞에 관사 the가 붙어야 한다.

고난도 POINT 35 병렬 구조는 동일한 형태로 나온다.

and나 but으로 연결된 병렬 구조의 문장은 앞뒤가 동일한 형태로 연결된다는 것이 중요한 포인트이다. 병렬 구조의 문제가 출제될 경우, 먼저 동일한 형태로 연결되어야 하는 것이 무엇인지 파악한다. 이 문제에서는 앞에 나온 the power와 and 뒤에 나온 the power가 병렬 구조로 연결된 문장이므로 빈칸에는 앞에 나온 the power 뒤에 이어지는 형태와 동일한 형태가 나와야 한다.

26 유형 접속사

Analysts said today's trading was typical of end-of-year trading, _____ did not indicate what is to come next year.
(a) and
(b) but
(c) furthermore
(d) that

[해석] 분석가들은 오늘의 거래가 전형적인 연말거래 양상이었지만 그것이 내년의 상황을 암시하지는 않았다고 말했다.
[해설] 오늘의 거래가 연말거래 양상이지만 그것이 내년의 상황을 암시하지 않는다고 말하므로 내용상 전환을 뜻하는 접속사가 나와야 한다.

27 유형 동사

They are debating what _____ the causes of air pollution.
(a) comprises
(b) is comprised of
(c) comprises of
(d) comprises in

[해석] 그들은 무엇이 대기오염의 원인을 구성하고 있는지 의논하고 있다.
[해설] comprise는 '~을 구성하다, 차지하다'라는 의미의 타동사로 A comprises B의 형태로 쓴다. 따라서 (a)가 적합하다. (b)는 '~로 구성되다'는 의미로 of 뒤에 나오는 부분이 주어의 구성요소임을 설명하므로 내용상 맞지 않다.

28 유형 시제

The Internet _____ user rate in Korea, reaching eighty percent of the entire population according to the recent survey.

(a) have an incredible
(b) had an incredible
(c) has an incredible
(d) has incredible

[해석] 최근의 조사에 따르면, 한국의 인터넷 사용자 수가 전체 인구의 80%에 이른다는 엄청난 수치가 나왔다.

[해설] 최근의 조사를 언급하므로 현재시제가 적절하고, rate는 가산명사이므로 앞에 관사와 함께 써야 한다.

29 유형 시제/문장의 형식

The Monsoon Company _____ when the auditors released the results.

(a) closed
(b) be closed
(c) closing
(d) will close

[해석] 몬순 회사는 감사원들이 결과를 발표하자 문을 닫았다.

[해설] 이때의 회사는 다분히 의인화된 존재로, 수동태가 아니라 능동태를 써도 상관이 없다. 그래서 1형식으로 표현해도 괜찮다. (d)는 시제가 맞지 않는다.

30 유형 접속사

Grameen believes that charity is not an answer to poverty _____ it creates dependency and takes away individual's initiative to break through the wall of poverty.

(a) and
(b) so
(c) since
(d) provided

[해석] 그라민은 구호금이 의존심을 낳고 가난을 이겨내고자 하는 개인의 자발성을 앗아가기 때문에 가난에 대한 해결책이 아니라고 믿는다.

[해설] 빈칸 앞뒤의 내용이 원인과 결과로 이어지고 있으므로 '~ 때문이다'를 나타내는 since나 because가 적합하다. provided는 조건을 나타낸다.

[어휘] break through 헤치고 나가다, 극복하다
initiative 솔선, 자발적인 행동

31 유형 한정사

_____ thousand Korean soldiers took part in the Vietnam war.

(a) Several
(b) Few
(c) Every
(d) Many

[해석] 수천 명의 한국군이 베트남 전쟁에 참여했다.

[해설] thousand 앞에 수를 나타내는 한정사로서 a, two, three 등 숫자와 several, a few 등이 가능하므로 (a)가 적합하다.

32 유형 명사

_____ of carbohydrates, at least three should be from whole grain foods.

(a) Among six of the eleven daily servings
(b) Of the six to eleven daily servings
(c) Daily serving of six to eleven
(d) With serving daily six of eleven

[해석] 탄수화물 섭취에 있어서 여섯에서 열 끼 중에서 최소한 세 끼는 통곡물 식품에서 섭취해야 한다.

[해설] 문장의 주어는 three이고 선택지에 나온 six, eleven의 일부분이라는 것을 알 수 있다. 따라서 '~중에서'를 의미하는 of를 써서 three를 꾸며주는 수식어구가 되어야 한다.

[어휘] daily serving 끼니

33 유형 전치사/관사

He was able to pay $1000 a month into an installment savings account when he was _____.
(a) in the office
(b) in office
(c) in the bank
(d) at bank

해석 그는 재직 중에 매달 1000달러씩 적금을 넣을 수 있었다
해설 in이 들어간 관용 표현으로 in office는 '재직 중에'라는 뜻이다.
어휘 installment savings 적금

34 유형 수 일치

Technological improvements in the industry, combined with significant reductions in the expenses associated with transport, _____ to remove these commodities more efficiently and at a much lower cost, resulting in an extraction rate that many experts consider to be unsustainable.
(a) has made possible
(b) has made it possible
(c) have made possible
(d) have made it possible

해석 수송과 관련된 비용이 상당히 줄어드는 것과 함께 산업 기술 발전은 원자재들을 더욱 효과적이고 훨씬 더 낮은 비용으로 운반할 수 있게 만들면서 많은 전문가들이 지속 불가능하다고 여기는 채취율을 도출했다.
해설 주어가 technological improvements이므로 have가 와야 한다. 또한 possible하게 된 것은 to remove ~ 이하의 내용이므로 가목적어 it을 써야 한다.
어휘 commodity 원자재 extraction 채취, 추출

고난도 POINT 36 가목적어에 유의하자.

it은 여러 가지 역할을 하는데 그 중에서 가목적어는 시험에 자주 출제된다. 이 문제에서도 it이 가목적어로 쓰인 경우이다. make, find, think 등과 같은 동사 뒤에 to부정사가 목적어로 오고 그 뒤에 형용사 목적격 보어가 올 경우, 가목적어 it을 쓰고 to부정사 구문을 목적격 보어 뒤로 보내 make it possible to do, find it difficult to do 등과 같은 형태로 쓴다.

---

35 유형 부정사

The price has gone up higher _____ for much better service.
(a) to pay
(b) paying
(c) paid
(d) pay

해석 훨씬 더 나은 서비스에 대한 비용을 지불하기 위해 가격이 더 올라갔다.
해설 빈칸에는 '훨씬 더 나은 서비스를 위해서 비용을 더 지불했다'라는 의미가 되어야 하므로 부사적 용법의 to부정사가 와야 한다.

36 유형 형용사

In plenty of animals, _____ involves reflex action or involuntary response to stimuli.
(a) almost the behavior
(b) almost behavior
(c) most behavior
(d) the most behavior

해석 많은 동물들의 대부분의 행동은 자극에 대한 반사 작용, 즉 무의식적인 반응과 연관된다.
해설 most는 '대부분'이라는 의미로 형용사로 쓰여 명사를 수식할 수 있다. almost는 부사로서 바로 명사 앞에 쓰지 못한다. 또한 almost all 다음에는 almost all (the) boys와 같은 형태로 복수형 명사가 나오고, 정관사 the를 쓰는 경우가 많다.
어휘 reflex action 반사 작용

37 유형 관사/명사

Take _____ if you'd like to visit the downtown art gallery.
(a) Ivy Lane bus
(b) the Ivy Lane bus
(c) some Ivy Lane bus
(d) a Ivy Lane's bus

[해석] 시내에 있는 미술관에 가고 싶다면 Ivy Lane행 버스를 타세요.

[해설] 정해진 버스나 기차 노선을 나타낼 때는 정관사와 함께 쓴다. 즉, 'Ivy Lane행 버스'를 나타내려면 the bus to Ivy Lane이나 the Ivy Lane bus로 표현할 수 있다.

38 유형 전치사

All of the activities that students do in the language study camp are _____ an assistant's supervision.
(a) in
(b) under
(c) within
(d) with

[해석] 이 어학연수 캠프에서 학생들이 하는 모든 활동은 조교의 감독 하에 있다.

[해설] '감독, 관리'를 뜻하는 supervision은 구속이나 책임 등을 나타내는 전치사 under와 함께 쓴다.

39 유형 수동태

Make sure you _____ of the risks relating to this option.
(a) are fully apprised
(b) fully apprised yourself
(c) fully apprising you
(d) fully apprise you

[해석] 이 방법에 따르는 위험성을 충분히 알고 계셔야 합니다.

[해설] 위험성을 인식하다는 표현을 쓰기 위해서는 (동사) apprise를 활용하되, 목적어를 자기 자신을 쓰는 재귀대명사를 활용하든지, 아니면 수동태로 사용해야 한다. 따라서 (d)의 경우는 you가 아니라 yourself 를 써야 정답이 된다.

[어휘] apprise 알려주다

40 유형 병렬 구조

After a crime case is reported, the police investigate the suspects and _____ .
(a) photograph and fingerprint them
(b) photograph, fingerprint them
(c) photograph and fingerprint themselves
(d) photograph, fingerprint themselves

[해석] 범죄 사건이 보고되면 경찰은 용의자들을 조사하고 사진을 찍고 지문을 채취한다.

[해설] 여기서 photograph와 fingerprint는 둘 다 동사로서 빈 칸 앞에 나온 and에 의해 investigate와 병렬로 연결된다. 목적어는 the suspects를 받는 것이므로 재귀대명사를 쓸 필요가 없다. 따라서 (a)가 적절하다.

Part III Questions 41-45

41 유형 관계대명사

(a) A: May I ask who you were talking to?
(b) **B: She's the professor for which class I couldn't attend during summer vacation.**
(c) A: Why can't you attend the class?
(d) B: I am planning to do an internship.

해석 (a) A: 너 누구랑 이야기했는지 물어봐도 되니?
(b) B: 그녀는 여름방학 동안 내가 참석할 수 없는 수업의 교수님이셔.
(c) A: 왜 참석할 수 없는데?
(d) B: 인턴 사원으로 일할 계획이거든.

해설 (b)에서 선행사는 the professor이고 뒤의 내용은 교수의 수업이므로 소유격 관계대명사가 적절하다. which class → whose class

어휘 internship 실무 연수, 인턴직

42 유형 형용사

(a) A: Do you need any help?
(b) **B: It'd be grateful if you could move this box on second floor.**
(c) A: Sure. Anything else?
(d) B: No, that's enough for now.

해석 (a) A: 도움이 필요하세요?
(b) B: 이 박스를 2층에다 올려주시면 감사하겠는데요.
(c) A: 물론이죠. 또 도와드릴 게 있나요?
(d) B: 아니오, 지금은 그걸로 충분해요.

해설 형용사 grateful은 '감사하는, 고맙게 여기는'이라는 뜻으로 사람이 주어가 되어야 한다. It'd be grateful → I'd be grateful

43 유형 전치사

(a) A: Where are you going?
(b) B: I'm going out to meet my friends.
(c) A: I wouldn't go out if I were you since it's raining cats and dogs. When are you coming back home?
(d) **B: It doesn't matter. I will be back until 3.**

해석 (a) A: 어디 가니?
(b) B: 친구들 만나러 가요.
(c) A: 비가 많이 오는데 내가 너라면 나가지 않을 거야. 언제 집에 오니?
(d) B: 상관없어요. 8시까지 올게요.

해설 전치사 until은 어느 시점까지 계속된다는 의미이고 by는 어느 시점까지 완료된다는 의미이다. 8시까지 온다는 것은 완료를 나타내므로 by로 써야 한다. until → by

44 유형 가정법

(a) A: You look so pale. What's wrong with you?
(b) **B: You are, too, if you had eaten rotten food like me.**
(c) A: That's a pity.
(d) B: I have to go see the doctor.

해석 (a) A: 너 매우 창백해 보여. 무슨 일이야?
(b) B: 네가 나처럼 썩은 음식을 먹었다면 너도 그랬을 거야.
(c) A: 저런.
(d) B: 나 의사에게 가봐야겠어.

해설 가정법 문장이므로 if절과 주절의 시제를 파악해야 한다. 썩은 음식을 먹은 것은 과거의 일이므로 if절은 가정법 과거완료가 되어야 하고, 주절은 현재 사실을 의미하는 것이므로 가정법 과거가 되어야 하는 혼합가정법 문장이다. 따라서 시제를 가정법 과거로 고쳐야 한다. You are → You would be

45 유형 관계대명사

(a) A: How is your grade for this semester?
(b) **B: It's not as good as I thought. I don't know that I've done wrong.**
(c) A: I suggest you meet the professor and ask about your grade.
(d) B: I agree. I should go and see her.

해석
(a) A: 이번 학기 성적 어때?
(b) B: 내가 생각했던 것만큼 좋지 않아. 뭐가 문제인지 모르겠어.
(c) A: 교수님 만나서 성적에 대해 물어보는 게 좋겠어.
(d) B: 맞아. 나도 가서 만나봐야겠어.

해설 I've done wrong에서 do의 목적어가 없으므로 선행사를 포함하면서 목적어 역할을 할 수 있는 관계대명사 what이 적절하다. that I've done → what I've done

Part Ⅳ Questions 46-50

46 유형 관계대명사

(a) People perceived as the most likely to succeed might also be the most likely to crumble under pressure. (b) A new study finds that individuals with high working-memory capacity, which allows them to excel, do worse on simple exams. (c) The pressure causes verbal worries, like 'Oh no, I can't screw up.' **(d) Negative thoughts take up space what would otherwise be pondering the task at hand.**

해석 (a) 가장 성공할 것 같다고 여겨지는 사람들이 또한 스트레스를 받으면 가장 무너지기 쉽다. (b) 새로운 연구조사에 따르면 탁월한 실력을 발휘할 수 있도록 해 주는 활성기억력이 뛰어난 사람들은 간단한 시험에서 더 잘하지 못한다고 한다. (c) 스트레스는 '이런, 나 망치면 안 되는데.' 처럼 말로 내뱉는 걱정을 유발시킨다. (d) 그런 걱정이 아니라면 당장 닥친 문제에 대해 고민할 공간을 부정적인 생각이 차지하게 된다.

해설 what은 선행사를 포함하는 관계대명사이다. (d)에서 앞에 선행사인 space가 나와 있으므로 what 대신 that을 써야 한다. what would otherwise → that would otherwise

어휘 crumble 무너지다
working memory 활성기억, 작동기억 excel 뛰어나다
screw up 망치다 ponder 생각하다

47 유형 시제

(a) This is to confirm that Mark Stephens was employed by the City of Drisdale and served as a Building Inspector for 8 years. (b) During his tenure of employment, he displayed a unique ability to identify and solve problems. (c) He ensured that structures built in Drisdale were constructed in a manner which guaranteed they were safe to live and or work in. **(d) Countless times, Mark had to perform his tasks despite physical strains.**

해석 (a) 이 편지는 Mark Stephens가 드리즈데일 시에서 8년간 건물 검사관으로 일했다는 것을 확인해 드리기 위한 것입니다. (b) 직무 기간 동안 그는 문제를 찾아내고 해결하는 데 대단한 능력을 보여주었습니다. (c) 그는 드리즈데일에 지어진 구조물들이 주거 및 근무에 안전하다고 보증할 수 있는 방법으로 건설되었는지 확인했습니다. (d) 셀 수 없을 정도로 여러 번 Mark는 신체적인 어려움에도 불구하고 자신의 일을 수행해야 했습니다.

해설 strain이 '긴장, 과로' 등을 뜻할 때는 불가산명사로 쓰이므로 단수형으로 쓴다. physical strains → physical strain

어휘 tenure 재직기간, 임기 unique 굉장한, 비길데 없는

48 유형 전치사/접속사

(a) **The Civil War between the states of north, where capitalism had developed on the basis of wage labor, or the southern states, where capitalism was based on the slave labor, became transformed into a revolutionary war.** (b) It was thanks to this terrible war that the U.S. definitively won its national unity. (c) It also allowed the democratic and independent road of the development of capitalism to triumph over the oligarchic and dependent road. (d) Hence, the current United States is exists.

[해석] (a) 임금노동자 기반의 자본주의를 발전시킨 북쪽의 주들과 노예들의 노동력에 기반하여 자본주의를 발전시킨 남쪽의 주들 사이의 전쟁은 혁명적 전쟁이 되었다. (b) 미국이 확실히 국가적인 통일을 이룬 것은 이 끔찍한 전쟁 덕분이었다. (c) 또한 자본주의의 발전을 가져온 민주적이고 자주적인 방식이 남북전쟁으로 인해 과두정치와 종속적인 방식을 극복할 수 있었다. (d) 그렇기에 지금의 미국이 존재하는 것이다.

[해설] between A and B 구문이다. where로 이어진 수식어구를 빼면 the states of north와 the southern states 사이에서 일어난 전쟁 즉, 남과 북 간의 싸움이라는 것을 알 수 있다. or the southern states → and the southern states

[어휘] oligarchic 과두정치의

49 유형 부사

(a) Easter is an annual festival observed throughout the Christian world. (b) The date for Easter shifts every year within the Gregorian Calendar. (c) The Gregorian Calendar is the standard international calendar for civil use. **(d) In contrast, it regulates the ceremonial cycle of the Roman Catholic and Protestant churches.**

[해석] (a) 부활절은 전체 기독교 세계에서 지내는 연례 축일이다. (b) 부활절 날짜는 그레고리력에 따라 매년 바뀐다. (c) 그레고리력은 일반 용도로 사용되는 국제 표준 달력이다. (d) 또한 로마 가톨릭과 신교도 교회들의 행사도 그레고리력에 따라 지켜진다.

[해설] 기독교에서 지내는 부활절을 그레고리력에 따르고 있고, 로마 가톨릭과 신교도 교회들도 역시 그 달력에 따라 행사일을 지킨다고 해야 하므로 첨가의 의미를 나타내는 부사가 적합하다. In contrast → In addition 혹은 Moreover

[어휘] civil (천문력에 대해) 상용(常用)의
regulate 규제하다, 조정하다

50 유형 관계사

(a) Cambridge University has announced that it will be introducing a scholarship program to encourage women in the engineering program. **(b) $500,000 has been set out over the next five years to be awarded to first-year university women which show promise in engineering.** (c) Cambridge hopes to re-balance the ratio of men and women in the program, from its current imbalance of eight to one. (d) Many women have shied away from pursuing an engineering degree due to the intimidation of a male-dominant field.

[해석] (a) 캠브리지 대학은 공과 계열의 여학생들을 장려하기 위해 장학금 제도를 도입할 것이라고 발표했다. (b) 공과 계열에서 전도유망한 신입 여학생들에게 앞으로 5년간 수여될 장학금 50만 달러가 책정되었다. (c) 캠브리지는 현재 8:1의 불균형 상태에서 장학제도로 남녀 학생의 비율이 다시 균형을 이루기를 바라고 있다. (d) 많은 여학생들이 남성 위주의 분야라는 어려움 때문에 공학 학위 취득을 꺼리고 있다.

[해설] (b)에서 선행사가 women이므로 관계대명사 who가 와야 한다. women which show → women who show

[어휘] promise 전도유망함 shy 겁을 먹다, 주춤하다
intimidation 협박, 위협

고난도 Actual Training 07

1. (a)	2. (b)	3. (a)	4. (c)	5. (d)	6. (c)	7. (a)	8. (d)	9. (b)	10. (b)
11. (b)	12. (c)	13. (d)	14. (c)	15. (b)	16. (b)	17. (a)	18. (b)	19. (a)	20. (a)
21. (c)	22. (a)	23. (c)	24. (a)	25. (c)	26. (b)	27. (b)	28. (c)	29. (d)	30. (a)
31. (c)	32. (a)	33. (c)	34. (d)	35. (b)	36. (a)	37. (c)	38. (a)	39. (c)	40. (b)
41. (d)	42. (d)	43. (d)	44. (d)	45. (a)	46. (a)	47. (b)	48. (b)	49. (d)	50. (d)

Part I Questions 1-20

1 유형 접속사

A: Ken is always of good manner _____ anyone annoys him.
B: I know. He seems to be out of this world.
(a) even though
(b) as if
(c) even
(d) as

해석 A: Ken은 누가 짜증나게 해도 늘 좋은 매너를 유지해.
B: 맞아. 그는 이 세상 사람이 아닌 것 같아.
해설 빈칸의 앞뒤 내용이 반대되므로 이를 나타내는 접속사 even though가 적합하다.

2 유형 부정사/조동사

A: Do we have to go to Namsan as part of the tour schedule?
B: No, we don't _____, the guide said.
(a) have
(b) have to
(c) have to go
(d) have to go it

해석 A: 여행 일정으로 남산에 가야 하나?
B: 아니, 가이드가 그럴 필요 없다고 했어.
해설 원래는 No, we don't have to go to Namsan.이 되어야 하는데 반복되는 부분은 생략하고 대부정사 to만 남긴다.

3 유형 부정사

A: _____ of the new strategy.
B: Sure. It is a brilliant idea!
(a) You seem to approve
(b) It seems you to approve
(c) You seem to be approving
(d) It seems you are approving

해석 A: 넌 새로운 전략에 대해 동의하는 거 같아.
B: 물론이지, 기발한 아이디어잖아!
해설 가주어 it이 주어일 때는 seem 뒤에 that절이 오며 사람이 주어로 오면 seem 뒤에 to부정사가 온다. 한편 know, approve 등 사고에 관한 동사는 진행형으로 표현할 수 없다.

4 유형 전치사

A: Is she watching the movie with you?
B: I couldn't talk her _____ with me.
  (a) to go
  (b) of go
  (c) into going
  (d) that she go

해석
A: 그녀랑 영화 같이 볼 거니?
B: 함께 가자고 설득 못했어.

해설 talk A into -ing는 'A를 설득하여 ~하게 하다'의 구문이다. '~에게 말하다'고 할 때는 'talk to A'의 형태로 쓴다.

5 유형 전치사

A: Why are you so sad?
B: I have an assignment but I am _____.
  (a) behind two days
  (b) behind schedule two days
  (c) two days behind
  (d) two days behind schedule

해석
A: 왜 그렇게 우울하니?
B: 과제가 있는데 이틀이나 밀렸어.

해설 '예정보다 늦게'를 나타낼 때는 behind schedule을 쓴다. 또한 늦은 정도를 표현하는 말은 behind schedule보다 앞에 써야 한다.

6 유형 형용사

A: _____ came to the party.
B: You must have had a lot of fun.
  (a) Many a students
  (b) The many students
  (c) A great many students
  (d) Many a great students

해석
A: 많은 학생들이 파티에 왔었어.
B: 재밌었겠네.

해설 a great many는 '많은'이라는 의미로 뒤에 복수명사가 온다. many a는 뒤에 단수명사와 함께 쓰므로 (a)와 (d)는 적절하지 않다.

7 유형 형용사/명사

A: When I watched the ceremony with the _____, I was too nervous.
B: Me, too. I hardly remember the winner of the ceremony.
  (a) authority figure present
  (b) present authority figure
  (c) figure authority present
  (d) authority present figure

해석
A: 권위 있는 사람이 참석한 시상식을 봤을 때, 난 너무 긴장이 되더라.
B: 나도 그랬어. 나는 시상식의 수상자도 거의 생각이 나지 않아.

해설 'with+목적어+목적보어' 구문이다. 목적어 authority figure는 '권위 있는 인물'이라는 의미로 쓰이고, '참석한'을 뜻하는 목적보어 present는 목적어인 명사 뒤에 와야 한다. present는 '현재의'라는 의미를 나타낼 때는 명사 앞에 올 수 있고 '참석한'이라는 의미로 쓸 때는 명사/대명사 뒤나 be동사 뒤에 온다.

8 유형 태

A: You don't need to prepare anything in advance since the registration process will _____ the program here.
B: That's cool.
  (a) facilitated by
  (b) facilitate by
  (c) be facilitating by
  (d) be facilitated by

해석
A: 등록 절차는 이곳 프로그램을 쓰면 쉬울 테니 사전에 아무 것도 준비하지 않으셔도 됩니다.
B: 정말 좋네요.

해설 facilitate는 '용이하게 하다'라는 뜻으로 타동사이다. 프로그램에 의해 절차가 쉬워질 것이므로 수동태가 되어야 한다.

9 유형 명사

A: Finally, I succeeded in joining the company that I have always prayed for.
B: _____!
(a) That's a good news
(b) That's good news
(c) It's a good news
(d) It's the good news

해석 A: 마침내 내가 항상 원하던 회사에 입사했어.
B: 좋은 소식이네!
해설 news는 셀 수 없는 명사이다. 부정관사와 함께 쓸 수 없으므로 that's a good news 나 it's a good news를 쓸 수 없다. 또한 앞에 나온 상황이 전제되거나 지칭하는 대상이 정해지지 않았기에 정관사 the와 함께 쓰지 않는다.

10 유형 형용사/명사

A: Why didn't you take part in the farewell dinner in the Ritz Carlton hotel?
B: Because I had _____ to finish.
(a) too much assignment
(b) a lot of assignments
(c) many assignment
(d) a assignment

해석 A: 리츠칼튼호텔에서 있었던 송별연에 왜 참석하지 못했니?
B: 끝내야 할 일이 너무 많았어.
해설 '할당된 일이나 과제'의 의미로 쓰일 때 assignment는 가산명사이다.

11 유형 부정사

A: I don't want him _____.
B: But he is always late to work and has embezzled the company's money.
(a) to discharge
(b) discharged
(c) to be discharging
(d) to been discharged

해석 A: 난 그가 해고되지 않았으면 좋겠어.
B: 하지만 그는 항상 지각하고 이번에 회사 돈을 횡령했잖아.
해설 want 뒤에 올 수 있는 형태는 to부정사 또는 분사이다. 그가 해고당하는 것이므로 수동형으로 to be discharged라고 쓸 수 있다. 여기에서는 to be를 생략하고 discharged만 썼다.

12 유형 조동사/시제

A: I took my parents to Thailand during the summer vacation.
B: That _____.
(a) must be nice
(b) must having been nice
(c) must have been nice
(d) must have nice

해석 A: 여름휴가 동안 부모님을 모시고 태국에 갔어.
B: 그거 참 좋았겠구나.
해설 이미 지난 과거에 대해 말하고 있으므로 과거에 대한 강한 추측을 나타내는 must have p.p. 구문이 적합하다.

고난도 POINT 37 '조동사+have+p.p.'를 알아두자.

이 문제에 나온 must have p.p.는 자주 나오는 표현으로 과거에 대한 강한 추측을 나타내서 '~했음에 틀림없다'는 의미를 띤다. 이 외에 may have p.p.는 '~했을지도 모른다'라는 의미로, cannot have p.p.는 '~했을 리가 없다'라는 의미로 쓰인다. 또한 should have p.p.는 '~했어야 했는데 (하지 못했다)'의 의미로 과거에 대해 후회를 나타내고 시험에 자주 출제된다.

13 유형 대명사

A: Those convertibles look luxurious. Do you know _____?
B: I heard that they are not as expensive as they look.
(a) how much cost them
(b) what do they cost
(c) they cost how much
(d) what they cost

[해석] A: 저 컨버터블 고급스러워 보여. 얼마인지 아니?
B: 보이는 것만큼 비싸지 않다고 들었어.
[해설] know의 목적절을 이끌면서 cost의 목적어와 접속사 역할을 동시에 하는 것은 의문대명사 what이다. 간접의문문이므로 '의문사+주어+동사' 순으로 쓴다.

14 유형 의문사

A: How come _____ all the risk?
B: That's because no one else will take it.
(a) did you try to take
(b) did you try taking
(c) you tried to take
(d) you tried taking

[해석] A: 왜 이 모든 위험을 네가 떠안으려고 하니?
B: 아무도 그것을 하려 들지 않으니까.
[해설] how come은 '왜, 어째서'란 의미의 의문사이지만 일반 의문사처럼 뒤에 주어와 동사가 도치되어 나오지 않는다는 점에 유의해야 한다. 문맥상 떠안으려고 노력한다는 의미가 되어야 하므로 '시험 삼아 해보다'라는 의미인 try taking이 아니라 try to take가 적절하다.

15 유형 시제

A: How are you doing these days?
B: _____ better days.
(a) I had had
(b) I've had
(c) I'd have
(d) I had

[해석] A: 요즘 어때?
B: 이보다 더 좋은 때도 있었어.
[해설] these days가 현재를 나타내지만, '이보다 더 좋은 때도 있었다'라는 대답이므로 과거부터 지금까지 연결되는 현재완료가 적절하다. B의 대답은 지금의 상태가 별로라는 의미이다.

16 유형 조동사

A: Finally, we are here on schedule.
B: What you did was very reckless. We _____ gotten into a car accident!
(a) would
(b) might have
(c) should
(d) must have

[해석] A: 드디어 제시간에 도착했어.
B: 네가 한 짓은 너무 무모했어. 하마터면 차 사고 날 뻔했잖아!
[해설] 사고가 날 뻔했다는 가능성을 나타내는 불확실한 추측 might have p.p.가 와야 한다.
[어휘] reckless 무모한

17 유형 관계대명사

A: Why has he changed so much?
B: I don't know. He is not _____.
(a) what he was
(b) who he used to
(c) what he would be
(d) what he is

[해석] A: 그는 왜 그렇게 많이 변했니?
B: 나도 모르겠어. 그는 이제 과거의 그가 아니야.
[해설] '과거의 그가 아니다'라는 표현으로 what he was 또는 who he was, what[who] he used to be를 쓴다.

| 고난도 **POINT 38** | **what을 이용한 관용 표현을 알아두자.** |

what은 의문사와 관계대명사의 두 가지 역할을 하는데 관계대명사일 경우가 문제에 많이 출제된다. 관계대명사 what은 선행사를 포함하고 있다는 것이 가장 큰 특징이고 이를 이용한 관용 표현도 많이 쓰인다. 이 문제에서처럼 what one is[was]는 사람의 상태를 나타내는 말로 '지금의[과거의] 사람'이라는 의미로 쓴다. 또한 what one has는 '사람이 가진 것'의 의미로 재산을 나타낸다. A is to B what C is to D는 'A와 B의 관계는 C와 D의 관계와 같다'는 의미이다.

18 유형 형용사

A: Our player has been sent off.
B: The team will have to operate _____.
 (a) a player shortly
 (b) a player short
 (c) a short player
 (d) a shortly player

[해석] A: 우리 선수가 퇴장당했어.
B: 우리 팀은 한 명이 부족한 상태로 경기를 해야 되겠군.

[해설] 부족하다는 의미의 형용사 short는 일반적으로 명사 뒤에서 서술적인 형태로 쓴다.

19 유형 명사

A: When Henny stayed in Boston, he used to play _____ on weekends.
B: Yes. We joined together.
 (a) baseball
 (b) a baseball
 (c) the baseball
 (d) baseball game

[해석] A: Henny가 보스턴에 있었을 때 그는 주말에 야구를 하곤 했어.
B: 맞아. 나도 함께 했어.

[해설] 일반적으로 운동명은 추상명사이고 불가산명사이므로 a 또는 an과 함께 쓰지 않는다. 특정 종류의 게임을 의미할 경우엔 보통명사로 앞에 관사를 쓴다. 선택지에서 적절한 것은 (a) baseball이다. (d)의 경우 관사가 있었다면 정답이 될 수 있다.

20 유형 관계대명사

A: He told me he loved me, _____ was a pure fabrication.
B: Really? That's a big surprise.
 (a) as
 (b) that
 (c) who
 (d) what

[해석] A: 그는 나에게 사랑한다고 해지만 순 거짓말이었어.
B: 정말? 정말 놀라운데.

[해설] as는 유사관계대명사로 앞 문장 전체가 선행사일 경우 쓸 수 있고 계속적 용법으로도 쓸 수 있다. he loved me의 내용을 모두 선행사로 받고 있으므로 as가 적합하다.

[어휘] a pure fabrication 새빨간 거짓말

| 고난도 **POINT 39** | **as는 다양한 역할을 한다.** |

as는 전치사, 부사, 접속사, 유사관계대명사의 다양한 역할을 하므로 자주 출제된다. '~처럼, ~로서'이라는 뜻의 전치사, '~만큼, ~하듯이'이라는 뜻의 부사, '~하는 동안에, ~ 때문에, ~대로, ~이긴 하지만'이라는 뜻의 접속사로 쓴다. 그리고 이 문제에 나온 것처럼 유사관계대명사로도 쓰이는데, 앞 문장 전체가 선행사이거나 선행사에 as, the same, such가 포함되어 있을 때 쓸 수 있다.

Part II Questions 21-40

21 유형 접속사

_____ no one has any further inquiries, I would like to conclude today's session.
(a) Notwithstanding
(b) Considering
(c) On condition that
(d) Just in case

해석 만약 더 이상 추가 질문이 없다면 오늘 회의를 마치도록 하겠습니다.

해설 조건의 의미를 나타내는 접속사가 필요하므로 (c)가 적합하다.

어휘 notwithstanding ~에도 불구하고
considering ~을 고려하면
just in case ~할 때를 대비해서

22 유형 접속사

Nevertheless, critics of globalization claim that the beneficiaries of IT are _____ the developed nations and that the inhabitants of developing countries are deprived of the advances in IT.

(a) those living in
(b) ones living in
(c) those living
(d) ones living

해석 그렇지만 세계화를 비판하는 사람들은 IT의 수혜자들은 선진국의 사람들이고 개발도상국의 국민들은 IT의 진보를 박탈당하고 있다고 주장한다.

해설 '~한 사람들'을 표현할 때는 those who를 쓴다. 그리고 live는 자동사이므로 장소를 목적어로 취하기 위해서는 전치사 in과 함께 사용한다. 원래 those who are living in이었으나 주격 관계대명사와 be동사를 생략하여 those living in이 된다.

고난도 POINT 40 one(s)과 those의 쓰임을 구별해야 한다.

one(s)과 those는 둘 다 막연한 대상을 나타낼 때 쓰며 특히 복수형인 ones로 쓸 경우 '~한 사람들'의 의미를 나타내는 those와 혼동될 수 있다. 하지만 those는 뒤에 어떤 사람들인지를 나타내는 수식어가 함께 나오며 ones의 경우 이미 앞에 그 대상이 나온다는 점에서 차이가 있다.

---

23 유형 관계사/전치사

Steven Jobs is currently the CEO of the company _____ he was once fired.
(a) which
(b) whatever
(c) from which
(d) of which

해석 Steven Jobs는 현재 해고당했던 회사의 사장이다.

해설 선행사가 the company이고 원래 문장은 he was once fired from the company가 되므로 from을 관계대명사 앞에 쓴 (c)가 정답이다.

24 유형 유사 관계대명사

When people first meet a person, they must see him _____, and not judge by his appearance.
(a) as he is
(b) what he is
(c) how he is
(d) as is he

해석 사람을 처음 만날 때, 그 사람 자체를 보아야 하며, 겉모습으로 판단해서는 안된다.

해설 see A as B는 'A를 B로 보다, 여기다'라는 뜻이다. 여기서 as는 접속사라기보다 유사 관계대명사로 쓰였다.

25 유형 시제/태

The rent fee for the apartment _____ by 10%, which forced the tenants to move out.
(a) was increased
(b) has increased
(c) had increased
(d) has been increased

해석 그 아파트의 임대료가 10퍼센트 상승했는데, 이 때문에 세입자는 이사를 가야만 했다.

해설 세입자들이 이사를 갈 수밖에 없는 점으로 보아 그 전부터 임대료가 상승되었다는 것을 알 수 있다. 따라서 과거완료가 적절하며 능동형으로 써야 한다.

26 유형 부사

The cars _____ delivered at the port today will arrive next week in Los Angeles.
(a) have
(b) just
(c) were
(d) itself

해석 지금 막 항구에 배달된 자동차들은 다음 주에 LA에 도착할 것이다.

해설 주어는 cars이고 이에 대한 동사는 will arrive다. delivered는 과거분사의 형태로 형용사처럼 명사 cars를 수식한다. 따라서 부사인 just밖에 들어갈 수 없다. have나 were를 넣을 경우 주어 하나에 동사가 두 개가 되어 오답이다. (d)는 themselves가 된다면 정답이 될 수 있다.

27 유형 전치사/한정사

If someone asks me a question, I will answer him _____.
(a) at some circumstances
(b) under any circumstances
(c) on certain circumstances
(d) in no circumstances

해석 만약 누군가가 나에게 질문을 하면 나는 어떤 상황에서라도 그에게 대답해 줄 것이다.

해설 '어떤 상황에서도'라는 표현은 under any circumstances로 쓴다.

28 유형 도치/강조구문

_____ his death that he was acknowledged as a great poet.
(a) Not until it was
(b) That was not until
(c) It was not until
(d) Not until it were

해석 그가 죽은 후에야 그는 위대한 시인으로서 인정받게 되었다.

해설 not until구문을 강조하여 문장 앞으로 보내면 뒤에 주어와 동사가 도치되어야 하므로 (a)는 적절하지 않다. 따라서 not until의 강조구문인 It was not until이 적합하다.

29 유형 전치사/명사

Meet me _____ to see the musical which begin at 7 o'clock.
(a) of Oxford Street
(b) on the Oxford Street
(c) along Oxford Street
(d) on Oxford Street

해석 오후 7시에 시작하는 뮤지컬을 보러 갈 때 Oxford Street에서 만나자.

해설 서수 앞엔 정관사가 붙지만 Oxford Street는 고유명사이므로 정관사와 관사를 모두 다 쓰지 않는다. 또한 막연한 길거리의 의미일 경우 전치사 in과 함께 쓰지만 특정 지명의 Street는 on과 함께 쓴다.

30 유형 부사

The game was _____ moving in the Beijing Olympics I want to visit there.

(a) so
(b) such
(c) that
(d) very

[해석] 베이징 올림픽에서의 그 게임은 아주 감동적이어서 나는 그곳을 방문해보고 싶다.

[해설] '아주 ~해서 ~하다'의 구문은 so ~ that 구문이다. 그런데 여기서 that은 구어체에서 자주 생략된다. 따라서 (a)가 적절하다.

고난도 POINT 41 구어체에서 that이 생략되는 경우가 있다.

so ~ that 용법을 모르는 TEPS 학습자는 없을 것이다. 하지만 이 용법이 구어체에서 쓰일 경우 that을 생략할 수 있다는 점이 중요하다. TEPS는 spoken English를 선호하기 때문에 구어체 표현 역시 함께 알아두는 것이 중요하다. 이 문제에서처럼 that이 생략되었다는 것을 빨리 파악하지 못한다면 문장 구조가 어색해서 정답을 쉽게 고를 수 없으므로 TEPS 학습시 spoken English도 함께 공부해야 한다.

---

31 유형 전치사

Claimants _____ an estate are part of the wealthy class of the country.

(a) for
(b) by
(c) to
(d) towards

[해석] 부동산에 대한 소유권을 주장하는 사람들은 그 나라의 부유층에 속한다.

[해설] 부동산에 대한 소유권 주장이므로 '~에 대한'이라는 전치사 to가 적절하다. claimants to an estate라는 구문을 알아두는 것도 좋다.

[어휘] claimant 요구자, 권리주장자

---

32 유형 전치사

When spring comes after winter, flowers start to be _____ full blossom.

(a) in
(b) on
(c) to
(d) of

[해석] 겨울이 가고 봄이 오면 꽃들이 만발하기 시작한다.

[해설] in이 들어간 관용 표현으로 in full blossom은 '꽃이 만발한'이라는 의미이다.

---

33 유형 태

All things considered, fat is the most _____ nutrient you can consume.

(a) fill
(b) filled
(c) filling
(d) full

[해석] 모든 것을 고려해볼 때 지방은 섭취할 수 있는 영양소 중 가장 포만감을 주는 영양소이다.

[해설] 동사 fill을 제외한 나머지 선택지는 모두 명사를 수식할 수 있다. 과거분사 filled는 '채워진, 배부른'의 의미가 있고 full은 '어떤 것이 가득 찬'이라는 뜻이다. 여기서는 배부르게 하는, 채우는' 뜻인 filling이 가장 적절하다.

34 유형 수 일치

Twenty _____ in the city.
(a) percents of the people lives
(b) percents of the population live
(c) percent of the people lives
(d) percent of the population lives

[해석] 인구 중 20%가 도시에 산다.
[해설] percent는 항상 단수로 쓴다. 또한 퍼센트 뒤에 오는 명사와 동사를 수 일치시키므로 (d)가 정답이다.

35 유형 관계대명사 whom / 분수

City bank has 600 employees, among _____ Asians.
(a) that a fourth is
(b) whom a fourth are
(c) which a fourth is
(d) that a fourth are

[해석] 시티 은행은 600명의 근로자가 있는데 그 중 4분의 1은 아시아인이다.
[해설] 우선 근로자들이므로 관계대명사 whom이 적절하고 4분의 1은 a fourth로 표현한다. 여기서 a가 있다고 단수로 취급하지 않고 600명의 4분의 1, 150명을 가리키므로 are를 쓴다.

36 유형 관계부사

Try to reach your ultimate goals, _____ much people try to discourage you.
(a) however
(b) notwithstanding
(c) disregarding
(d) no matter

[해석] 아무리 사람들이 너를 포기하게 할지라도, 너의 궁극적인 목표에 도달할 수 있게 노력해라.
[해설] much를 수식할 수 있는 관계부사를 찾는 문제이다. 문맥상 의미를 파악하여 보기에 있는 단어를 헷갈리지 않도록 한다. no matter how와 however는 같은 의미로 쓰일 수 있다.

37 유형 일치/명사

_____ grow best in well-drained soils.
(a) Most kinds of corns
(b) Most kind of corns
(c) Most kinds of corn
(d) Most kind of corn

[해석] 대부분의 옥수수 종류는 배수가 잘되는 땅에서 제일 잘 자란다.
[해설] 우선 대부분의 종류라는 의미로 most 다음에 kinds가 나와야 한다. 또한 옥수수는 물질명사이므로 corn에 s를 붙이지 않는다.

38 유형 전치사

The referee warned the players _____.
(a) against risky tackles
(b) that risky tackles
(c) on risky tackles
(d) of tackles risky

[해석] 심판은 위험한 태클에 대해 선수들에게 경고했다.
[해설] 'warn+사람+of[about]'을 기본 형태로 한다. (d)의 경우 risky와 tackles의 위치가 적절하지 않아 정답이 될 수 없다. of의 의미를 대신하는 against와 함께 쓴 (a)가 적합하다.

39 유형 형용사

A singer _____ the Billboard Chart will have no concerns about competing with other new singers.

(a) atop spending 37 weeks
(b) spending atop 37 weeks
(c) spending 37 weeks atop
(d) 37 weeks atop spending

[해석] 37주 동안 빌보드 차트 정상을 차지한 가수는 다른 새로운 가수들과 경쟁하는 것에 관한 걱정은 없을 것이다.
[해설] a top은 전치사로 뒤에 명사와 함께 쓰며 spend는 뒤에 시간이 함께 나오므로 (c)가 적절하다.
[어휘] atop ~의 꼭대기에, ~의 정상에

40 유형 전치사

We have to go up 50 meters _____ the ground to bungee jump.

(a) on
(b) above
(c) off
(d) to

[해석] 우리는 번지점프를 하기 위해 지상에서 50미터 올라가야 한다.
[해설] 땅으로부터 50미터 떨어진 것이므로 above가 적절하다. 혹은 from을 쓸 수도 있다. above는 주로 '해발'을 나타낼 때 above sea level처럼 쓴다.

Part III Questions 41-45

41 유형 형용사

(a) A: Did you know that the rate of suicide of young men is the highest in Korea among the OECD countries?
(b) B: Really? It is a striking fact.
(c) A: What do you think about it?
(d) B: It's a shame that such many people lose their lives when they are young.

[해석]
(a) A: 한국이 OECD 국가 중에 젊은이들의 자살률이 가장 높다는 거 알고 있었어?
(b) B: 정말? 충격적인 사실인데.
(c) A: 이거에 대해 어떻게 생각해?
(d) B: 많은 사람들이 젊었을 때 목숨을 잃는다니 정말 부끄러워.

[해설] such가 '대단히, 매우'라는 의미일 때 뒤에 '형용사+명사'가 온다. 하지만 many와 much의 경우에는 항상 so를 동반하여 so many people, so much money처럼 쓴다. such many → so many

42 유형 관사/명사

(a) A: This dress is too small for me.
(b) B: Really? Where did you purchase it?
(c) A: At the department store.
(d) B: Do you have a receipt? You need it when you are getting a refund.

[해석]
(a) A: 이 드레스가 저한테 너무 작아요.
(b) B: 정말요? 어디서 구입하셨나요?
(c) A: 백화점에서요.
(d) B: 영수증 있나요? 환불받을 때 영수증이 필요합니다.

[해설] 환불을 받으려면 영수증이 필요한데 이때 영수증은 구입한 드레스에 대한 것이므로 the receipt가 적절하다 a receipt → the receipt

43 유형 분사

(a) A: For how long have you been living in this city?
(b) B: I was born here.
(c) A: How is the city? I'm planning to move to this city.
(d) B: I think you need to consider moving a little bit more since I want to get out of this bored city.

해석
(a) A: 이 도시에서 얼마나 살았어?
(b) B: 난 여기에서 태어났어.
(c) A: 이 도시 어때? 여기로 이사할 계획인데.
(d) B: 나는 이 지겨운 마을을 벗어나고 싶기 때문에 내 생각엔 이사하는 걸 좀 더 생각했으면 해.

해설 마을이 사람에게 지겨움을 주는 것이므로 능동형을 써야 한다. this bored city → this boring city

---

고난도 POINT 42 감정동사의 형태에 유의해야 한다.

이 문제에서 나온 bore와 surprise, amaze, frighten, please, satisfy, embarrass, confuse, disappoint, interest 등 감정을 나타내는 동사는 문맥에 따라 형태가 바뀐다. 예를 들어 surprise는 '놀라게 하다'는 의미이므로 '그 뉴스는 너무 놀랍다'를 표현하려면 그 뉴스가 놀라게 하는 것이므로 능동의 현재분사를 써서 The news is so surprising으로 표현한다. 반면에 '난 너무 놀랐어'를 표현하려면 내가 다른 것에 의해 놀라게 된 것이므로 수동의 과거분사를 써서 I was so surprised처럼 쓴다. 이처럼 문맥에 따라서 감정동사의 형태를 결정해야 한다.

---

44 유형 형용사/대명사

(a) A: How did you do on your test?
(b) B: It was so terrible that I don't want to think about it.
(c) A: Was it that bad?
(d) B: I was so upset and frustrated that I cried all night for a week.

해석
(a) A: 시험 어땠어?
(b) B: 너무 못 봐서 다시는 생각하고 싶지 않아.
(c) A: 그렇게 나빴어?
(d) B: 너무 우울하고 좌절해서 일주일 동안 밤마다 울었어.

해설 every와 all의 차이점을 묻고 있다. every night는 '밤마다'라는 뜻이고 all night는 '밤새도록'이라는 뜻이다. 대화의 흐름상 일주일 동안 매일 밤에 울었다는 의미이므로 every night가 적절하다. all night → every night

---

45 유형 시제

(a) A: Do you overcome the hard times?
(b) B: No, not yet.
(c) A: I knew it. You look depressed.
(d) B: I think I might go see the psychotherapist.

해석
(a) A: 힘든 시기 극복했니?
(b) B: 아니, 아직.
(c) A: 그럴 줄 알았어. 너 우울해 보여.
(d) B: 나 심리치료사를 만나봐야 할 것 같아.

해설 과거에 있었던 힘든 시기에 대해 묻고 있으므로 과거시제를 써야 한다. 현재시제는 반복적, 일반적 사실에 대해 쓰므로 대화의 흐름상 부적절하다. Do you overcome → Did you overcome

Part IV Questions 46-50

46 유형 관계대명사

(a) **A heap of debris taken from quarry trash in Mexico has yielded a stone block inscribed with that researchers believe is the oldest writing ever found in the New World.** (b) Researchers say the serpentine block dates back almost 3000 years and was created by people from the Olmec civilization. (c) Broken pieces of pottery and ground stone made the experts believe the block and its text date to the Lorenzo phase. (d) This period was 400 years earlier than any previous writing in the Western Hemisphere.

[해석] (a) 멕시코의 한 채석장 쓰레기에서 나온 한 더미의 파편에서 연구조사자들이 생각하기에 신대륙에서 발견된 것 중 가장 오래된 것으로 추정되는 글이 새겨진 돌덩어리가 나왔다. (b) 연구조사자들에 따르면 나선형의 이 돌덩어리는 거의 3천년 전의 것으로 올멕인들에 의해 만들어졌다고 한다. (c) 전문가들은 도자기 파편과 깨진 돌 조각들을 근거로 그 돌덩어리와 문자가 로렌조 시대의 것으로 추정했다. (d) 이 시기는 서반구에서 이전에 나온 글보다 400년 더 오래되었다.

[해설] (a)에서 with 뒤에는 명사가 와야 하므로 선행사를 포함한 관계대명사가 필요하다. with that → with what

[어휘] heap 덩어리 debris 부스러기, 잔해 quarry 채석장 yield 생산하다 inscribe 새기다 serpentine 나선형의 date back 시간을 거슬러 올라가다 pottery 도자기류 phase 단계, 시기 hemisphere 반구

47 유형 수 일치

(a) When I'm interested in something, I might spend so much time immersed in it that I forget to eat or sleep! (b) **The autistics share these characteristic with me, becoming obsessed with what the world might see as unimportant things.** (c) When I am immersed in an obsession, it is absolutely wonderful. (d) Time seems to stop, and nothing bothers me while I'm pursuing my "obsession."

[해석] (a) 나는 뭔가에 관심이 있을 때, 너무나 많은 시간을 거기에 빠져 지내서 먹거나 자는 것을 잊어버릴 정도다! (b) 많은 자폐증 환자들도 나와 비슷한 이런 특성을 가지고 있으면서, 세상이 중요하지 않게 여길지도 모르는 것에 집착한다. (c) 내가 무언가에 푹 빠져 있다는 것은 아주 멋진 일이다. (d) 시간이 멈춘 것 같고, 몰두해 있는 동안에는 그 무엇도 나를 방해할 수 없다.

[해설] 여기서 언급하는 특징은 앞에 필자가 이야기한 하나의 특징을 가리키는 것이므로 복수형이 아닌 단수형이 와야 한다. these characteristic → this characteristic

[어휘] immersed in ~에 빠진 autistic 자폐증의 obsessed with ~에 집착하는 obsession 집착, 강박관념

48 유형 동사의 형식/부정사

(a) The roots of a tree make it strong because they bring water and food from the soil to the tree. (b) **The tree's roots help it stayed straight in wind and rain.** (c) A human being's roots come from his or her culture. (d) One generation passes them on to the next.

[해석] (a) 나무의 뿌리는 토양에서 나무로 물과 영양분을 제공하기에 나무를 강하게 만든다. (b) 그 나무의 뿌리는 바람과 비에도 나무가 꼿꼿이 서있게 도와준다. (c) 인간의 뿌리는 문화로부터 온다. (d) 한 세대가 다음 세대에게 그것을 전해준다.

[해설] help는 뒤에 목적어와 목적격 보어를 취할 수 있는 동사로, 목적격 보어에 동사원형이나 to부정사가 올 수 있다는 특징이 있다. stayed → stay 혹은 to stay

[어휘] soil 토양 generation 세대

49 유형 관계대명사 whose

(a) When you're ready for the closure that only a divorce can provide, we can give you a reliable and affordable alternative to high priced lawyer fees and mind-numbing do-it-yourself divorce kits. (b) Our experienced team of legal professionals has prepared thousands of divorce documents which have been accepted by courts across the country. (c) If you and your spouse cannot agree on the terms of the divorce, you need to consult a lawyer. **(d) However, if you are among the 90% of Canadians who divorce is uncontested, our services are ideal.**

해석 (a) 이혼을 유일한 해결책으로 선택하셨다면, 저희는 비싼 변호사 비용이나 정신없이 혼자서 준비해야 하는 이혼 관련 서류들 대신에 믿을 만하고 저렴한 대안을 제시할 수 있습니다. (b) 당사의 노련한 법률 전문가 팀은 전국 법정에서 인정받고 있는 수천 개의 이혼 서류를 준비해 두었습니다. (c) 만약 귀하와 귀하의 배우자가 이혼 조건에 대해 합의할 수 없다면 변호사와 상담해야 합니다. (d) 하지만 두 분이 90%의 캐나다 사람들처럼 이혼에 관해 논쟁이 없다면 당사의 서비스가 이상적일 겁니다.

해설 90%의 캐나다 사람들의 이혼이므로 소유격 관계대명사를 써야 한다. who divorce → whose divorce

어휘 closure 종결 affordable 저렴한 mind-numbing 정신이 멍해질 만큼의 do-it-yourself 스스로 하는 uncontested 명백한, 논쟁의 여지가 없는

50 유형 일치

(a) Why does the most sophisticated communications technology suffer the most primitive forms of advertising? (b) Internet banner ads are little more than billboards flashing at us with garish, distracting messages. (c) Pop-ups are like carnival callers trying to muscle you into their show. **(d) One of the most unique benefits of the Web is that they give individuals tremendous autonomy and freedom.**

해석 (a) 왜 가장 정교한 의사소통 기술이 가장 원시적인 형태의 광고로 고생을 하고 있을까? (b) 인터넷 배너 광고는 우리에게 화려하고 정신을 산만하게 만드는 메시지가 달린 번쩍거리는 광고판에 지나지 않는다. (c) 팝업창은 카니발에서 당신을 쇼로 끌어들이려고 부르는 사람과 같다. (d) 인터넷의 가장 특별한 장점 중 하나는 그것이 개인에게 막대한 자치권과 자유를 준다는 것이다.

해설 (d)에서 that 뒤에 나오는 주어는 앞에 나오는 the Web을 가리키는 것이므로 단수로 써야 한다. of the Web is that they give → of the Web is that it gives

어휘 sophisticated 정교한 primitive 원시적인
garish 현란한 distracting 주의를 흩뜨리는
muscle ~에 억지로 끼어들다, 힘으로 밀고 나가다

고난도 Actual Training 08

1. (d)	2. (d)	3. (b)	4. (c)	5. (c)	6. (d)	7. (a)	8. (b)	9. (b)	10. (d)
11. (b)	12. (a)	13. (a)	14. (a)	15. (c)	16. (c)	17. (b)	18. (a)	19. (d)	20. (b)
21. (b)	22. (d)	23. (b)	24. (a)	25. (d)	26. (a)	27. (b)	28. (a)	29. (b)	30. (c)
31. (d)	32. (b)	33. (a)	34. (c)	35. (d)	36. (b)	37. (b)	38. (a)	39. (c)	40. (d)
41. (c)	42. (a)	43. (d)	44. (b)	45. (d)	46. (d)	47. (d)	48. (c)	49. (d)	50. (d)

Part I Questions 1-20

1 유형 대명사

A: I think these shoes are really pretty.
B: You can _____ if you want.
 (a) put on them
 (b) put it on
 (c) put on it
 (d) put them on

[해석] A: 이 신발 정말 예쁜 것 같아.
B: 신어보고 싶으면 신어 봐도 돼.
[해설] 옷을 입어보거나 신발을 신어볼 때 put it on 또는 put them on이라고 한다. 대명사가 아닌 shoes가 나왔을 경우에는 put on these shoes 등과 같이 쓸 수 있지만 대명사인 경우에는 꼭 put them on의 형태로 써야 한다.

2 유형 동사의 형식/접속사

A: Do you think I have to confess that I like her?
B: I'd prefer _____.
 (a) it you did
 (b) if you didn't
 (c) it you didn't
 (d) it if you didn't

[해석] A: 내가 그녀에게 좋아한다고 고백해야 할 것 같니?
B: 그러지 않는 게 좋겠어.
[해설] prefer는 타동사이므로 목적어가 필요하다. 가정을 나타내는 if절은 명사절이 아니라 부사절이기 때문에 타동사의 목적어로 바로 올 수 없다. 따라서 it이 삽입된 (d)가 적합하다.

3 유형 대명사

A: Do you want to drink some water or juice?
B: _____, thank you.
 (a) Either does well
 (b) Either will do
 (c) each one is good
 (d) each will be fine

[해석] A: 물 마실래, 아님 주스 마실래?
B: 아무거나 괜찮아. 고마워.
[해설] '둘 중 어느 쪽이든 괜찮다'라는 표현으로 either will do를 쓴다. (a)는 do well의 표현이 어색하고, (c), (d)에서는 무엇이든지 좋다는 의미가 되지 않는다.

4 유형 관계대명사

A: Where is my key?
B: Is _____ you're looking for?
   (a) this on which
   (b) this which
   (c) this the thing which
   (d) which this

[해석] A: 내 열쇠 어디 있지?
B: 이게 네가 찾고 있는 거니?

[해설] 빈칸 앞에 Is만 제시되어 있어서 빈칸에는 주어가 필요하다. this가 주어로 적합하고 is 뒤에 나와야 하는 보어는 빈칸 뒤의 you're looking for와 관계대명사로 연결되어야 하므로 선행사와 관계대명사가 필요하다. 따라서 (c)가 적합하다.

5 유형 병렬 구조

A: What am I supposed to do when my meeting is interrupted by an unexpected visitor?
B: Do not show displeasure. Just whisper to the person with whom you are talking, and _____.
   (a) left
   (b) leaving
   (c) leave
   (d) having left

[해석] A: 갑자기 찾아온 사람 때문에 회의를 방해받을 땐 어떻게 해야 하죠?
B: 불쾌한 내색은 하지 마세요. 이야기 중이던 사람에게 귀띔을 하고 나가면 돼요.

[해설] 회의 중에 예고 없이 찾아온 사람으로 인해 방해를 받는다면 어떻게 할지에 대한 대화이다. and를 중심으로 whisper와 빈칸이 병렬 구조를 이루고 있다.

[어휘] displeasure 불쾌감

6 유형 관사/형용사

A: I saved $1000 a month for 10 years and finally I bought _____.
B: Great! I really wanted to buy that cabin too.
   (a) a two-stories mountain cabin
   (b) a two-story mountain cabin
   (c) the two-stories mountain cabin
   (d) the two-story mountain cabin

[해석] A: 한 달에 1000달러씩 10년간 저금해서 드디어 2층짜리 산장을 하나 샀어.
B: 우와! 나도 그 산장 사고 싶었는데.

[해설] 대화를 통해서 서로 공통적으로 알고 있는 산장이므로 the를 써야 한다. 또한 two-story가 뒤에 오는 명사를 수식하는 것이므로 형용사로 취급해야 한다. 그러므로 복수인 stories의 형태로 쓰지 않는다.

7 유형 태

A: How is your new girlfriend _____?
B: She is prettier and has a great body.
   (a) contrasted with your ex-girlfriend
   (b) contrasted with ex-girlfriend
   (c) contrasting with ex-girlfriend
   (d) contrasting with the ex-girlfriend

[해석] A: 예전 여자 친구랑 비교해서 지금 여자 친구는 어때?
B: 더 예쁘고 몸매도 좋아.

[해설] 여자 친구들이 대조되는 것이므로 수동형으로 써야 한다. 또한 명사 앞에 관사나 소유격이 와야 한다.

8 유형 대명사+일치

A: Where did I leave my bat?
B: _____ at home.
   (a) Yours are
   (b) Yours is
   (c) Your one is
   (d) Your ones are

[해석] A: 야구방망이를 내가 어디 뒀더라?
B: 네 것은 집에 있어.

[해설] '너의 야구방망이'라는 의미의 your bat를 소유대명사 yours로 표현할 수 있으며 bat가 하나이므로 단수이다. 따라서 빈칸에는 yours is 또는 your bat is가 와야 한다.

9 유형 동사의 형식/전치사

A: I heard that he got a position at Samsung at the first half recruitment.
B: I take _____ that he can have many opportunities to succeed.
 (a) as promising job
 (b) it as a promising job
 (c) as promising a job
 (d) it a promising job

해석 A: 그가 이번 상반기 채용에서 삼성에 취직했다고 들었어요.
B: 성공할 수 있는 기회를 많이 얻을 수 있으니 아주 전망이 좋다고 봐요.

해설 take A as B의 구문으로 that 이하의 명사절을 받는 가목적어 it이 필요하고, job은 가산명사이므로 부정관사와 함께 쓴다. 원래 문장은 I take that he can have many opportunities to succeed as a promising job.이다.

10 유형 한정사/형용사

A: We had _____ we could have a party outside.
B: Really? I should have gone there.
 (a) a very good weather
 (b) very good weather
 (c) such a good weather
 (d) such good weather

해석 A: 야외에서 파티할 만큼 날씨가 좋았어.
B: 진짜? 갈 걸 그랬나봐.

해설 weather는 불가산명사이므로 부정관사와 함께 쓰지 않는다. 날씨에 대해 수식하는 절이 뒤에 오므로 정도를 의미하는 such가 적절하다.

11 유형 도치

A: Jerry, are you the one who glued Robert to his chair?
B: What do you mean? Under no circumstances _____!
 (a) will I do such mean thing
 (b) will I do such a mean thing
 (c) I will do such a mean thing
 (d) I will do such a means

해석 A: Jerry, 네가 Robert를 그 아이 의자에 접착제로 붙였니?
B: 무슨 말이에요? 무슨 일이 있어도 그런 나쁜 짓은 하지 않아요!

해설 부정의 의미를 나타내는 부사구가 문장 앞부분에 있으므로 주어와 동사가 도치된다. 그리고 thing은 보통명사로 관사를 취해야 하므로 such a ~ thing 형태로 쓴다.

12 유형 관사/고유명사

A: Boss, there is _____ waiting in the room.
B: I will be there in a minute.
 (a) a Mr. Park
 (b) the Mr. Park
 (c) Mr. Park
 (d) the Mr. Park's

해석 A: 사장님, Mr. Park이라는 분이 방에서 기다리고 있습니다.
B: 곧 갈게요.

해설 고유명사 앞에는 관사를 일반적으로 쓰지 않지만 서로 잘 모르는 '어떤 Mr. Park'이라고 할 때는 Mr. Park 앞에 부정관사 a를 함께 쓴다.

13 유형 부사

A: What are you _____ these days?
B: Nothing much, just helping out my father's business.

(a) up to
(b) up at
(c) doing up
(d) do

해석 A: 요즘 뭐하고 지내?
B: 특별한 건 없고, 아버지 사업을 도와드리고 있어.

해설 up to는 '~을 하고 있는, ~에 달려 있는, ~정도에 미치는'의 의미로 쓰인다. 여기서는 '~을 하고 있는'에 해당하고 What are you up to?는 관용적으로 자주 쓰는 표현이다.

14 유형 조동사

A: Should we do some more work or leave some work for tomorrow?
B: Let's call it a day, _____?

(a) shall we
(b) should we
(c) will we
(d) would we

해석 A: 지금 일을 더 할까 아니면 내일을 위해 남겨둘까?
B: 그냥 여기까지 하자, 어때?

해설 보통 명령문의 부가의문문은 will you를 쓰지만 Let's로 시작하는 부가의문문의 경우에는 shall we를 쓴다.

15 유형 일치

A: What's the result of the meeting?
B: Dentists agree that brushing your teeth three times a day _____ and a more attractive smile.

(a) promote good dental health
(b) should promote good dental health
(c) promotes good dental health
(d) should promote dental good health

해석 A: 그 회의의 결과는 무엇이에요?
B: 치과 의사들은 하루에 세 번 이를 닦는 것이 치아 건강과 더 매력적인 미소를 증진시킨다는 데 공감하고 있어요.

해설 agree는 주장, 제안의 동사가 아니어서 뒤에 반드시 should가 와야 하는 것은 아니다. 또한 brushing이 주어이므로 단수 동사가 와야 한다.

16 유형 형용사

A: How is the class? There is a rumor that the professor is _____ picky.
B: I think he is OK except for his tedious talk.

(a) sort a
(b) sorts of
(c) sort of
(d) a sort of

해석 A: 수업 어때? 그 교수님이 좀 까다롭다는 소문이 있던데.
B: 교수님의 지루한 이야기 빼고는 괜찮은 것 같아.

해설 sort of는 '어느 정도, 다소의'라는 의미로 형용사를 수식할 때 쓰고 명사를 수식할 때는 a sort of와 같이 쓴다.

어휘 picky 까다로운, 별스러운 tedious 지루한

17 유형 동사

A: When is the plane for Seoul departing?
B: It _____ 14:30 over the electronic display. Please refer to it.
  (a) is announced
  (b) says
  (c) said
  (d) announced

[해석] A: 서울행 비행기가 언제 떠나죠?
B: 오후 2시 30분이라고 전광판에 써 있어요. 참고하세요.
[해설] say는 자동사로 '~라고 적혀 있다'는 뜻으로 쓰인다. announce는 말로 어떤 내용을 공표할 때 사용된다.
[어휘] electronic display 전광판

18 유형 수 일치/전치사

A: What's the situation on TV?
B: While the farmers are trying to increase pesticide use, government _____ its use prevent natural disasters.
  (a) controls on
  (b) control for
  (c) control on
  (d) controls for

[해석] A: TV에서 상황이 어떻다고 하는 거예요?
B: 농부들은 살충제 사용을 늘리려고 하지만 정부의 살충제 사용 억제책은 자연 재해를 막아준단 얘기에요.
[해설] prevent라는 동사로 보아 선택지에 나온 control은 명사로 쓰였음을 알 수 있고 따라서 복수형으로 써야 한다. '~에 대한 통제'라는 의미로 쓸 때는 전치사 on과 함께 쓴다.

> **고난도 POINT 43** 긴 주어와 동사를 파악하는 것이 중요하다.
> 이 문제에서처럼 주어가 길 경우 먼저 주어가 어디까지인지 그리고 동사가 무엇인지 파악해야 한다. 주어에 따라서 동사의 수 일치가 달라지므로 주어를 묻는 문제일 경우 동사 파악은 중요하다. 여기서는 전치사구 on its use가 수식하는 이중명사 government controls가 주어 역할을 하고 있고 prevent가 동사 역할을 한다. prevent가 현재동사로 쓰이고 주어가 복수형임을 빨리 파악했다면 쉽게 정답을 고를 수 있다.

19 유형 시제

A: This is ridiculous. I have been waiting for the bus for over an hour.
B: I heard a traffic accident _____.
  (a) took place in
  (b) have been taken place
  (c) to be taken place in
  (d) took place

[해석] A: 이건 말도 안돼요. 버스를 한 시간 넘게 기다렸어.
B: 교통사고가 났다고 들었어.
[해설] 과거에 일어난 사실을 들었다는 의미이므로 빈칸 역시 과거형이 와야 한다. take place in은 '개최하다'라는 의미이므로 문맥상 맞지 않다.

20 유형 형용사

A: About how many people are coming to the concert?
B: _____ 10,000 people are lined up to enter the concert hall.
  (a) Approximate
  (b) An estimated
  (c) The estimating
  (d) Approximated

[해석] A: 콘서트에 몇 명 정도 올 것 같니?
B: 약 만 명의 사람들이 콘서트홀에 들어오려고 줄을 섰어.
[해설] 10,000 people을 수식하기 위해 형용사 역할을 하는 분사가 사용되어야 한다. 사람들이 추정되는 것이므로 estimated의 형태로 쓰고 관사를 함께 쓴다. approximate는 approximately의 형태로 써야 정답이 될 수 있다.

Part II Questions 21-40

21 유형 동사

The new decision will make North Korea prepare for and _____ the shortage of food supplies.

(a) confront for
(b) confront
(c) confront to
(d) confront with

[해석] 새로운 결정은 북한으로 하여금 식량부족을 준비하고 대응하도록 영향을 줄 것이다.

[해설] and로 연결된 병렬구조의 문장이다. 앞에 prepare for에 맞춰 confront for를 정답으로 고르지 않도록 하자. confront는 '직면하다, 맞서다'라는 의미로 쓰일 때는 전치사를 동반하지 않는다.

[어휘] shortage 부족

22 유형 전치사

Theorists typically proposed some sort of sudden and violent catastrophic event, _____ a collision of the Sun with another stellar body or comet.

(a) while
(b) but
(c) so
(d) such as

[해석] 이론가들은 태양이 또 다른 별이나 혜성과 충돌하는 것과 같은 급작스럽고 격렬한 대이변설을 일반적으로 주장해왔다.

[해설] 문맥상 a collision of the Sun ~ comet는 catastrophic event의 예에 해당하므로 '예를 들어, ~같은'을 나타내는 such as가 적절하다.

[어휘] catastrophic 대이변의

23 유형 비교

Weather lore represented _____ a haphazard collection of proverbs derived from stories of personal experience.

(a) much more than
(b) little more than
(c) a little more than
(d) a few more than

[해석] 날씨에 대한 구전지식은 개인적 경험담에서 나온 무계획적 속담 모음집에 지나지 않았다.

[해설] weather lore가 haphazard collection이라는 의미이므로 '단지, ~에 지나지 않는'을 나타내는 little more than이 적절하다. a few는 셀 수 있는 명사에 쓰고, (a)와 (c)는 '그 이상'을 나타내므로 적절하지 않다.

[어휘] haphazard 무계획적인, 되는 대로의
derived 유래된, 파생된

24 유형 부정사

_____ accumulate the vast volumes of data required to create an accurate picture of the weather, contemporary meteorologists employ a wide range of devices.

(a) In order to
(b) In pursuance of
(c) In contrary to
(d) In conclusion to

[해석] 날씨에 대한 정확한 그림을 만들기 위한 방대한 자료를 축적하기 위해서, 현대 기상학자들은 다양한 장치들을 이용한다.

[해설] 문맥상 '~하기 위해라'는 의미가 와야 한다. (b)도 '~하기 위해'의 의미가 있지만 of라는 전치사 때문에 accumulating이 되어야 하므로 여기서는 적절하지 않다.

25 유형 형용사/명사

This is one _____ houses that they are selling off.
(a) of them
(b) of those
(c) of this
(d) of their

해석 이것은 그들이 처분하려는 그들 소유의 집들 중 하나이다
해설 houses라는 명사의 한정사로 올 수 있는 건 지시형용사와 소유형용사이다. (b)는 두 그룹 이상의 house가 제시되고 그 중에 한 그룹을 가리킬 때 사용된다.

26 유형 축약

The criminal must have broken into our house by the window, _____, how else would he get in?
(a) if not
(b) if he were not
(c) if he's not
(d) were it not

해석 범인은 창문으로 우리 집에 침입했던 게 틀림없다. 그렇지 않다면 달리 어떻게 들어왔을까?
해설 if not은 if the criminal didn't break into our house by window가 축약된 형태로 앞에 나온 내용에 대한 반대를 나타낸다. 이 구문의 주어는 the criminal이므로 t으로 쓴 (d)는 적절하지 않다.

27 유형 부정사/전치사

All members are compelled _____ the rules of the conclave.
(a) to conform
(b) to conform to
(c) conforming
(d) to conforming to

해석 모든 회원들은 비밀회의의 규칙에 따를 것이 강요된다.
해설 be compelled to 다음에는 동사원형이 나와야 한다. 따라서 (a)나 (b)가 타당한데, conform이 자동사로서 뒤에 to가 와야 하므로 정답은 (b)이다.

28 유형 부사

_____ of the accuracy of computer models with respect to the state of the atmosphere, they would be of limited value without some means to estimate future weather patterns based on the information.
(a) Regardless
(b) Although
(c) In spite
(d) Nonetheless

해석 대기상태에 대한 컴퓨터 모델들의 정확성과 관계없이, 그 모델들은 정보를 바탕으로 한 미래의 날씨 패턴을 예상할 수단이 없다면 가치가 제한적일 것이다.
해설 긴 문장의 연결어 문제일 경우 문맥을 잘 파악해야 한다. Although는 접속사이므로 적절하지 않고, Nonetheless는 부사이되로 빈칸 뒤의 of와 어울리지 않는다. 문맥상 '~와 관계없이'라는 의미의 Regardless of가 적합하다.

29 유형 접속사

Few vitamins and minerals are absorbed so fluently in our body _____ are those made in natural foods.
(a) that
(b) as
(c) which
(d) than

해석 비타민과 미네랄은 자연음식 상태에서 만들어지는 것만큼 우리 체내에서 원활하게 흡수되는 것이 별로 없다.
해설 'so+형용사(또는 부사)+as'의 구문으로 원래 as 뒤에 those made in the natural foods are (absorbed)였는데 문장이 도치되었다.
어휘 synthetic 인조의, 인공적인

30 유형 부정사

Our company would like to confirm our decision _____ the catering service from your company.
(a) in purchasing
(b) for purchasing
(c) to purchase
(d) purchasing

[해석] 자사는 귀사로부터 음식 공급 서비스를 구입하고자 하는 결정을 확인하고 싶습니다.

[해설] 명사인 decision을 수식하는 형태를 묻는 문제로, 앞으로 할 행동을 의미하는 문구이므로 to부정사의 형용사적 용법을 쓰는 것이 적절하다.

[어휘] catering 음식 공급

31 유형 관계사

The critics suggested many opinions, _____ is often the case.
(a) what
(b) that
(c) who
(d) as

[해석] 비평가들은 종종 그렇듯이 여러 의견을 제시했다.

[해설] 일반적으로 선행사가 문장 전체일 경우 관계대명사 which를 쓰지만, 여기서는 which를 대신할 수 있는 유사 관계대명사 as가 적합하다. as 역시 문장 전체가 선행사일 경우 관계대명사로 쓴다.

32 유형 문장의 형식

The Pope _____ in the meeting on New Year's Day.
(a) wished well everyone
(b) wished everyone well
(c) everyone well wished
(d) well wished everyone

[해석] 교황은 신년 집회에서 모든 이에게 평안을 기원했다.

[해설] 여기서 well은 부사가 아니라 '평안, 안녕'을 나타내는 명사이다. wish는 뒤에 '사람+사물'을 써서 '(사람)에게 (사물)을 기원하다'를 뜻한다.

33 유형 동사의 형식

Neither these gold rings nor this pearl necklace _____ with my crown.
(a) goes
(b) go
(c) becomes
(d) become

[해석] 이 금반지들도 이 진주목걸이도 모두 내 왕관과 어울리지 않는다.

[해설] neither A nor B 구문에서 동사의 형태는 동사에서 가까운 쪽에 있는 B에 일치시켜야 한다. become은 전치사 없이 뒤에 바로 목적어를 취하여 '~와 어울리다'란 의미를 나타낸다.

> **고난도 POINT 44** 다양한 표현을 숙지해야 한다.
> 이 문제는 '~와 어울리다'를 나타내는 표현을 묻고 있다. become은 전치사 없이 뒤에 바로 목적어를 취하고, 이와 동일한 표현으로 go with가 쓰인다. 이 표현을 숙지하고 있었다면 쉽게 정답을 고를 수 있다.

34 유형 대명사

Ben and Jenny, _____ much younger than Michael, were not allowed to see the performance with him.
(a) who
(b) are
(c) both
(d) whose

[해석] Michael보다 훨씬 어렸던 Ben과 Jenny는 그와 함께 그 공연을 보는 것을 허락받지 못했다.

[해설] Ben과 Jenny 모두 Michael보다 나이가 어린 것이므로 빈칸에는 둘다를 나타내는 both가 적합하다. (a)와 (d)의 관계대명사는 각각 빈칸 뒤에 동사와 주어가 없으므로 적절하지 않고, (b)는 빈칸 뒤에 동사 were not이 나왔으므로 정답이 될 수 없다.

35 유형 수 일치/시제

The very book I wanted to read being at a loss to break through the struggle _____ "The Gulliver's travels."
(a) is
(b) are
(c) were
(d) was

[해석] 고난을 어떻게 헤쳐 나가야 할지 어찌할 바를 모르고 있었을 때 읽고 싶었던 책이 바로 '걸리버 여행기'였다.

[해설] 이 문장에서 주어는 The very book이므로 단수이고 wanted로 보아 과거임을 알 수 있다.

> **고난도 POINT 45** 동사 문제일 경우 시제에 우의해야 한다.
> 동사 유형에서 자주 출제되는 문제는 수 일치, 형식, 태, 시제이다. 일반적으로 수 일치를 묻는 경우가 많으므로 자칫 이 문제도 수 일치 문제로만 오해할 수 있지만 문제에서 요구하고 있는 것은 The very book I wanted를 통해 과거이면서 단수를 나타내는 답을 고르는 것이다. 이처럼 단순히 한 가지단 묻기보단 두 유형을 섞어 복합적으로 묻는 경우가 많으므로 단순하게 생각하지 말고 요소도 살펴보아야 한다.

36 유형 관사

I was too sad of my friend's death to do _____ as playing golf leisurely.
(a) any such a thing
(b) any such thing
(c) such any a thing
(d) such any thing

[해석] 친구의 죽음으로 너무 슬퍼서 한가롭게 골프나 치는 그런 일은 할 수가 없었다.

[해설] any나 some은 그 자체가 관사의 성격이 있다. 따라서 관사 a를 함께 쓰지 않는다. 그리고 such와 같이 쓸 때는 any such의 어순으로 쓰인다.

37 유형 조동사/문장의 형식

The manager suggests _____ or we might be moved away.
(a) us that we get rid of bad customs
(b) that we get rid of bad customs
(c) us to get rid of bad customs
(d) that we might get rid of bad customs

[해석] 매니저는 우리가 나쁜 구습을 없애야 하고 그렇지 않으면 전근을 가게 될 것이라고 한다.

[해설] '~에게 제안하다'라고 표현할 때는 suggest to라고 쓴다. 따라서 (a)와 (c)는 적절하지 않다. 그리고 주장, 제안의 동사이므로 that 이하의 동사는 '(should)+동사원형'으로 쓴다.

38 유형 수사

The salary raise in the motor company was $8,000 per year, _____.

(a) double the payment of last year
(b) the payment double of last year
(c) the double payment of last year
(d) the last year double payment

해석 그 자동차 회사에서 봉급인상은 일 년에 8,000달러였는데, 그것은 작년 지급액의 두 배이다.

해설 배수사는 관사보다 앞에 쓴다. 이 문제에서 double은 '두 배'라는 의미의 배수사이다. 따라서 어순에 충실한 (a)가 적절하다.

39 유형 관계대명사/삽입절

Tom, a twelve year old boy, invented a gadget _____ can bring rain when activated. Actually, it was just a piece of junk metal.

(a) who he said
(b) when he said
(c) which he said that
(d) he said it which

해석 12살짜리 Tom은 자칭 비를 오게 할 수 있다는 물건을 발명했는데 그건 단지 고철덩어리에 불과했다.

해설 a gadget을 선행사로 하는 관계대명사가 필요하므로 (a)와 (b)는 정답이 될 수 없다. 그리고 '그가 말하기를'이라는 의미의 삽입절이 필요하므로 he said가 관계대명사 뒤에 와야 한다. 따라서 (c)가 적합하다. which와 that은 둘 다 앞에 나온 a gadget을 선행사로 받는 관계대명사이다.

40 유형 접속사/도치

_____ today did I realize she had a boyfriend, so that made me stop chasing her.

(a) Hardly
(b) However
(c) Notwithstanding
(d) Not until

해석 그녀가 남자 친구가 있다는 걸 오늘에서야 깨닫고 그녀를 쫓아다니는 것을 그만두었다.

해설 빈칸 뒤에 did I로 도치가 되어 있다. 따라서 빈칸엔 부정어가 들어간다. 선택지 중 Hardly와 Not until이 해당되지만 Hardly는 접속사 역할을 못하므로 Not until이 정답이다.

Part III Questions 41-45

41 유형 대명사/도치

(a) A: What happened last night? Did you fail the breathalyzer test?
(b) B: Unfortunately yes.
(c) A: How you are going to tell your father about it?
(d) B: I don't know. I might not tell anyone and solve the problem.

해석 (a) A: 어젯밤에 무슨 일 있었어? 음주단속에 걸렸어?
(b) B: 불행하게도 그래.
(c) A: 아버지한테 어떻게 말할 거야?
(d) B: 모르겠어. 말하지 않고 내가 일을 처리할까 봐.

해설 의문문의 어순은 '의문사+동사+주어'의 순서로 쓴다. How you are going → How are you going

어휘 breathalyzer test 음주단속

42 유형 동명사/부정사

(a) A: The doctor told me to lose weight to stop to snore.
(b) B: I need a diet, too.
(c) A: What are you going to do?
(d) B: First of all, I might reduce the amount of food I ingest everyday.

해석
(a) A: 의사가 나에게 코고는 것을 멈추기 위해서 살을 빼라고 했어.
(b) B: 나도 다이어트해야 하는데.
(c) A: 어떻게 할 건데?
(d) B: 우선 매일 먹는 양을 줄여야 할 것 같아.

해설 'stop+to부정사'는 '~하기 위해 멈추다', 'stop+동명사'는 '~하던 것을 멈추다'라는 뜻이다. 코고는 것을 그만두는 것이므로 동명사 형태로 써야 한다. stop to snore → stop snoring

어휘 snore 코골다 ingest 섭취하다

43 유형 명사

(a) A: Are you going somewhere?
(b) B: Yeah, I decided to move to a new studio apartment.
(c) A: Is the studio apartment equipped with all the household goods?
(d) B: No, not yet. I need to buy some furnitures.

해석
(a) A: 어디 가니?
(b) B: 응, 나 새로운 오피스텔로 이사가기로 했어.
(c) A: 거기는 가구가 다 갖춰져 있니?
(d) B: 아니, 아직. 가구를 사야 해.

해설 some은 뒤에 셀 수 있는 명사와 셀 수 없는 명사 둘 다 올 수 있지만 furniture는 셀 수 없는 명사이다. some furnitures → some furniture

어휘 studio aprtment 작은 부엌, 욕실이 딸린 원룸형 아파트

고난도 POINT 46 빈출 불가산명사를 암기해야 한다.

영어의 명사는 가산명사와 불가산명사로 나뉘는데, TEPS에서는 주로 불가산명사가 출제된다. 이 문제에 나온 furniture 역시 집합적 물질명사로 불가산명사에 속한다. 이 외에도 information, cash, change(잔돈), baggage, clothing, equipment, jewelry, machinery 등이 있다. 불가산명사이므로 복수형으로 쓰지 않는다는 점을 명심하자.

---

44 유형 의문사

(a) A: Excuse me. You need to show me your identification to see this movie.
(b) B: What is that necessary?
(c) A: Since this movie is an X-rated movie, people under the age of 18 are not allowed to watch it.
(d) B: I guess I should choose another one.

해석
(a) A: 죄송합니다. 이 영화를 보려면 신분증을 보여주셔야 돼요.
(b) B: 왜 그래야 하나요?
(c) A: 19세 이상 관람가라서 18세 이하인 영화를 못 봅니다.
(d) B: 그럼 다른 걸 봐야겠네요.

해설 신분증을 제시해달라고 했는데 왜 그래야 하는지 묻고 있다. 그때는 Why is that necessary?라고 되어야 적절하다.

어휘 X-rated 성인용의

45 유형 태

(a) A: Did you choose your food?
(b) B: Not yet. What would you recommend?
(c) A: We specialize in steaks.
(d) B: Then, I would like my steak rarely to cook.

[해석]
(a) A: 메뉴 고르셨어요?
(b) B: 아직 못 골랐어요. 무엇을 추천해주시겠어요?
(c) A: 저희는 스테이크를 전문으로 합니다.
(d) B: 그럼 살짝 익힌 스테이크로 주세요.

[해설] 스테이크는 요리된 것이므로 수동형으로 써야 한다. to cook → cooked

Part IV Questions 46-50

46 유형 병렬 구조

(a) "I would describe it as a reinvention and a move away from the work I've done in the past," says Hilary Duff, in a description of her newest album. (b) Just a child herself, at 19, Duff hardly seems capable of 'reinvention.' (c) However, given her remarkable fame and constant media attention, anything from dyeing her hair to a slight wardrobe change warrants some degree of Hollywood news coverage. **(d) For someone so young with so much media hype, Duff appears surprisingly ground and modest about her music.**

[해석] (a) Hilary Duff는 최신 앨범을 설명하면서 "나는 그것을 과거의 제 작품들로부터 벗어난 새로운 창조라고 부르고 싶어요."라고 한다. (b) 단지 아이일 뿐인 19살의 Duff가 '새로운 창조'를 할 수 있을 것 같지는 않다. (c) 하지만 놀랄 만한 명성과 그녀에 대한 언론의 지속적인 관심을 고려해 본다면 머리를 염색하고 의상을 살짝 바꾸는 등 그녀가 하는 것은 무엇이든 할리우드 뉴스에 어느 정도 보도되는 것이 당연하다. (d) 그런 떠들썩한 언론보도를 몰고 다니는 젊은이치고 Duff는 놀라울 만큼 감정에 흔들리지 않으며 자신의 음악에 대해서도 겸손해 보인다.

[해설] (d)에서 ground는 appear의 보어이면서 and 뒤에 나오는 modest와 병렬로 연결되어야 하므로 형용사가 와야 한다. 문맥상 grounded가 적합하다. ground → grounded

[어휘] wardrobe 옷장, 의상 hype 과대광고
grounded 감정에 잘 흔들리지 않는, 현실적인

47 유형 접속사

(a) PD Ports wants to build a new deep-sea container terminal on Tees side that would bring goods directly to the North from the Far East. (b) If that happens, it can reduce road congestion in the South and revitalize the economy of the Tees Valley. (c) But Felixstowe, Harwich, and Thamesport, have already submitted applications to the government, which said it was ready to approve Thamesport and would make a decision about the others soon. **(d) If all three are approved, Teesport's plans become unviable because of the port capacity shortage in the UK will have been met.**

[해석] (a) PD Ports는 극동지역으로부터 북쪽 지역까지 직접 상품을 가져올 심해 컨테이너 터미널을 Teesside에 짓기를 원했다. (b) 만약 그렇게 된다면, 남부의 교통 정체를 줄이고 Tees Valley의 경제를 다시 활성화할 수 있을 것이다. (c) 그러나 Felixstowe와 Harwich, Thamesport는 이미 정부에 신청서를 제출했고 정부는 Thamesport를 승인할 채비를 갖추었고 곧 다른 지역들에 대해 결정을 내릴 것이라고 한다. (d) 만약 이 세 가지가 모두 승인된다면, 영국에서의 항구 용량 부족이 충족될 것이기 때문에 Teesport의 계획은 실행이 불가능해진다.

[해설] (d)에서 because of는 전치사이다. 뒤에 나오는 will have been met을 보아 주어와 동사를 갖춘 절이기 때문에 접속사를 써야 한다. because of → because

[어휘] revitalize 부활시키다 unviable 실행 불가능한

48 유형 병렬 구조

(a) The microclimate is the variations in localized climate around a building and a building's microclimate is affected by its orientation, the location of neighboring objects, and the surrounding landscape. (b) It has a very important impact on both the energy and environmental performance of a building. **(c) The microclimate can also determine the shape of the building and it sits on the site.** (d) For an ideal site, you would want to maximize solar access to the south facade as solar energy is greatest and most intense from the south.

[해석] (a) 미기후는 건물 주위에서 일어나는 한정된 기후 변화이고 건물의 미기후는 건물의 방향, 주위에 있는 사물들의 위치, 그리고 주변경관의 영향을 받는다. (b) 미기후는 건물의 에너지와 환경 적응능력 둘다에 아주 중요한 영향을 끼친다. (c) 미기후는 또한 건물의 모양과 건물이 어떻게 위치하게 될지를 결정할 수 있다. (d) 이상적인 집의 위치는, 남쪽에서 들어오는 햇빛이 가장 많고 강렬하기 때문에, 남쪽으로 들어오는 태양열을 최대한 이용할 수 있는 곳이라고 할 수 있다.

[해설] (c)에서 determine의 목적어는 and로 연결된 두 두 가지 사항이다. 병렬구조이므로 and 뒷부분은 앞부분의 the shape of the building처럼 명사가 와야 한다. 따라서 it sits on the site을 명사절로 만드는 의문사가 필요하고 문맥상 how가 적절하다. it sits on the site → how it sits on the site

[어휘] microclimate 아주 작은 지점의 기후, 미기후 localize 국한하다 maximize 극대화하다 facade 건물정면, 겉, 외관

49 유형 명사

(a) Teachers need the ability to understand a subject well enough to convey its essence to a new generation of students. (b) The goal is to establish a sound knowledge base on which students will be able to build as they are exposed to different life experiences. (c) The passing of knowledge from generation to generation allows students to grow into useful members of society. **(d) Good teachers are able to translate informations, good judgments, experiences, and wisdoms into a significant knowledge of a subject that is understood and retained by the student.**

[해석] (a) 선생님들은 과목을 충분히 숙지하여 그 핵심을 새로운 세대의 학생들에게 전할 능력이 필요하다. (b) 그것의 목적은 학생들이 다양한 삶의 경험을 접할 때 의지할 수 있는 건전한 지식 기반을 확립하는 것이다. (c) 한 세대에서 다른 세대로의 지식 전수는 학생들이 사회의 유용한 구성원으로 성장하게 한다. (d) 좋은 선생님은 정보와 훌륭한 판단력, 경험 지혜를 학생들이 이해하고 기억할 수 있는 중요한 학과 지식으로 바꿀 수 있어야 한다.

[해설] (d)에서 information은 불가산명사이다. 그러므로 s를 붙이면 안 된다.

[어휘] build on 발판으로 삼다

50 유형 형용사

(a) When Sam Walton founded Wal-Mart more than 40 years ago, his stores were chaotic, with goods piled high on tables and the company's success rested on "Mr. Sam's" formula of scouring the marketplace for the best prices and keeping a relentless rein on expenses. (b) The stores charged unparalleled low prices and crowds flocked to them. (c) But the retailer, recognizing the importance of efficient systems, also led a technology revolution, installing computerized ordering and distribution that others quickly imitated. **(d) Little would have imagined that Wal-Mart would become such a controversial issue as it has become today.**

[해석] (a) 40여년 전 Sam Walton이 월마트를 창립했을 때 그의 가게는 탁자 위에 높이 쌓인 물건들 때문에 정신이 없을 지경이었고 최고의 가격을 위해서 시장을 샅샅이 뒤지고 잔인할 정도로 비용 유지를 하는 'Mr. Sam의' 법칙에 기반해서 성공했다. (b) 이 가게들이 그 누구도 따라올 수 없을 정도로 저렴한 가격을 제공하자 사람들이 몰려들었다. (c) 하지만 효율적인 시스템의 중요성을 깨달은 이 월마트 소매점은 기술적인 혁명까지 이루어내 컴퓨터로 주문하고 유통하는 방법을 채택했는데, 이를 다른 곳에서도 재빨리 모방하게 되었다. (d) 월마트가 지금처럼 큰 화제를 일으키는 존재가 될 거라고 상상한 사람은 아무도 없었다.

[해설] little은 '거의 없는'이라는 뜻으로 숫자가 아닌 양이 거의 없을 때 쓰는 단어이다. 여기서는 상상하는 사람들을 말하는 것이므로 few가 적절하다. Little → Few

[어휘] chaotic 혼란스런 scour for ~을 찾아 돌아다니다
keep a rein on ~을 통제하다
relentless 가차 없는, 잔인한, 혹독한

고난도 Actual Training 09

1. (a)	2. (d)	3. (b)	4. (c)	5. (b)	6. (a)	7. (d)	8. (c)	9. (b)	10. (a)
11. (b)	12. (a)	13. (d)	14. (a)	15. (a)	16. (a)	17. (b)	18. (d)	19. (b)	20. (a)
21. (d)	22. (c)	23. (c)	24. (b)	25. (b)	26. (a)	27. (b)	28. (b)	29. (a)	30. (a)
31. (d)	32. (c)	33. (a)	34. (a)	35. (d)	36. (a)	37. (c)	38. (b)	39. (c)	40. (c)
41. (c)	42. (c)	43. (a)	44. (b)	45. (c)	46. (d)	47. (d)	48. (b)	49. (c)	50. (b)

Part I Questions 1-20

1 유형 조동사/비교

A: How is the party?
B: _____ be better.

 (a) Couldn't
 (b) Shouldn't
 (c) Mustn't
 (d) Wouldn't

해석 A: 파티 어때?
B: 최고야.

해설 '더할 나위 없이 좋다.' '그 이상 좋을 수 없다'는 couldn't be better로 표현한다.

2 유형 분사

A: Oh, my gosh! My purse _____ gone!
B: Don't you remember where you last left it?

 (a) was
 (b) be
 (c) had
 (d) has

해석 A: 오, 이런. 내 지갑이 사라졌어!
B: 그걸 마지막으로 어디에 두었는지 기억 안 나니?

해설 현재 '~이 사라지고 없다'는 것을 표현할 때 have[has] gone과 같이 현재완료 형태로 쓴다.

3 유형 형용사

A: Why did you go home so early last night from the party?
B: I had to finish my assignment but I returned home _____.

 (a) drunk
 (b) drunken
 (c) being drunken
 (d) to be drunken

해석 A: 지난 밤 파티 때 왜 집에 일찍 갔어요?
B: 과제를 끝내야 해서요. 그런데 취한 상태로 집에 갔지 뭐예요.

해설 I returned home은 주어와 return이라는 동사가 결합된 완벽한 문장에 부사 home이 붙은 것이다. 이때 뒤에 형용사 drunken을 써서 취한 상태로 집에 돌아갔다는 뜻으로 쓰인다. 흔히 문법 용어로는 유사 보어라고 부른다.

111

4 유형 태

A: I'm disappointed with the new representative _____ in my constituency.
B: Tell me about it.
   (a) to have elected
   (b) electing
   (c) elected
   (d) to be elected

해석 A: 우리 선거구에서 선출된 새 국회의원에게 실망했어.
    B: 내 말이 그 말이야.

해설 선출되는 것은 수동의 의미이므로 과거분사인 elected가 정답이다. (d)는 '앞으로 선출될'이라는 의미로 문맥상 맞지 않는다.

5 유형 동사

A: Mmm. The food _____ delicious!
B: Don't you dare touch it before your sister comes home.
   (a) is smelling
   (b) smells
   (c) smelling
   (d) has smelle

해석 A: 음. 맛있는 음식 냄새가 나는데요!
    B: 네 여동생이 집에 오기 전까진 손댈 생각도 하지 마.

해설 smell, taste, feel 등의 지각동사는 격식체에서는 현재진행형이 아닌 현재형으로 쓰인다. 비격식체에서는 종종 표현을 위해 현재형을 쓰기도 한다. 생일케이크를 샀는데 먹지 않고 며칠 지난 경우 상했는지 아닌지를 알아보기 위해 냄새를 맡는다면 I'm smelling the cake.와 같은 식으로 표현한다.

6 유형 간접의문문

A: What's the matter with your car?
B: I don't know _____ it — all I remember is parking it in front of my house.
   (a) what has happened to
   (b) whether it has happened to
   (c) whatever has happened
   (d) what it had happened

해석 A: 네 차 왜 그래?
    B: 무슨 일이 있었는지 잘 모르겠어. 내가 기억하는 건 집 앞에 주차해 놓은 일밖엔 없는데.

해설 (b)의 경우에는 it의 의미가 불분명하다. 따라서 무엇이 일어났는지의 의미를 띠는 (a)가 정답이 되어야 한다. (d)의 경우는 시제는 별개로 생각해도 우선 happened 다음에 to가 오지 않아서 적합하지 않다.

7 유형 명사

A: What is the assignment for today's class?
B: You need to write _____ by this Friday.
   (a) paper
   (b) lost of paper
   (c) any paper
   (d) some papers

해석 A: 오늘 수업 과제가 뭐야?
    B: 이번 주 금요일까지 리포트를 좀 써야 해.

해설 paper가 '종이'라는 의미일 때는 셀 수 없지만 신문이나 리포트를 나타낼 때는 셀 수 있다. 문맥상 paper는 종이가 아니라 보고서를 나타낸다.

8 유형 조동사

A: I really don't like this kind of weather It's so humid!
B: You _____ as well get used to it since we are going to be staying here for another year.
  (a) should
  (b) could
  (c) might
  (d) need

해석 A: 이런 날씨 정말 싫어! 너무 습해.
B: 일 년을 더 여기에 있어야 하니까 날씨에 적응하는 게 좋을 거야.

해설 might as well은 '~하는 편이 낫다'라는 의미로 문맥상 어울린다.

9 유형 동사의 형식

A: Do you have any idea where we are?
B: _____ me. I have never been here before.
  (a) Beating
  (b) Beats
  (c) Beat
  (d) Beaten

해석 A: 여기가 어디인지 알겠어?
B: 도저히 모르겠어. 전에 여기 온 적이 없어.

해설 원래는 앞에 가주어 it이 붙어 it beats me라고 해야 하나 it이 생략되어 '모른다'라는 뜻의 관용어구 Beats me로 쓴다.

10 유형 의문사 how / 형용사

A: How _____ more pairs of shoes are necessary?
B: A hundred would be enough.
  (a) many
  (b) a large number of
  (c) by far
  (d) a plethora of

해석 A: 몇 켤레의 신발이 필요해요?
B: 100켤레면 될 것 같아요.

해설 how old와 같이 how 뒤에는 형용사나 부사가 온다. 뒤에 오는 pair는 셀 수 있는 가산명사이므로 how many가 적합하다.

어휘 plethora of 넘쳐나는

11 유형 접속사/병렬구조

A: I got free tickets to the baseball game tonight! Do you want to join us?
B: Thanks, but I'd rather stay home _____.
  (a) than going out
  (b) than go out
  (c) than to go out
  (d) than to going out

해석 A: 오늘 밤 농구경기 공짜 표가 생겼어! 우리랑 같이 갈래?
B: 고맙지만, 오늘은 나가는 것 보단 집에 있는 게 낫겠어.

해설 would rather ~ than 이후에는 바로 동사원형을 쓴다. '~하느니 차라리 ~ 하다'의 의미이다.

12 유형 부사/분사구문

A: What's the earliest and most primitive link in mythology?
B: It was surely that of hunter and prey with _____ the fatal role of victim.

(a) humans possibly playing
(b) playing possibly humans
(c) possibly humans playing
(d) possibly playing humans

해석 A: 신화에 있어서 가장 초기의 그리고 가장 원시적인 연관성은 무엇이지?
B: 그것은 분명히 사냥꾼과 먹이감의 관계야. 아마도 인간이 숙명적인 희생자 역할을 담당했을 거야.

해설 'with+명사+분사'의 부대상황구문이다. possibly는 부사로서 동사를 꾸며주어야 하므로 playing과 가까이 있어야 한다.

13 유형 비교

A: I heard that you were sick for a week! Have you gotten _____ better?
B: I'm fine now.

(a) lots
(b) very
(c) some
(d) any

해석 A: 너 일주일 동안 아팠다고 들었어! 좀 좋아졌어?
B: 지금은 괜찮아.

해설 비교급을 수식할 때는 일반적으로 much, far, still, a lot을 써서 '훨씬, 더욱'의 의미를 나타내지만 조금이라도 더 나아졌는지의 여부를 물을 땐 any를 사용할 수 있다. 조금 나아졌다고 평서문으로 말을 할 때는 some better를 사용한다.

14 유형 형용사의 어순

A: What did they serve for the official dinner?
B: The authorities prepared _____ for us.

(a) authentic Chinese food
(b) Chinese authentic food
(c) authentically Chinese food
(d) Chinese authentical food

해석 A: 공식 만찬으로 뭐가 나왔어?
B: 주최측은 우리에게 정통 중국요리를 내주었어.

해설 형용사가 여러 개 나올 경우, 소속을 나타내는 Italian이나 Korean 등이 바로 명사 앞에 나오고 그 앞에 상태나 성질을 나타내는 형용사가 나온다. 따라서 (a)가 적절하다. 일반 형용사의 경우 '성질, 상태+대소+신구+색상+소속+재료'의 순으로 쓰인다.

고난도 POINT 47 여러 형용사를 나란히 쓸 경우, 일정한 규칙의 어순이 있다.

일반적으로 형용사가 여러 개 나올 경우, '전치 한정사(all, both, such, quite, 배수, 분수)+중위 한정사(관사, 소유격, this, that)+후치한정사(서수, 기수)+일반 형용사'의 어순을 따른다. 또한 일반 형용사 역시 성질에 따라 종류가 많으므로 일반 형용사는 '주관적 성질(beautiful, ugly)+대소(small, big, tall)+신구(old, new)+모양(square, round)+색상(red, yellow)+소속(Italian)+재료(metal)'와 같은 어순으로 쓴다.

---

15 유형 비교/형용사

A: How do you think of him or his company?
B: He is expected to get a good deal of income, if not _____.

(a) many as again
(b) as many again
(c) again as many
(d) as again many

해석 A: 그나 그의 회사에 대해서 어떻게 생각해?
B: 그는 곱절은 아니라도, 상당한 소득을 거둘 것이 예상돼.

해설 as many again은 '곱절'이라는 뜻이다. 특히 이 때의 again은 '다시'의 의미보다는 '두 배'라는 의미이다.

16 유형 형용사

A: Why are you busy working even on weekends?
B: I need _____ more money for traveling eastern Europe during this summer vacation.
  (a) some
  (b) any
  (c) a few
  (d) a lot of

해석 A: 왜 주말에도 일하느라 바쁜 거야?
B: 이번 여름방학 동안에 동유럽 여행을 가기 위해서 더 많은 돈이 필요하거든.

해설 긍정문에 쓰이는 some이다. 특히 이때의 some은 any와 비교해서 어감상 '상당한 정도(의 돈)'라는 느낌이 있다. a few는 수에 사용된다.

17 유형 대명사

A: How could you find these nice cooks?
B: Once I decided to, I advertised for _____ in the classified news.
  (a) ones
  (b) them
  (c) they
  (d) those

해석 A: 어떻게 넌 이렇게 훌륭한 요리사들을 뽑았니?
B: 결정을 내리고 난 후에, 신문 광고란에 요리사들을 뽑는다는 광고를 실었지.

해설 광고를 통해서 뽑은 these nice cooks를 가리키는 말이므로 them이 타당하다.

18 유형 동명사

A: I knew he couldn't pay back the debt he got for using a credit card.
B: You're right. _____ he couldn't reimburse the money.
  (a) No denying is that
  (b) It is not to deny that
  (c) Not to deny there that
  (d) There is no denying that

해석 A: 나는 그가 신용카드를 사용하면서 얻은 빚을 못 갚을 줄 알았어.
B: 맞아. 그가 돈을 못 갚는다는 것은 부인할 수 없지.

해설 There is no -ing는 '~하는 것은 불가능하다'라는 표현으로 동명사 관용표현이다. 'It is impossible+to부정사'로도 쓸 수 있다.

어휘 reimburse 상환하다

19 유형 부사/비교

A: What's the lesson of this story?
B: _____ well-established system can collapse by a single lean woman.
  (a) Even more
  (b) Even the most
  (c) The most even
  (d) More even

해석 A: 이 이야기의 교훈은 무엇이니?
B: 가장 잘 확립된 제도조차도 한 명의 가녀린 여성에 의해서 붕괴될 수 있다는 거야.

해설 even은 비교급을 수식하는 부사로 쓰일 수도 있지만 또한 '~조차도'의 의미로도 쓰인다. 여기서는 '가장 잘 확립된 제도마저도'란 의미가 적절하므로 well-established 앞에 최상급 the most를 연결하고 그 앞에 even을 써야 한다.

고난도 POINT 48 even의 역할에 유의해야 한다.

even은 '~조차도'라는 양보의 의미와 함께 '훨씬'이라는 의미로 비교급을 강조한다. 두 가지 의미가 달라서 TEPS 고난이도 시험에서 빈번하게 출제된다. 이 문제에서는 (a) Even more처럼 비교급 앞에 even을 썼지만, 문제에서 요구하는 바가 아니므로 정답으로 고르지 않도록 주의해야 한다.

20 유형 형용사

A: What should I do if I can't carry the luggage?
B: You can ask me for help at _____ times.

(a) all
(b) much
(c) some
(d) any

해석 A: 그 짐을 들 수 없으면 어떻게 해요?
B: 언제든지 저에게 도움을 청하시면 됩니다.

해설 any와 all은 유사한 의미가 있지만 어감과 뒤에 나오는 명사의 단수, 복수에 차이가 있다. times가 복수이므로 all이 적절하다. 반대로 any일 때는 at any time과 같이 쓴다.

Part II Questions 21-40

21 유형 시제/태

Hyundai Motors announced in the press conference that its car _____ first in 1975.

(a) has manufactured
(b) had been manufactured
(c) has been manufactured
(d) was manufactured

해석 현대 자동차는 기자회견에서 1975년에 그들의 자동차가 처음 만들어졌다고 발표했다.

해설 뒤에 1975년도라는 특정 시점이 왔기에 문장의 시제는 과거이다. 또한 문맥상 자동차가 생산을 하는 것이 아니라 생산이 되는 것이기에 수동으로 표현한다.

22 유형 관계대명사

The professor provided me with a lot of tips for my paper, _____ was quite unnecessary.

(a) many of which
(b) many of them
(c) much of which
(d) much of what

해석 교수님은 내 논문에 필요한 많은 조언을 해주셨는데, 대부분은 매우 불필요한 것이었다.

해설 두 개의 문장을 연결하면서 tips를 선행사로 취하는 관계대명사 구문이다. 원래 문장은 Much of the tips was ~ 이므로 the tips 부분을 관계대명사로 고친 (c)가 정답이다.

23 유형 관계대명사

Please pay attention to the presentation given, _____ will be of interest to you.

(a) for which I'm confident
(b) what I'm confident
(c) which I'm confident
(d) that I'm confident of

해석 이 발표에 집중해주세요. 당신이 관심이 있을 것이라고 확신합니다.

해설 관계대명사의 계속적 용법이므로 that은 쓸 수 없다. 선행사가 presentation이므로 what도 쓸 수 없고 which가 적절하다.

24 유형 동사/시제

Animals which _____ to produce a lot of offspring show a tendency to breed early.

(a) have been evolved
(b) have evolved
(c) evolved
(d) evolves

해석 많은 새끼들을 낳도록 진화한 동물들은 번식을 빨리 하는 경향을 보인다.

해설 evolve는 자동사로 5형식으로 못 쓰이고 특별히 부정사와 결합하는 타동사 용법이 없기 때문에 수동태가 될 수 없다. 그러므로 (a)는 답이 될 수 없고 (d)는 발달해온 것이기 때문에 현재시제는 적절하지 않다. (c) 역시 단순히 과거시제로 끝나므로 적절하지 못하다.

25 유형 대명사

_____ continue to pollute the ocean with all forms of contamination such as plastic containers remains a mystery to environmentalists.

(a) People that
(b) Why people
(c) Those people that
(d) Although people

[해석] 환경 운동가들에게 사람들이 플라스틱 용기와 같은 온갖 오염물질로 바다를 오염시키는 이유는 아직도 수수께끼이다.

[해설] (a)와 (c)는 동사 remains와 문법적으로 어울리지 않는다. 문맥상 바다를 오염시키는 원인이 a mystery인 것이므로 의문사 why가 명사절을 이끌어 주어 역할을 하는 (b)가 정답으로 적절하다.

26 유형 부정사

In the past, it was considered adequate for a building _____ during an earthquake, now insurance companies and even clients are demanding buildings that will be able to maintain their structural integrity through an earthquake and remain sound after the earthquake.

(a) not to collapse
(b) not to be collapsed
(c) to not collapse
(d) to not be collapsed

[해석] 과거에는 지진이 일어나도 건물이 무너지지 않는 것만으로 충분하다고 여겼지만 지금은 보험사뿐만 아니라 고객들까지 지진이 일어나는 동안 건물이 구조적으로 온전하고 그 후에도 멀쩡하게 있을 수 있는 건물을 요구하고 있다.

[해설] 부정사의 부정에 관한 문제이다. 부정사를 부정할 때는 부정사 앞에 not을 써서 'not+to부정사, ought not+to부정사, in order for+목적격+not+to부정사'처럼 쓴다. 또한 collapse는 자동사이므로 수동형으로 쓰지 않는다.

27 유형 접속사

The theory of Adam Smith is that, _____ intact by government, competition in the market will bring benefits to the greatest number of people.

(a) were left
(b) if left
(c) if that's left
(d) it is left

[해석] Adam Smith의 이론은, 정부에 의해 간섭받지 않으면, 시장 경쟁은 최대 다수에게 이익을 가져다 줄 것이라는 것이다.

[해설] 주어인 the theory의 보어인 that절이 다시 두 개의 절로 이루어져 있다. 완전한 문장인 두번째 절로 보아 앞부분에 종속접속사가 필요하고, 접속사 뒤의 주어와 동사는 생략할 수 있으므로 '접속사+분사' 구문 형태인 (b)가 정답이다.

[어휘] intact 전혀 다루지 않은, 온전한

28 유형 명사/형용사/관계대명사

When I went to the lost and found, the assistant asked me _____ I had when I checked in at Incheon Airport.

(a) how many baggages
(b) how much baggage
(c) how many bags of baggages
(d) how many pieces of baggages

[해석] 분실물 신고 센터에 갔더니 도우미가 나에게 인천공항에서 짐을 부칠 때 가방이 몇 개였는지 물어보았다.

[해설] baggage는 집합명사로 쓰이므로 복수형이 될 수 없다. 셀 수 없으므로 much를 붙여서 쓴다.

29 유형 분사

The second crusade, _____ enough, was defeated severely.

(a) not prepared to fight
(b) preparing not to fight
(c) prepared not to fight
(d) would prepare to fight

[해석] 2차 십자군은 싸울 수 있도록 충분히 준비가 되지 않았기에 철저히 패하였다.

[해설] 빈칸 뒤에 was라는 전체 문장의 동사가 있기에 빈칸은 분사가 들어가야 한다. 문맥상 수동의 과거분사를 써야 하고 부정은 앞에서 한다.

30 유형 접속사

_____ she didn't like to play the piano for her children.

(a) Not that
(b) No that
(c) Not because
(d) No because

[해석] 그녀가 아이들을 위해 피아노를 연주하기 싫어서 그런 게 아니다.

[해설] not that A but that B는 not because A but because B와 같은 구문으로 'A 때문이 아니라 B 때문이다'라는 의미이다. 이 문제에서는 'but that B' 부분을 밝히지 않은 형태이다. 하지만 not because A but because B 구문으로 쓸 경우에는 뒤에 but because B 부분을 생략할 수 없다.

31 유형 분사

_____, the Russian chemist Dmitri Mendeleev also used a tabular method to group all known elements (sixty-five at the time) into vertical columns based on their chemical properties in the order of ascending atomic weights.

(a) Worked contemporaneously
(b) Worked contemporaneous
(c) Working contemporaneous
(d) Working contemporaneously

[해석] 같은 시기에 연구하던 러시아 화학자 Dmitri Mendeleyev 또한 표를 만드는 방법을 사용하여, 알려진 모든 원소(당시 65개)를 화학적 특성에 따라 원자량의 오름차순으로 세로 열로 배열하였다.

[해설] Dmitri Mendeleyev가 동시대에 같이 일을 한다는 의미이므로 능동의 분사구문이 와야 한다. 또한 work를 수식하는 부사가 와야 한다.

32 유형 관사

_____ scientist, Einstein, discovered the neutron in the nucleus of an atom, which was actually the beginning of nuclear physics.

(a) There is
(b) It is
(c) The
(d) It is the

[해석] 과학자인 Einstein은 원자의 핵에서 중성자를 발견하였고, 그것은 실제로 핵물리학의 시작이었다.

[해설] Einstein과 discovered로 보아 주어와 동사가 모두 있는 문장이다. 따라서 scientist는 Einstein을 설명하는 동격으로 볼 수 있으므로 앞에 관사만 넣으면 된다.

33 유형 문장의 형식/부정사

The researchers found _____ counterfeited.

(a) surprising facts to be
(b) surprising facts being
(c) it surprising facts to be
(d) it surprising facts being

[해석] 연구원들은 놀라운 사실들이 위조됐다는 걸 발견했다.

[해설] find가 '~을 알게 되다'의 의미로 쓰일 때 뒤에 목적어와 목적격 보어를 동시에 취한다. 여기서는 surprising facts가 목적어로 쓰이고 뒤에 to부정사를 목적격 보어로 쓴 형태이다. 목적어가 길지 않으므로 가목적어 it은 필요 없다.

34 유형 접속사

We should stop clearing wilderness land for construction, _____ the deer population keeps decreasing.

(a) **otherwise**
(b) even if
(c) supposing
(d) however

[해석] 우리는 건설을 위한 황무지 개발을 중단해야 한다. 그렇지 않으면 사슴 수가 계속 줄어들 것이다.

[해설] 문맥상 앞에 언급한 것과 반대의 경우를 가정하는 '만약 ~하지 않으면'이 적합하다. 따라서 otherwise가 정답이다.

35 유형 수 일치/태

By and large, the first half of our youth _____ studying, and the other half by constantly working.

(a) are spent
(b) were spent
(c) become spent
(d) **is spent**

[해석] 대체로 우리는 젊은 시절의 전반부는 공부하느라 보내고 나머지 반은 계속 일하느라 보낸다.

[해설] 문맥상 spend의 목적어인 시간이 주어로 나왔으므로 수동형으로 쓰고 the first half에 맞춰 단수동사가 와야 한다.

[어휘] by and large 대부분, 대체로

36 유형 관사

_____ are the indigenous people of Australia.

(a) **The Aborigines**
(b) The Aborigine
(c) An Aborigine
(d) Aborigine

[해석] Aborigines는 호주의 토착부족이다.

[해설] 부족 이름을 사용할 때는 부족명 앞에 the를 붙이거나 Aborigine people처럼 써야 한다. 여기서는 여러 부족을 일컬으므로 (a)가 적절하다.

[어휘] indigenous 토착의

37 유형 조동사/가정법

The labor union argued that the recent deaths of the workers _____ if the previous recommendations by the union had been accepted by the company.

(a) might be averted
(b) should be averted
(c) **could have been averted**
(d) should have been averted

[해석] 노동조합은 최근 노동자들의 죽음은 회사가 조합의 이전 권고사항들을 받아들였다면 피할 수 있었을 것이라고 주장했다.

[해설] if 구문의 had been으로 보아 가정법 과거완료 문장임을 알 수 있다. 문맥상 could have p.p.가 적절하다.

[어휘] avert 피하다, 막다

38 유형 양보 구문

Pope Peter said, "I will not accept any forceful method _____."

(a) anything
(b) **no matter what**
(c) what matter is
(d) however

[해석] 교황 Peter는 "나는 어떠한 강제적인 수단에도 동의하지 않는다."고 말했다.

[해설] '그 어떤 것이라도'라는 의미가 되어서 강조를 나타내는 no matter what이 알맞다.

39 유형 접속사/대명사

I can swim quite a long distance, _____.
(a) but neither can John
(b) and so John can
(c) **but John can't**
(d) or so John may

해석 나는 꽤 먼 거리를 수영할 수 있지만 John은 할 수 없다.

해설 can go와 can't go의 상반된 내용을 연결하려면 but이 쓰여야 한다. (a)는 neither 앞에 부정이 나왔을 때만 쓸 수 있고 (b)는 and so can John이 되어야 하고 (d)는 병렬일 경우 조동사가 일치해야 하므로 적절하지 않다.

40 유형 조동사

The new production, starting last year, proved to be a little less than we wished it _____.
(a) would be
(b) should be
(c) **would have been**
(d) should have been

해석 작년에 시작된 새로운 생산은 우리가 그럴 거라고 기대했던 것보다 조금 적었던 것으로 밝혀졌다.

해설 우리가 기대했던 것이므로 과거의 사실에 대한 것이고 따라서 가정법 과거완료를 써야 한다. 당위보다는 예정에 가깝기에 would를 써야 한다.

Part Ⅲ Questions 41-45

41 유형 관사+명사

(a) A: I have a very important meeting tomorrow at 8 o'clock in the morning.
(b) B: Wow. You must get up early.
(c) **A: Of course. Can you give me wake-up call at six tomorrow morning?**
(d) B: Sure, I will arrange that for you.

해석 (a) A: 내일 아침 8시에 중요한 회의가 있어.
(b) B: 와, 일찍 일어나야겠네.
(c) A: 당연하지. 내일 아침 6시에 모닝콜 해줄 수 있어?
(d) B: 물론이지, 하지만 너무 믿지는 마.

해설 단순한 부름이 아닌 모닝콜의 의미로 wake-up call은 가산명사이므로 a wake-up call로 써야 한다. me wake-up call → me a wake-up call

42 유형 대명사/숙어

(a) A: I think it is a terrific idea to design a T-shirt to promote good teamwork.
(b) B: I will create the design then.
(c) **A: OK. Should we have anything special written it on?**
(d) B: No, just a good picture would be fine.

해석 (a) A: 팀 단합을 위해 단체 티셔츠를 제작하는 아이디어가 아주 좋은 것 같아.
(b) B: 그럼 내가 디자인할게.
(c) A: 그래. 특별한 메시지를 티셔츠에 적어야 할까?
(d) B: 아니, 그냥 하얀색 티가 괜찮을 것 같아.

해설 '동사+부사'로 이루어진 숙어의 경우 목적어로 대명사가 오면 pick it up처럼 동사와 부사 사이에 대명사를 써야 한다. 하지만 '동사+전치사'로 이루어진 숙어의 경우 look at it처럼 전치사 뒤에 전치사의 목적어인 대명사 it이 와야 한다. written it on → written on it

43 유형 형용사

(a) A: **We need to do a great deal of things to get a job.**
(b) B: I agree. Where should we start from?
(c) A: What do you say about signing up for a foreign language institute?
(d) B: OK. Let's get moving.

해석
(a) A: 취업하려면 정말 많은 걸 해야 할 것 같아.
(b) B: 맞는 말이야. 어디서부터 시작할까?
(c) A: 어학원에 등록하는 거 어때?
(d) B: 좋아. 움직이자.

해설 things처럼 셀 수 있는 명사는 a number of, many 등으로 수식해야 한다. a great deal of, much, a large amount는 셀 수 없는 명사의 많은 양을 나타낼 때 쓰이는 말이다. a great deal of → a number of 혹은 many

44 유형 접속사/분사

(a) A: Where did you learn to speak English so well?
(b) B: **I just studied myself while watch CNN.**
(c) A: You must have tried very hard.
(d) B: Not really. I can just have a basic everyday conversation in English.

해석
(a) A: 그렇게 영어를 잘하는 것은 어디서 배웠니?
(b) B: 그냥 CNN 보면서 혼자서 공부했어.
(c) A: 정말 열심히 노력했겠구나.
(d) B: 그렇지도 않아. 일상적인 대화밖에 못해.

해설 접속사 뒤에 대명사 주어와 be동사가 생략되고 형용사, 전치사구, 분사 등이 올 수 있다. 여기서는 원래 while I was watching CNN에서 I was가 생략된 형태이므로 watch를 현재분사인 watching으로 바꿔야 한다. while watch → while watching

45 유형 일치

(a) A: Can we get a non-smoking table?
(b) B: I'm sorry. It's full right now.
(c) A: **Then we will wait because neither of us smoke.**
(d) B: OK. I will get you a seat as soon as possible.

해석
(a) A: 우리 금연석 주시면 안 될까요?
(b) B: 죄송합니다. 지금은 다 차 있어요.
(c) A: 우리 둘다 담배를 피우지 않으니까 기다릴게요.
(d) B: 알겠습니다. 최대한 빨리 자리를 마련해 드릴게요.

해설 neither는 '둘다 ~ 아니다'라는 뜻이지만 단수 취급을 한다. 그러므로 neither of us smokes로 바꿔야 한다. neither of us smoke → neither of us smokes

Part IV Questions 46-50

46 유형 전치사

(a) The course of American history was drastically changed by the Vietnam War. (b) The American policies on foreign affairs, domestic policies and cultural and social history were greatly changed by this event. (c) The Vietnam War was a military attempt by the US to halt Communist aggression in Southeast Asia. **(d) In January 23, 1973 the US and the North Vietnamese agreed to cease-fire arrangements.**

[해석] (a) 미국 역사는 베트남 전쟁으로 급격하게 바뀌었다. (b) 미국의 외교정책, 국내정책, 문화·사회적인 역사는 이 사건으로 큰 변화를 겪었다. (c) 베트남 전쟁은 미국에 의한 군사적 시도로서 동남아시아를 겨냥한 공산주의 침략을 저지하려는 것이었다. (d) 1973년 1월 23일 미국과 북 베트남은 정전협정에 동의하였다.

[해설] 날짜를 나타낼 때 월 앞에는 on이라는 전치사가 적절하다.
In January 23 → On January 23

[어휘] halt 멈추다　cease-fire 휴전, 정전

47 유형 수 일치

(a) The peasant is the class of character most commonly represented smoking. (b) There are countless examples of low-life smokers in Dutch 17th-century art. (c) Tobacco, with its mind-dulling narcotic capacities, was ideally suited to such representations. **(d) His character ranged from naive, earthy simpleton to diligent worker to aggressive brute.**

[해석] (a) 농부들은 담배 피우는 모습의 인물로 가장 흔히 제시되는 계층이다. (b) 17세기 네덜란드 예술 작품에는 하류층 흡연자의 예가 수없이 많다. (c) 정신을 흐리게 하는 마약과 같은 능력이 있는 담배는 하류층의 모습과 이상적으로 잘 맞아 떨어졌다. (d) 그런 인물에는 순진하고 순박한 숙맥에서부터 열심히 일하는 일꾼, 공격적이고 잔인한 인간까지 다양했다.

[해설] 문맥상 (d)에서 언급하는 His character는 앞에 나온 smokers를 가리키는 것이므로 their characters로 고쳐야 한다. 또한 뒤에 여러 종류의 인물의 예를 나열하고 있으므로 복수가 적절하다. His character → Their characters

[어휘] peasant 농부　low-life 하류층(의)
mind-dulling 정신을 흐리게 하는
narcotic 최면성의, 마취성의　earthy 순박한
simpleton 숙맥, 바보　brute 짐승, 잔인한 사람

48 유형 사역동사

(a) We've noticed that your contact information has changed. **(b) When you read this email, please let us to know your new address and telephone number as soon as possible.** (c) You can do this by visiting our Web site, by calling our toll-free phone number or by writing. (d) If you write to us, please be sure to sign the letter and include your social insurance number.

[해석] (a) 저희는 귀하의 연락처 정보가 바뀌었음을 알게 되었습니다. (b) 이 이메일을 읽으면, 저희에게 귀하의 새로운 주소와 전화번호를 가능한 한 빨리 알려 주시기 바랍니다. (c) 당사의 웹사이트를 방문하시거나 무료 전화로 전화하시거나 편지를 주셔도 됩니다. (d) 편지를 쓰실 거면 꼭 편지에 서명을 하시고 귀하의 사회보험 번호도 알려 주십시오.

[해설] let은 사역동사로서 뒤에 목적보어로 동사원형을 취한다.
let us to know → let us know

49 유형 분사

(a) A new study shows mechanical heart pumps designed for adults may be used in children whose bodies are large enough to accomodate the devices. (b) The ventricular assist devices maintain heart function in critically ill patients while they are waiting for a heart transplant. **(c) Researchers examined the cases of 99 children who received a mechanical heart pump between January 1993 and December 2003 and their prognoses were very promised.** (d) Seventy-eight percent of the cases successfully adapted to the transplanted organ.

[해석] (a) 새로운 연구에 따르면 성인용으로 만들어진 인공 심장 펌프를, 이 장치를 달 수 있을 정도로 체격이 큰 아이들에게 사용할 수도 있다고 한다. (b) 이 심실 보조 장치는 심장 이식을 기다리는 동안 상태가 위독한 환자들의 심장 기능을 유지시켜 준다. (c) 연구 조사자들은 1993년 1월부터 2003년 12월 사이에 인공 심장 펌프를 한 아이들 99명을 조사했는데, 그들의 예후가 매우 좋았다는 것을 알았다. (d) 그 중 78퍼센트가 이식받은 장기에 잘 적응했다.

[해설] 그들의 prognoses가 좋은 것이므로 능동형을 써야 한다. promised → promising

[어휘] ventricular 심실의 transplant 이식, 이식하다
prognosis 예후

50 유형 어순

(a) As for women, one shouldn't drive alone at night and always try to avoid areas where there are few people. **(b) Buddy's creator, Sheilas' Wheels, launched the blow-up man for the purpose of women making feel less nervous about driving at night.** (c) Women who don't like driving alone at night can purchase a blow-up to place in the passenger seat. (d) When they are finished with the "Buddy on Demand," they can deflate it by flicking a switch and the "passenger" is even small enough to fit in the car's glove box.

[해석] (a) 여성들의 경우, 밤에 혼자 운전해서는 안 되고 항상 인적이 드문 지역을 피해야 한다. (b) 버디를 만들어 낸 실라스 휠 사는 여성들이 밤에 운전하는 동안 덜 초조감을 느끼도록 바람을 넣으면 남자의 모습으로 부풀어오르는 인형을 출시했다. (c) 밤에 혼자 운전하기 싫은 여성들은 바람을 넣으면 부푸는 남자 인형을 구입하여 조수석에 둘 수 있다. (d) 휴대용 버디의 역할이 끝나면 스위치를 눌러 바람을 뺄 수 있고 심지어 이 승객은 크기가 작아서 자동차 앞좌석의 함에 넣기에도 딱 알맞다.

[해설] (b)에서 여성들이 덜 초조하게 느끼게 만드는 것이므로 make 뒤에 목적어 women이 오고 그 뒤에 목적격 보어 feel이 와야 한다. women making feel → making women feel

[어휘] buddy 친구 launch 시장에 내다
blow-up 바람을 넣으면 부푸는
on demand 주문형 deflate 바람을 빼다
flick 찰싹 치다
glove box 자동차 앞좌석 앞의 잡동사니 넣는 곳

고난도 Actual Training 10

1. (c)	2. (a)	3. (c)	4. (b)	5. (b)	6. (d)	7. (d)	8. (d)	9. (a)	10. (b)
11. (a)	12. (a)	13. (b)	14. (c)	15. (c)	16. (a)	17. (b)	18. (a)	19. (d)	20. (d)
21. (a)	22. (b)	23. (c)	24. (a)	25. (b)	26. (c)	27. (a)	28. (b)	29. (b)	30. (b)
31. (b)	32. (a)	33. (d)	34. (b)	35. (a)	36. (a)	37. (b)	38. (c)	39. (d)	40. (b)
41. (d)	42. (c)	43. (c)	44. (b)	45. (d)	46. (d)	47. (a)	48. (d)	49. (d)	50. (a)

Part I Questions 1-20

1 유형 접속사/시제

A: Bill, don't forget you lend me a chemistry book.
B: I don't have it _____ at school.
  (a) as I miss the book
  (b) missed the book
  (c) as I missed the book
  (d) cause I had missed the book

해석 A: Bill, 나에게 화학책을 빌려주는 것 잊지 마.
B: 학교에서 그 책을 가져오지 않아서 지금은 갖고 있지 않아.

해설 지금 가지고 있지 않은 것은 현재이지만 학교에 책을 놓고 온 것은 과거의 일이므로 과거시제를 쓰며, 이유를 나타내는 접속사 as가 적합하다.

2 유형 동사/부정사

A: How did you do on your presentation?
B: It was close. I couldn't get the computer _____ at first.
  (a) to work
  (b) working
  (c) to working
  (d) work

해석 A: 발표는 어떻게 됐어?
B: 큰일 날 뻔했어. 처음에 컴퓨터를 작동시킬 수가 없었거든.

해설 get은 목적보어로 to부정사를 취한다.
어휘 close 아슬아슬한

3 유형 부가의문문

A: Pass me that salt, _____?
B: There's another one beside you.
  (a) won't you
  (b) can't you
  (c) will you
  (d) couldn't you

해석 A: 거기 있는 소금 좀 줄래?
B: 네 옆에도 있어.

해설 명령문 뒤에 오는 부가의문문의 형태는 will you이다.

4 유형 분사

A: A drug addict was killed.
B: Where is the dead body of the _____ guy?
  (a) murder
  (b) murdered
  (c) murdering
  (d) murderer

[해석] A: 마약중독자가 살해당했어요.
B: 살해당한 그 사람의 시체는 어디 있나요?
[해설] guy가 살해를 당한 것이므로 수동형인 murdered가 적합하다.
[어휘] addict 중독자

5 유형 명사

A: Excuse me, but do you _____ a ten dollar bill?
B: I'm sorry. We don't have any cash at the moment.
  (a) have enough changes break
  (b) have enough change to break
  (c) have enough a change break
  (d) have change enough breaking

[해석] A: 실례합니다만 10달러를 바꿔주실 만큼 잔돈이 충분히 있나요?
B: 미안합니다. 지금은 현금이 없습니다.
[해설] change는 '잔돈'이라는 의미일 때 부정관사를 함께 쓰지 않고 복수형으로도 쓰지 않는다. 또 '~하기에 충분한 ~'이라는 표현은 'enough+명사+~to부정사' 형태를 쓴다.

6 유형 시제

A: What are you planning to do after graduation?
B: Well, when I _____ undergraduate school, I plan to study more.
  (a) will graduate
  (b) will have graduated
  (c) graduate
  (d) have graduated from

[해석] A: 졸업 후에 뭐 할 계획이니?
B: 음, 학부를 졸업하면 공부를 더 할 예정이에요.
[해설] when이 시간이나 조건을 나타내는 접속사이므로 이러한 접속사가 있는 절에서는 의미상으로는 미래에 일어날 일일지라도 현재형이나 현재완료형으로 나타낸다. 또 graduate는 자동사이므로 전치사 from과 함께 써야 한다.

7 유형 시제

A: Which school _____ ?
B: Actually, I work now.
  (a) have you been in
  (b) have you attended
  (c) did you go to
  (d) do you go to

[해석] A: 어느 학교에 다녀?
B: 사실, 지금은 일하고 있어.
[해설] 현재의 습관이나 상태를 말할 때는 단순 현재형을 쓴다. B의 대답에서 미루어 보면 A가 묻는 것이 현재 상태임을 알 수 있다.

8 유형 태

A: Any news on the next conference?
B: I heard that the conference _____ next year.
  (a) is held
  (b) is to be held
  (c) is to be hold
  (d) holds

[해석] A: 다음 회의에 관한 소식 있니?
B: 내가 듣기로 다음 회의는 내년에 열릴 예정이야.
[해설] hold는 '모임 등을 개최하다'라는 뜻으로 문맥상 수동태로 써야 한다. next year에 맞게 미래를 나타내기 위해 'be+to부정사'를 사용할 수 있다.

9 유형 접속사

A: Will you join us today at the baseball park?
B: No, I can't. I have an appointment with John _____ we can go to the fish market.

(a) so that
(b) unless
(c) if only
(d) even if

해석　A: 오늘 우리랑 야구장에 같이 갈래?
　　　B: 아니, 못 가. 수산시장에 가려고 John하고 약속을 했어.

해설　약속이 되어 있다는 말과 어울리기 위해서는 수산시장에 간다는 것이 일종의 목적이 되어야 한다. 그래서 목적적 의미를 띠는 접속사 so that 과 어울려 써야 한다.

10 유형 시제

A: How long has it been since _____ your science textbook?
B: Over a year.

(a) had you last opened
(b) you last opened
(c) you have last opened
(d) last you open

해석　A: 네가 마지막으로 과학 교과서를 펼쳐본 지 얼마나 되었니?
　　　B: 일 년 넘었어.

해설　since는 과거의 어느 시점을 나타내어 '~(한) 이래로'라는 의미를 나타내므로 과거시제를 쓴다. (c)는 last의 어순은 조동사와 본동사 사이라서 맞지만 시제가 적절하지 않다.

11 유형 시제

A: Mike, what's going on with your teammates nowadays?
B: Never worry. I _____ control.

(a) have it under
(b) am having them under
(c) have been them over
(d) had had it over

해석　A: Mike, 요즈음 네 팀원들과 어때?
　　　B: 걱정하지 마. 잘 지내고 있어.

해설　요즈음 어떠냐고 물었으므로 폭 넓은 시간개념인 현재형을 이용하여 have를 쓰면 일종의 현재의 습관이나 상태를 나타낸다. 요즈음의 전반적인 상황은 it으로 표현하고, 그러한 상황을 잘 통제한다는 의미이므로 under가 적합하다.

12 유형 특수구문

A: How many candles do I have to light up?
B: I _____ 10.

(a) believe she has just reached
(b) just believe she reached to
(c) just believe she has reached
(d) believe she has reached to just

해석　A: 촛불 몇 개 켜야 돼?
　　　B: 이제 갓 열 살이 되었을 거야.

해설　just는 빈도 부사에 준해서 has와 reached 사이에 써야 한다. 여기서 reach는 '어떤 수량이나 정도에 이르다'라는 의미의 타동사이므로 전치사와 함께 쓰지 않는다. (c)는 just가 believe를 수식하므로 문맥상 맞지 않다.

13 유형 부정사/태

A: The inauguration speech was fantastic, don't you think?
B: Yes, especially the part where the president emphasized how the strengthening elementary education policy is crucial if no child _____.
(a) is left out
(b) is to be left out
(c) is to left out
(d) lefts out

[해석] A: 취임식 연설은 대단했어, 그렇지 않니?
B: 응, 특히 대통령이 어떤 아이들도 낙오되지 않도록 초등 교육 정책을 강화하는 것이 얼마나 중요한지 강조하는 부분이 그랬어.

[해설] '어떠한 어린아이도 낙오되지 않도록'의 의미가 와야 하므로 수동형이 적절하다. 또한 의도를 나타내고 있으므로 be to 용법으로 써야 한다.

[어휘] inauguration 취임식

14 유형 접속사

A: What, _____, solutions do you have for this matter?
B: I will have one as soon as possible.
(a) if ever
(b) nonetheless
(c) if any
(d) nevertheless

[해석] A: 만약 있다면, 이 상황에 대한 어떤 해결책이 있니?
B: 빠른 시일 내에 알아 올게.

[해설] if any는 '설사 있다 해도'라는 의미로 다소 부정적이거나 '만일 있다면'의 작은 희망을 나타낼 때 쓰인다. 즉, 양이나 수가 얼마 되지 않을 때 쓰며 문장 끝 또는 명사 앞에 온다. if ever는 '있다고 해도'의 의미로 동사 앞에 He rarely, if ever, goes to church(그는 교회에 가는 일이 있다고는 해도 좀처럼 가지 않는다).와 같은 형태로 쓰인다.

15 유형 too ~ to

A: John and I had a big fight yesterday.
B: Again! Are you guys at the point where you two are too upset with each other _____ have a normal conversation?
(a) that you can
(b) that we can
(c) to be able to
(d) unable to

[해석] A: 나 어제 John이랑 크게 싸웠어.
B: 또! 너희는 이제 서로에게 너무 화가 나서 제대로 된 대화조차 할 수 없는 상태가 된 거니?

[해설] too upset를 보아 too ~ to 구문임을 알 수 있다. 따라서 빈칸에는 to부정사가 와야 하며 too에 이미 부정의 의미가 포함되어 있으므로 not을 함께 쓰지 않는다. (a)와 (b)의 경우 형용사 so와 함께 쓴다.

16 유형 분사

A: What did you do when the monitor blacked out?
B: _____ no time, I wrote down what was coming out of the speakers.
(a) There being
(b) Being
(c) Having been
(d) As there is

[해석] A: 모니터가 갑자기 꺼졌을 때 어떻게 했어?
B: 시간이 없어서 스피커에서 나오는 소리를 받아 적었지 뭐.

[해설] 원래 As there was no time 또는 Because there was no time인데 분사구문으로 고치면 There being no time이 된다. 여기서 There는 주절의 주어와 다르므로 생략할 수 없다.

[어휘] black out 정전되다, (모니터·화면 등이) 꺼지다

17 유형 동명사/태

A: I really appreciate _____ the time to explain everything to me.
B: Anytime.
  (a) you will take
  (b) your taking
  (c) you taken
  (d) you being taken

해석 A: 저에게 모두 설명해주시느라 시간을 내주셔서 정말 감사합니다.
B: 언제든지요.

해설 appreciate는 뒤에 '사람+동명사' 형태로 쓰며 일반적으로 동명사의 의미상 주어는 소유격 형태로 쓴다. 또한 뒤에 the time이라는 목적어가 나온 것으로 보아 능동형이 적합하다. (a)는 appreciate 다음에 that이 생략된 형태라고 볼 수 있지만, 문맥상 미래시제를 쓸 수 있는 상황은 아니다.

18 유형 수사

A: What do you have to do in the afternoon?
B: I must peruse _____ as the first assignment of the class.
  (a) chapter one
  (b) first chapter
  (c) chapter first
  (d) the chapter one

해석 A: 오후에는 무엇을 해야 해?
B: 첫 번째 수업 과제로 1장을 정독해야 해.

해설 1장은 순서로도, 고유번호로도 처음, 1이므로 서수와 기수 둘 다 사용 가능하다. chapter one 혹은 the first chapter로 쓸 수 있다.

어휘 peruse 정독하다

19 유형 태

A: What happened? You are so early and you don't look good.
B: I _____ everyone at the prom because of a silly action that I did.
  (a) laughed at
  (b) was laughed at
  (c) was laughed by
  (d) was laughed at by

해석 A: 무슨 일이야? 매우 일찍 왔는데 얼굴이 안 좋아 보이네.
B: 내가 한 멍청한 짓 때문에 졸업식 파티에서 모든 애들에게 놀림받았어.

해설 laugh at은 '~을 비웃다'라는 의미이다. 문맥상 놀림을 받았다는 수동형으로 써야 한다. laugh at이 하나의 단위로 전치사 at도 같이 쓰며 그 뒤에 수동태 전치사 by를 쓴다.

20 유형 태/시제

A: There is a rumor that you are being dispatched to Vietnam?
B: Are you sure? I thought you _____ as a suitable person.
  (a) consider
  (b) considered
  (c) were considering
  (d) were being considered

해석 A: 네가 베트남으로 파견된다는 소문이 있던데?
B: 확실해? 난 네가 적합한 사람으로 고려되고 있는 줄 알았는데.

해설 상대방이 고려되는 상황이기 때문에 수동태로 쓴다.

어휘 dispatch 파견하다

Part II Questions 21-40

21 유형 부정사

I studied as hard as I could everyday _____ fail.

(a) **in order not to**
(b) in order to not
(c) in not order to
(d) not in order to

해석 나는 실패하지 않으려고 매일 열심히 노력했다.
해설 to부정사의 부정은 to 앞에 부정형을 쓴다. 따라서 in order not to fail이 적합하다.

22 유형 지각동사

When I entered his study, I _____ in the breeze over the window.

(a) have been seeing swayed
(b) **saw a beech tree sway**
(c) have seen a a beech tree swayed
(d) was seeing a beech tree have been swayed

해석 그의 서재에 들어갔을 때 나는 창문 너머로 너도밤나무가 산들바람에 흔들리는 걸 보았다.
해설 see는 지각동사로 뒤에 목적어와 목적격 보어를 취한다. 이때 목적격 보어는 원형부정사나 현재분사가 온다.

23 유형 관계부사

You haven't been sleeping for days. You should get some sleep _____ much reading you have to do.

(a) no matter
(b) despite
(c) **however**
(d) regardless

해석 넌 며칠째 안 자고 있다. 아무리 읽을 게 많이 남았어도 좀 자야 한다.
해설 형용사 much를 수식하는 관계부사로 적절한 것은 however 또는 no matter how이다.

24 유형 명사

One reason that the coach was fired was he said beforehand that even a _____ against Brazil would be tough.

(a) **draw**
(b) drawing
(c) drawal
(d) drawer

해석 그 코치가 해임된 한 가지 이유는 그가 그 전에 브라질고는 무승부조차 힘들 것이라고 말한 것이다.
해설 문맥상 특히 빈칸 앞에 관사가 있는 것으로 보아 빈칸에는 '무승부'라는 뜻의 명사가 들어가야 한다. 따라서 draw가 적절하다.

25　유형　명사/관사

Surprisingly, although most age groups are known to be influenced by the new H1N1 virus, _____ affected.

(a) the aged is least
(b) the aged are least
(c) least the aged is
(d) least the aged are

해석 거의 모든 연령대가 새로운 H1N1 바이러스에 영향을 받는다고 알려져 있으나 놀랍게도 가장 적게 영향을 받는 연령대는 고령자들이다.

해설 the aged는 'the+형용사' 형태의 복수명사로 복수동사와 함께 쓰고 least는 little의 최상급 표현으로 affected를 수식한다.

26　유형　비교

After he passed his bar examination, his credit was _____ as before.

(a) twice
(b) more than twice
(c) twice as much
(d) twice more

해석 그가 변호사 시험을 통과한 후, 그의 신용은 예전보다 두 배로 올랐다.

해설 '~배나 ~한'이라는 표현은 '수사+times+as ~ as' 또는 '수사+times+비교급 than' 형태를 쓴다. two times =twice이므로 twice as much as before 또는 twice more than before이라고 쓰면 된다.

27　유형　수사/명사

The demonstration against war was supported by _____ from all over the world.

(a) a million people
(b) millions people
(c) a million peoples
(d) millions of peoples

해석 전쟁에 반대하는 시위는 전 세계적으로 백만 명의 지지를 받았다.

해설 사람들이라는 뜻의 people은 복수형이 될 수 없으며 백만 명은 a million people, 수백만 명은 millions of people로 나타낸다. 따라서 (a)가 적절하다.

28　유형　동사

She has studied English since she was ten years old, and _____ of English.

(a) it seem she is a now good speaker
(b) now it seems she is a good speaker
(c) now she is a good she seems speaker
(d) it is a good she seems speaker now

해석 그녀는 10살 때부터 영어 공부를 해왔고 지금은 영어를 잘 하는 것 같다.

해설 동사 seem은 뒤에 절이 올 때 일반적으로 'it seems (that) +주어+동사'의 어순으로 사용한다. now는 문장 앞이나 뒤에 위치할 수 있다.

29　유형　동사/재귀대명사

We just have to leave grandma's coat beside the door, and she _____.

(a) dresses
(b) dresses herself
(c) gets dressed herself
(d) dresses her

해석 우리가 그냥 할머니의 외투를 문 옆에 걸어 놓으면 할머니가 혼자 입으신다.

해설 '스스로 옷을 입다'라는 표현은 dress oneself를 쓴다.

30 유형 분사

When I traveled around the world, _____ to go with me, I had to go alone.

(a) as there being no one
(b) there being no one
(c) as is no one there
(d) there is no one as

[해석] 전 세계를 여행할 때 나는 같이 갈 사람이 없어서 혼자 가야 했다.

[해설] 문장의 동사가 2개(travel, had to go)이고 접속사가 1개 있으므로 접속사가 필요 없고 부사절의 축약 형태인 분사가 들어있는 (b)가 정답이다.

31 유형 가정법

Stella sometimes tells you stories some would rather you _____ about.

(a) don't know
(b) didn't know
(c) hadn't known
(d) haven't known

[해석] Stella는 가끔씩 누군가가 알리고 싶지 않은 이야기들을 이야기한다.

[해설] would rather 가정법에 관한 문제이다. 원래 some would rather you didn't know about stories.에서 stories를 관계대명사로 연결한 문장이다. 목적격 관계대명사는 생략되었다.

[어휘] would rather A did B A가 B했으면 하다

32 유형 의문대명사/수 일치

_____ the MOSFET and its characteristics according to the studies in the conference?

(a) What is
(b) What are
(c) How come
(d) How about is

[해석] 회의에서 이루어진 연구에 의하면 MOSFET은 무엇이고 그 특징은 무엇인가?

[해설] 원래의 문장은 What is the MOSFET and what are the characteristics~?가 된다. 두 개를 하나로 합쳐도 자체의 의미와 특징을 따로 묻는 것이므로 are로 묶을 수는 없다. 따라서 What is가 되어야 한다.

33 유형 문장의 형식

It is important to work hard in your job; it is _____ to take care of your family.

(a) equally as importance
(b) equally to importance
(c) equally importance
(d) equally of importance

[해석] 일을 열심히 하는 것은 중요하다. 가족들을 돌보는 것도 똑같이 중요하다.

[해설] 'be동사+형용사' 형태로, important 또는 of importance가 형용사 자리에 올 수 있다. 여기서는 equally important 또는 of equal importance로 쓸 수 있다.

34 유형 관계대명사/접속사

He still works in the company as an understrapper _____ he always wanted to quit.

(a) which used to say that
(b) that he used to say that
(c) what he used to say
(d) he say used to

[해석] 그는 항상 때려치우고 싶다던 그 회사에서 아직도 말단 직원으로 일한다.

[해설] 두 문장을 연결하기 위해서 접속사나 관계사가 필요하다. 그러므로 (d)는 합당하지 않고 (c) 역시도 앞에 선행사가 나와 있음에도 불구하고 선행사 포함 관계대명사 what이 있으므로 적절하지 않다. (a)는 문맥상 타당하지 않다.

[어휘] understrapper 말단 직원

35 유형 전치사/동명사

My mother objected _____ at my house.

(a) to my friends sleeping over
(b) to my friends to sleep over
(c) my friends sleeping over
(d) my friends to sleep over

[해석] 엄마는 내 친구들이 우리 집에서 자는 것을 반대했다.

[해설] object to는 '~에 반대하다'는 의미로 여기서 to는 전치사라서 뒤에 (동)명사를 수반한다. 동명사의 의미상 주어는 동명사 앞에 소유격이나 목적격 형태로 써준다.

36 유형 문장의 형식/대명사

_____ last night's terrible fire was started by a notorious arsonist.

(a) It is believed that
(b) They had believed that
(c) It believes that
(d) They believe as

[해석] 어젯밤 끔찍한 화재는 악명 높은 방화범이 저지른 것으로 생각된다.

[해설] '~라고 생각된다'를 나타낼 때 believe를 쓰면 they believe that이나 it is believed that으로 쓴다.

37 유형 태/동명사

I won't be _____ the mid-term exam if the exam starts early.

(a) prepared to taking
(b) prepared for taking
(c) preparing to take
(d) preparing for taking

[해석] 만약 시험이 앞당겨 시작되면 난 중간고사 시험 볼 준비가 되어 있지 않을 것이다.

[해설] 지금 준비 중이 아니라 내가 준비된 상태를 나타내므로 prepared가 적절하다. 또 '~할 준비가 되어 있다'라고 할 때는 prepared 뒤에 for -ing 혹은 to부정사가 온다.

38 유형 조동사

A class action lawsuit is a type of lawsuit in which claims of many people are decided in a single case, meaning that you _____ try to win the case with the best lawyers, although quite costly.

(a) have got
(b) would have to
(c) might as well
(d) may well

[해석] 집단소송은 많은 사람들의 주장이 한 번의 소송으로 결정되는 소송의 한 가지 방법으로, 비싸더라도 최고의 변호사들을 갖춰 소송에서 이기는 편이 낫다는 것을 의미한다.

[해설] 상대방에게 권고를 하는 내용이므로 might as well의 표현을 쓴다.

고난도 POINT 49 조동사의 의미를 정확히 알아두어야 한다.

조동사 유형의 문제가 출제될 경우 가정법 관련 문제나 관용 표현을 묻는 문제가 많다. 따라서 각 조동사의 쓰임과 의미, 관용 표현을 정확히 알고 있다면 정답을 쉽게 고를 수 있다. 위의 문제에서처럼 may는 '~일지도 모른다'라는 의미이지만 might as well의 관용 표현으로 쓰여 '~하는 게 낫다'라는 전혀 다른 의미로 쓰이는 경우를 묻는 문제들이 많이 나온다.

39 유형 전치사/동명사

When I was sick from food poisoning, I blamed my friend because she never visited me _____ my favorite snacks.

(a) bring
(b) to bring
(c) without to bring
(d) without bringing

해석 내가 식중독으로 아팠을 때 친구는 문병을 올 때마다 내가 제일 좋아하는 간식들을 들고 와서 내 타박을 받았다.

해설 never ~ without은 이중부정으로 긍정을 의미한다. 문맥상 '항상 ~ 하였다'라는 뜻임을 알 수 있다.

40 유형 명사

The cute Korean girl completed her performance on the ice far more wonderfully than _____ figure skater and won the gold medal.

(a) another
(b) any other
(c) each
(d) any

해석 그 귀여운 한국 소녀는 얼음판에서 다른 어떤 피겨스케이트 선수보다도 훨씬 더 멋지게 연기했고 금메달을 땄다.

해설 another, any other, each는 뒤에 단수명사가 나온다. 따라서 여기서는 뒤에 복수명사가 올 수 있는 any other가 정답이 되어야 한다.

Part Ⅲ Questions 41-45

41 유형 동사/태

(a) A: How much time do we have left?
(b) B: About an hour.
(c) A: An hour? We must hurry.
(d) B: Yeah, the time just seems to have been disappeared

해석
(a) A: 우리 시간이 얼마나 남았지?
(b) B: 한 시간 정도.
(c) A: 한 시간? 서둘러야겠어.
(d) B: 응. 시간이 그냥 막 사라지는 것 같아.

해설 occur, happen, collapse, appear, disappear 같은 자동사는 수동태를 쓸 수 없기 때문에 능동형으로 써야 한다.
have been disappeared → have disappeared

고난도 POINT 50 자동사는 수동태로 쓰지 않는다.

우리말에 자동사, 타동사의 개념이 불분명하여 영어에서 자동사와 타동사를 혼동하는 경우가 많다. 자동사는 수동태로 쓰지 않는다고 하지만 자동사와 타동사를 구분하지 못하면 오답을 고를 수 있다. 자주 출제되는 자동사 occur, happen, appear, disappear 등을 파악해두고 이 동사들은 수동태로 쓰지 않는다는 점을 항상 유의해야 한다.

42 유형 시제

(a) A: Who did you choose to go to the dance party?
(b) B: I think Mary is the proper partner for me.
(c) **A: Mary? I didn't get it. You must be kidding me.**
(d) B: Seriously. I have a crush on her.

해석 (a) A: 댄스파티에 누구랑 가기로 했어?
(b) B: Mary가 적당한 파트너인 거 같아.
(c) A: Mary? 이해가 안 돼. 장난치지 마.
(d) B: 진심이야. 나 그녀에게 반했어.

해설 대화의 흐름상 과거에 이해를 못했다는 뜻이 아니라 지금 이해가 안 된다는 의미이다. didn't get it → don't get it

어휘 have a crush on ~에게 반하다

43 유형 문장의 형식

(a) A: Did you know that Joe committed suicide in the army?
(b) B: That is very astonishing. What made him so foolish?
(c) **A: I know nothing of it, and I find that hardly to believe.**
(d) B: I think he lacks of filial piety to his parents.

해석 (a) A: Joe가 군대에서 자살했다는 거 알았니?
(b) B: 정말 놀라운데. 왜 그런 어리석은 짓을 했대?
(c) A: 전혀 모르겠어. 그리고 믿어지지가 않아.
(d) B: 내 생각에 그의 부모님한테 불효인 것 같아.

해설 hardly는 부사로 '거의 ~하지 않는'이라는 뜻이다. (c)에서 뒤 문장은 5형식 문장으로 'find+목적어+목적보어' 구문이므로 목적보어에 형용사를 쓴다. hardly to believe → hard to believe

어휘 filial piety 효도

44 유형 문장의 형식

(a) A: How was the presentation in your class?
(b) **B: It was fantastic, which made every student interesting in the presentation.**
(c) A: That's good news.
(d) B: Now, I am confident in giving a presentation.

해석 (a) A: 수업 때 발표 어땠어?
(b) B: 모든 학생들이 발표에 관심을 가질 만큼 환상적이었어.
(c) A: 좋은 소식이네.
(d) B: 이제는 발표하는 거 자신 있어.

해설 which 이하는 'make+목적어+목적보어' 구문이다. 학생들이 관심을 가지는 것이므로 interested가 되어야 한다. every student interesting → every student interested

45 유형 생략

(a) A: Are you coming to the airport to see Jenny off?
(b) B: Sure. I will go, and maybe one of my friends is coming along.
(c) A: Who's coming with you?
(d) **B: As far as I know, John has. Do you know who he is?**

해석 (a) A: Jenny 배웅하러 공항에 올 거야?
(b) B: 물론이지. 나도 가고 내 친구 한 명도 아마 같이 갈 거야.
(c) A: 누가 같이 오는데?
(d) B: 내가 알기론, John이 같이 갈 거야. 누군지 알아?

해설 Who's coming ~?을 사용해 묻고 있으므로 대답 역시 이에 맞게 써야 한다. 원래 John is coming with me라고 되어야 하는데 coming with me는 생략 가능하므로 John is가 되어야 한다. John has → John is

Part IV Questions 46-50

46 유형 시제

(a) In the early 1900s, the company wasn't known by its familiar fowl moniker and sold other foods in addition to tuna. (b) But fortune shined on it when it became the first food company to can 'light tuna.' (c) The mildly flavored fish became the company's trademark product, and its owners sought a catchier name for their canned fish. **(d) When asked about the flavor of the new light tuna, many customers remark, "it tastes like chicken," so the company began to market the light tuna as 'Chicken of the Sea.**

[해석] (a) 1900년대 초에 그 회사는 우리에게 익숙한 닭고기 별명으로 알려지지 않았고 참치 외에도 다른 음식들을 팔았다. (b) 하지만 그 회사에서 최초로 '저지방 참치'를 통조림으로 팔기 시작했을 때 운이 따랐다. (c) 부드러운 맛의 생선이 그 회사의 특징적인 제품이 되자, 그 회사의 소유주들은 통조림 생선에 좀 더 귀에 쏙 들어오는 이름을 붙이고 싶어 했다. (d) 새로운 저지방 참치의 맛에 대해 질문하자, 많은 고객들은 "닭고기 같은 맛이 나요"라고 했고 그래서 그 회사는 저지방 참치를 '바다의 닭고기'로 시장에 내놓기 시작했다.

[해설] 원래 When they were asked about ~으로 과거의 내용이므로 뒤에 연결되는 내용 역시 과거형이 와야 한다. many customers remark → many customers remarked

[어휘] fowl 닭고기, 새고기 moniker 별명, 인명
flavored ~의 맛이 있는 catchier 재미있고 외기 쉬운

47 유형 전치사

(a) Depending various biological and social factors, from insects to fish to small mammals and even humans scientists are finding examples of excellent fatherhood. (b) Some creatures have evolved adaptive qualities that ensure the male is raising his own offspring. (c) Female giant water bugs, for example, cement their eggs onto the dad's back immediately after they mate. (d) For weeks, the male cares for his bug eggs, stroking them with his hind legs.

[해석] (a) 과학자들은 다양한 생물학적, 사회학적 요인에 따라 곤충부터 어류, 작은 포유류와 심지어 인간에 이르기까지 대단한 부성애의 예를 찾아내고 있다. (b) 어떤 생명체들은 아빠가 자식들을 키우도록 하는 적응력을 키워 왔다. (c) 예를 들어, 물장군 암컷은 짝짓기를 한 직후에 수컷의 등에다 알을 낳는다. (d) 수주 동안 수컷은 뒷다리로 알들을 어루만지면서 돌본다.

[해설] depend는 자동사로 뒤에 전치사 on과 함께 쓴다. Depending various biological → Depending on various biological

[어휘] fatherhood 아버지임, 부권 adaptive 적응의
giant water bug 물장군
cement ~에 시멘트를 바르다; 굳게 결합하다
stroke 쓰다듬다 hind leg 뒷다리

48 유형 수 일치

(a) Marcel Proust said: "The only true voyage, the only Fountain of Youth, would be found not in traveling to strange lands but in having different eyes." (b) He also said, "In seeing the universe with the eyes of another, of a hundred others, is seeing the hundred universes each of them sees, which each of them is." (c) Whilst I agree with him in part, I think that traveling in strange lands is the eyes of another person. **(d) Growing beyond one's origins necessitate the departure from one's origins in every sense of the word, particularly in the physical sense.**

[해석] (a) Marcel Proust는 '유일한 젊음의 샘인 진정한 의미의 여행은 낯선 땅을 여행하는 게 아니고 다른 시각을 갖는 것이다.'라고 말했다. (b) 그는 또한 백 명의 다른 이들의 눈으로 우주를 보는 것은 그 백 명 각자이자 그들 각자가 보는 백 개의 우주를 보는 것이다.'라고 말했다. (c) 부분적으로 그의 말에 동의하기는 하지만, 나는 생소한 곳을 여행하는 것이 다른 사람의 눈이라고 생각한다. (d) 자신의 근원을 넘어 성장하는 것은 어느 의미로 보나 자신의 근원을 떠나야만 가능한 것이고, 특히 물리적 의미에서 더 그렇다.

[해설] 동명사와 to부정사가 주어로 제시될 경우 단수로 취급해야 한다. (d)에서 주어는 origins가 아닌 Growing이므로 necessitate가 아니라 necessitates로 고쳐야 한다. origins necesstate → origins necessitates

[어휘] whilst ~하는 반면

49 유형 접속사

(a) The Puritans were not susceptible to the charms of poetry. (b) The strenuous life of the pioneer left little time for cultivating any of the arts. (c) The spirit of New England was too serious and too stern to permit indulgence in what was merely pleasant or beautiful. **(d) What the Puritans were not without imagination, however, is abundantly proved by the forceful figures and impassioned rhetoric of the prose writers.**

[해석] (a) 청교도인들은 시의 매력에 빠질 여지가 없었다. (b) 개척자의 힘든 삶은 예술을 함양할 만한 시간을 거의 허용하지 않았다. (c) 기분 좋고 아름답기만 한 것에 빠지기에는 뉴잉글랜드 정신이 너무 심각하고 엄격했다. (d) 하지만 청교도인들에게 상상력이 없지 않았다는 사실은 산문 작가들의 힘찬 비유적 표현들과 열정적인 미사여구로 충분히 입증된다.

[해설] 관계대명사로서 what은 자체에 선행사를 포함하여 'the thing which'의 뜻으로 쓰이고 뒤에 불완전한 문장이 온다. 하지만 (d)에서 what 뒤에 완전한 문장이 나왔으므로 여기선 관계대명사가 아닌 접속사가 필요하다. 따라서 that으로 고쳐야 한다. What → That

[어휘] susceptible ~의 여지가 있는, 받아들이는
strenuous 정력적인, 열심인
cultivate 장려하다, 함양하다
indulgence 몰두, 탐닉 figure 비유, 비유적 표현
impassioned 정열적인 rhetoric 미사여구, 수사학

50 유형 분사

(a) We are so exciting you and your family will be coming to stay with us over the holiday season. (b) I wanted to let you know that we would like to pick you up at the airport, but we don't have your flight number, please call us as soon as possible with your travel plans. (c) June is really looking forward to meeting her cousins and Rob and I really want to hear about all you have been up to with that business of yours. (d) 985-1132 is Rob's cellphone, which is always with him, so you can reach us there too.

[해석] (a) 당신의 가족이 연휴 동안 우리와 함께 지내러 온다고 생각하니 정말 기쁩니다. (b) 공항에 마중가고 싶지만 항공기 번호를 모르니, 여행 계획을 가능한 빨리 전화로 알려주세요. (c) June은 사촌들을 몹시 만나고 싶어 하고 Rob와 저는 사업이 어떻게 되고 있는지 무척 궁금합니다. (d) Rob는 항상 휴대폰을 가지고 다니는데 번호는 985-1132이고, 그리로 전화하면 우리와 연락할 수 있을 거예요.

[해설] (a)에서 다른 가족들이 연휴기간 동안 놀러오는 것 때문에 우리가 기쁜 것이므로 과거분사 excited를 써야 한다. exciting → excited

고난도 TEPS in TEPS 문법 ANSWER BooK

고득점을 위한 point를 정확히 알려주는 학습서

TEPS 고득점을 위한 Actual Training
고만고만한 빈출 문제는 그저 그런 성적을 낳을 뿐이다. 한 차원 높은 고난도 문제가 실전 경쟁력을 높인다.

전략적인 학습을 유도하는 유형 표시
각 문제에서 묻는 문법 요소를 표기한 유형 분류 tag를 활용하여 자신의 취약 분야에 대한 전략적 학습이 가능하다.

고난도 문제의 핵심을 꿰뚫는 고난도 point
기본적인 해설에 덧붙여 심도 있는 '고난도 point' 해설로 고난도 문제 해법의 핵심을 제시한다.

ISBN 978-89-6049-240-0 13740
978-89-6049-239-4(세트)

₩15000